Star Trek and
Philosophy

Popular Culture and Philosophy®
Series Editor: George A. Reisch

Popular Culture and Philosophy®

Star Trek and Philosophy

The Wrath of Kant

Edited by

JASON T. EBERL

and

KEVIN S. DECKER

OPEN COURT

Chicago and La Salle, Illinois

Volume 35 in the series, Popular Culture and Philosophy®, edited by George A. Reisch

To order books from Open Court, call 1-800-815-2280, or visit our website at www.opencourtbooks.com.

Open Court Publishing Company is a division of Carus Publishing Company.

First printing 2008

Printed and bound in the United States of America.

Library of Congress Cataloging-in-Publication Data

Star Trek and philosophy : the wrath of Kant / edited by Jason T. Eberl and Kevin S. Decker.
     p. cm. — (Popular culture and philosophy ; 35)
    Summary: "Essays address philosophical aspects of the five television series and ten feature films that make up the Star Trek fictional universe" — Provided by publisher.
    Includes bibliographical references and index.
    ISBN 978-0-8126-9649-3 (trade pbk. : alk. paper)
    1. Star Trek television programs — History and criticism. 2. Star Trek films — History and criticism. I. Eberl, Jason T. II. Decker, Kevin S.
PN1992.8.S74S727 2008
791.45'75—dc22
                                  2008021531

Contents

Starfleet Directive Three

A United Federation: Social and Religious Values of the Future

Starfleet Directive Four

Multiple Enterprises: *Metaphysical Conundrums from A to E*

The Federation Council

It takes an enormous amount of work to get a *Star Trek* episode, not to mention a feature film, from idea to screen. It also takes a talented crew of hard-working, creative, and brilliant people, not unlike the Starfleet crews who've graced our screens for the past forty years. So we'd like to start by expressing our gratitude to everyone whose talent and dedication—both in front of and behind the camera—brought *Star Trek*, in its many incarnations, into our lives. We also wish to salute the equally dedicated officers and crew who helped bring this ship into port.

First of all, our contributors, who, when given strict deadlines, produced brilliant work in half the time, making us believe that they had taken a page from Scotty's "miracle worker" playbook. Next, of course, is the Command Staff at Open Court, Admirals David Ramsay Steele and George Reisch, who gave us the Prime Directive as editors that we, in true *Star Trek* fashion, always adhered to but sometimes had to bend to save innocent, backward planets from destroying themselves.

A number of sentient creatures from quadrants Alpha to Delta donated valuable time in reviewing drafts of various chapters or influencing the shape of this book in other important ways: Ralph Anske, Susan and Zoe Arp, Jay Ayer, Carole Berg, Ben Dixon, George Dunn, Dave Frisbee, Jason Gatliff, Karl Erbacher, Andy Glasser, Ben Jonson, Kathryn Julyan, Joseph Kapus, Rebecca Kemnitz, Terrance MacMullan, Mimi Marinucci, Randy McKinney, Frank Menetrez, John Muenzberg, Alice Nelson, Wilhelm Nightingale, Gabriel Rocklin, Bernard Rowan, Pam Schierman, Stephen Scott, Tonya Scott, Tim Shiell, Ven Srinivasan, and Ariadne Wilber.

Editing this book on a *Galaxy*-class starship, we were fortunate to have our wives and precocious, ship-saving children along to help guide us through the glittering cosmic sea of uncertainty. Our wives Jennifer and Suzanne have had to put up with more in-jokes about Vulcan sexuality and daily attempts at refining the "Picard Maneuver" with polo shirts than anyone should be required to, and we love them for it. We dedicate this book to our children, August, Kennedy, Ethan, and Jackson, who we're confident will make the final frontier an amazing place to live.

Ex Astris, Scientia

From the stars, knowledge is the motto for Starfleet Academy.[1] But what kind of "knowledge" is this? Certainly, it must mean the knowledge of starship operations, first contact procedures, and how to look your best in velour, spandex, or a form-fitting catsuit. Yet it also means a type of knowledge that's not accessible through LCARS.[2] Captain Picard obviously knows this, as he gives Starfleet cadet hopeful Wesley Crusher a book by the nineteenth century American philosopher William James ("Samaritan Snare," *TNG*). Neither Picard nor Wesley suffer from the delusion that Wesley will be tested on James's views on "the will to believe" for his Academy entrance exam, but Picard knows that being a Starfleet officer takes more than just knowing that the matter/antimatter ratio is always one-to-one or how to open hailing frequencies.

From its very beginning, philosophy, or the "love of wisdom," has seen the stars as a metaphor for the quest for knowledge. Thales (around 624–545 B.C.E.), widely credited as the first western philosopher, famously fell into a ditch as he walked the Greek countryside in rapt admiration of the stars. In his well-known "cave allegory," Plato took the sun as symbolic of the ultimate good and the source of all knowledge. Aristotle considered heavenly bodies to be unchanging and made of a unique, non-terrestrial substance—the "quintessence" or fifth element. More recently, Immanuel Kant demanded that the

---

[1] This is inspired by the motto for the Apollo 13 mission, *Ex luna, scientia* ("From the moon, knowledge").

[2] If you've picked up this book, it's safe to assume that you're probably familiar with this acronym. But just in case you've accidentally been zapped by a memory beam and are now living among transplanted Native Americans on some idyllic planet, it stands for 'Library Computer Access and Retrieval System.'

epitaph for his grave immortalize the wonder inspired in him by two things: the moral law within each person, and the starry heavens above us all.

There's something that draws us toward the stars, both literally in terms of space exploration, and figuratively in terms of the potential they represent for transcending the limits of human experience. At its best, the quest for transcendence is what *Star Trek* is about, as the intrepid crews of the *Enterprise* (all seven of them), *Voyager*, and Deep Space Nine impress us with their sense of wonder at these possibilities. Consider the following dilemmas that could confront you if you were a typical starship captain:

- Stuck on a planet with an alien who speaks an indecipherable language, you must decide whether to fight him or help him.

- Your android operations officer kills a Borg in anger and laughs uncontrollably at seven-year-old jokes. How can you help him learn to balance his newfound emotions?

- An old foe is out to chase you "'round Perdition's flames" and eventually kill you, and you must convince your nemesis that his being "superior" is incompatible with his self-destructive drive for vengeance.

- An omnipotent being has offered your first officer unlimited power to give himself and his friends anything they want. How can you convince him that it's better not to use that power and miss out on a Klingon sex romp?

- A socially awkward crewmember spends more time in the holodeck than on duty. How can you convince him that life is better in the real world, even if he must suffer an embarrassing nickname?

- Starfleet Command has started issuing unethical orders. Should you obey without question or investigate whether super-intelligent bugs have taken over the admiralty?

- You discover that your chief medical officer has been illegally genetically enhanced. Do you drum him out of the service or just out of the ship's racquetball tournament?

- Having been thrown back in time at a crucial moment in Earth's history, how can you do what's right, get back home, and avoid a visit from the Department of Temporal Investigations?

- The ship encounters a planet of sheepish aliens whose lives are directed by a computer that wants to sterilize imperfections and name a rogue as the planet's leader, all the while searching for its "creator." Deprived of your phaser, what's your best weapon?

Believe it or not—and if you don't, you're about to be convinced otherwise—similar dilemmas have confronted human beings, not three hundred years in the future, but since about 2,500 years in the past. Asking the question, for example, of whether you should show mercy to an enemy doesn't require your foe to wear a rubber lizard suit in the heat of the ubiquitous Vasquez Rocks. Nor does wrestling with your dualistic nature, inclined now toward good, now toward evil, necessitate being physically divided in two in a transporter mishap. Some of the most intriguing and intractable problems of the *Star Trek* universe have also been faced by philosophical adventurers at the "final frontier" of mind and spirit.

Canvassing the over seven hundred hours of *Star Trek* presented in five television series (six if you count the animated series) and ten feature films (thus far), our contributors have gone well beyond some of the familiar philosophical dilemmas that trouble starship captains from Archer to Kirk to Janeway: Does Captain Kirk "die" every time Scotty beams him up?[3] Should Vulcan logic or human passion (or both) inform the captain's plan of action?[4] Our authors have plotted a course to engage a variety of topics in epistemology, politics, language, culture, logic, psychology, spirituality—and yes, good ol' fashioned metaphysics and ethics, too.

First up are some significant philosophical themes that underlie the entire *Star Trek* mythos and our own human history. Paul

---

[3] This and other metaphysical questions are discussed in Richard Hanley's *Is Data Human?: Or, The Metaphysics of Star Trek* (New York: Basic Books, 1997).

[4] This and other ethical questions are discussed in Judith Barad's *The Ethics of Star Trek* (New York: HarperCollins, 2000).

Cantor explores how it's possible for two persons from different planets and cultural backgrounds to communicate with each other in the first place. Walter Robinson channels a Vulcan philosophy professor who shows us that living a logical life isn't as easy as it might seem. In a close look at the characters of Spock and Data, Hal Thorsrud finds value in the Stoic temperament; while William Devlin and Shai Biderman explore the motivation of revenge behind the wrath of Khan. Robert Arp, focusing on pleasure and its problems, gives us good reasons to prefer being human to being a Q.

Some particular moral quandaries follow that may make one want to live under Vaal's tender care. Jason Eberl asks what the ethics of genetic research and manipulation might look like in both the far and near future. Timothy Challans uses his joint experience in philosophy and the military to explore the morality of Starfleet. Sander Lee analyzes whether it was right for Odo to work for the Cardassians during the occupation of Bajor and to help cure the Founders of a fatal disease. Finally, Jacob Held asks if it's oxymoronic to be an ethical Ferengi.

Next are discussions of some of the values vital to life in the Alpha and Delta Quadrants. After reading Kevin Decker's chapter, followed by Jason Murphy and Todd Porter's, you can decide for yourself whether it's better to live in the Federation or be assimilated by the Borg Collective—of course, deciding *for yourself* kind of biases the whole thing. Or perhaps, like Reg Barclay, you've been considering living your life in the holodeck, but you should read the chapter by Philip Tallon and Jerry Walls first. Heather Keith offers a justification for Worf's belief in the Klingon "messiah," Kahless; and Marnie Nolton shows us why it's difficult, but maybe not impossible, for Cardassians and Bajorans to reconcile with each other.

At last, we come to some of the classic puzzles of metaphysics and logic ruled by the Vulcan Science Directorate to be unsolvable. Amy Kind explores the philosophy of time that underlies the paradoxes and pitfalls of temporal travel. Theodore Schick and Mahesh Ananth each try to infer the natures of humans, Vulcans, and Horta from the "facts" of mind melding and survival of various transporter mishaps. Jerry Kapus closes our "journey into a wondrous land whose boundaries are that of imagination" (wait, that's another classic TV show) with a how-to guide for destroying ill-programmed, tyrannical computers with a few well-planned, simple claims.

From celebrating the transcendence of intercultural boundaries to singing the praises of reason over superstition and false authority, in the end, every thinker who has tackled the depths of *Trek* in these pages agrees on one thing. *Star Trek*'s oft-touted vision of a better future is not a cliché, but instead carries a call to action beyond its entertainment value. Novelist James Branch Cabell famously (and cynically) stated, "The optimist proclaims that we live in the best of all possible worlds; and the pessimist fears this is true." Gene Roddenberry's vision that defines the *Star Trek* universe is occasionally scientistic, often humanistic, yet thoroughly *optimistic*. To face the final frontier is to be committed to the idea that one *can* make a difference. When Picard says of life in the twenty-fourth century, "The acquisition of wealth is no longer the driving force in our lives. We wish to better ourselves and the rest of humanity" (*Star Trek: First Contact*), he's describing a path for personal self-realization based on Aristotle's idea that "All human beings by nature desire to know."[5]

Unlike Cabell's starry-eyed optimists, however, the crews of *Voyager*, *Defiant*, and the various *Enterprises* are accustomed to the universe being a dangerous place that, as Q warns, "is not for the timid." Although the *Next Generation* writers found it impossible to kill off Tasha Yar entirely, and we've learned not to trust the teaser for any episode that begins with the *Enterprise* exploding before the opening credits, the world of *Trek* is full of genuine risks and losses. Like us, its characters struggle to find meaning in death, destruction, and chaos. On occasion, these threats issue from *within*, as *Star Trek* gives many of its characters the dramatic opportunity to face their dark side—from Kirk's literal double-take to Janeway's pursuit of vengeance against Captain Ransom.

Despite these threats, Starfleet officers see their missions as best carried out, not through violence and coercion, but by the force of their ideals. This they also share with the great philosophers, who from Socrates on have largely agreed that it's better to suffer the "slings and arrows of outrageous fortune" than to

---

[5] Aristotle, *Metaphysics*, Book I, Chapter 1, line 980a21.

do evil or embrace falsehood. The optimistic commitment to understand the world and ourselves that *Star Trek* represents thus requires self-criticism and commitment to what William James calls "the strenuous life."[6] As Kirk puts it poetically, "Maybe we weren't meant for paradise. Maybe we were meant to fight our way through. Struggle, claw our way up, scratch for every inch of the way. Maybe we can't stroll to the music of the lute, we must march to the sound of drums" ("This Side of Paradise," *TOS*).

Star Trek, like philosophy, encourages us to rely on and revise our ideals when the going gets tough. To find the strength to be a leader, Picard looks to poetry and history, while Janeway draw lessons from her background as a scientist, and Archer emulates the virtues of his personal heroes: Zefram Cochrane and his own father. Like German philosophers Arthur Schopenhauer and Friedrich Nietzsche, Spock finds enlighten-ment in art—specifically, Marc Chagall. Julian Bashir and Tom Paris embrace the influences of twentieth-century pop culture. And Data attempts, until his noble self-sacrifice, to understand what it means to be human by cultivating his abilities in nearly as many ways as there are *Next Generation* episodes.

Rather than mere escapism, all the incarnations of *Star Trek* ought to be seen as an entertaining, edifying preparation for thinking through the problems that the future will undoubtedly throw at us.[7] If the following chapters are successful in fulfilling this book's aim, each will offer sage advice on living by one's ideals, and will stand as a kind of a primer for how philosophy can be part of our ongoing, never-ending life education.

So consider this book a supplement to the standard Officer's Manual issued to every Academy graduate (and any serious role-playing gamer). The Great Bird of the Galaxy himself expresses our purpose:

---

[6] William James, "The Moral Philosopher and the Moral Life," in *The Writings of William James: A Comprehensive Edition* (Chicago: University of Chicago Press, 1977), p. 627.

[7] If you've gotten this far, it's likely that you think you're up to this task. If you still have doubts, remember that thanks to Picard and company, it was a loutish drunkard afraid of his own legacy—Zefram Cochrane—who first made human contact with an alien species.

Let me do what we always try to do on *Star Trek*. Hopefully, entertain you. Perhaps even make you laugh a couple of times. And
when your guard is down, slip in a heavy idea or two. Because science fiction is a remarkable device for looking at the human creature and into the human condition. Indeed, as Ray Bradbury has
often said, science fiction may be one of the last places in our society where the philosopher can roam just as freely as he chooses.[8]

Live long, *think well*, and prosper.

---

[8] From the "Inside *Star Trek* with Gene Roddenberry" bonus CD included with
the twentieth anniversary edition of the soundtrack to *Star Trek: The Motion
Picture* (Columbia/Legacy, 1998).

Starfleet Directive
ONE

Seek Out New Ideas: Major Philosophical Themes in Star Trek

1

From Shakespeare to Wittgenstein: "Darmok" and Cultural Literacy

PAUL A. CANTOR

In October, 2005, I saw a world-class production of *Othello* at the Shakespeare Theater in Washington, D.C., with Avery Brooks in the title role. The casting of the man who played Commander Sisko in *Deep Space Nine* seemed to be establishing a *Star Trek* tradition for Shakespeare in our nation's capital. Eight years earlier Patrick Stewart—who played Captain Picard in *The Next Generation*—had appeared as Othello on the same stage in an experimental production that reversed the racial roles—with a white Othello and a black Iago. I began to wonder if Brent Spiner—who played Data in *The Next Generation*—would soon be appearing as the first android Othello, with perhaps the Borg Collective as a particularly mean Iago.

The Brooks *Othello* was a good reminder of the longstanding connection between *Star Trek* and Shakespeare, and hence of the show's aspirations to cultural literacy. *Star Trek VI: The Undiscovered Country* takes its subtitle from *Hamlet* and is filled with quotations from Shakespeare.[1] The Klingon General Chang is played by Christopher Plummer, a famous Shakespearean actor perhaps best-known, as it happens, for the Iago he played opposite James Earl Jones's Othello on Broadway. What is less well-known is that early in Plummer's career, when he played Henry V in Stratford, Ontario, his understudy was a young ambitious Canadian actor named William Shatner, who of course

---

[1] See my essay, "Shakespeare in the Original Klingon: *Star Trek* and the End of History," in *Gilligan Unbound: Pop Culture in the Age of Globalization* (Lanham: Rowman and Littlefield, 2001).

went on to play Captain Kirk in the original *Star Trek*. No wonder his replacement at the helm of the *Enterprise* turned out to be Patrick Stewart, one of the greatest Shakespearean actors of his generation.

Stewart's familiarity with Shakespeare came in handy during the shooting of a third season *Next Generation* episode called "The Defector." It opens with a scene of Data learning more about being human by role-playing in the holodeck. Stewart suggested that Spiner do a scene from Shakespeare's *Henry V*, the one where the king passes among his soldiers the night before the decisive battle of Agincourt. After getting through the scene, Data tells Picard—in one of those typical *Star Trek* sequences of familiar and then unfamiliar names that assures us there will be life beyond the twentieth century: "I plan to study the performances of Olivier, Branagh, Shapiro and Kullnark." *Star Trek* likes to remind us of the timelessness of Shakespeare, and indeed *Henry V*—with its exploration of the problem of language and translation—turns out to be profoundly relevant to the series in all its incarnations.

Something very strange happens in the middle of the play— a couple of French people come out on stage and *start to speak in French:*

> **Katherine**: Alice, tu as été en Angleterre, et tu bien parles les langage.
> **Alice**: Un peu, madame.[2]

And much to our amazement—and initial consternation—the French princess and her attendant continue to speak in French for the entire scene. Shakespeare violates a theatrical convention that seems to be as old as drama itself. Ever since the characters in Aeschylus's *The Persians* spoke Attic Greek instead of Persian, it has been customary for drama to be written in the language of the audience viewing the play and not that of the land where it takes place.

Shakespeare being Shakespeare, he is able to make a scene in French work for an English audience. What we are witnessing turns out to be a little language lesson. Katherine antici-

---

[2] *Henry V*, Act III, scene 4, lines 1–3. All Shakespeare quotations and line references are from *The Riverside Shakespeare* (Boston: Houghton Mifflin, 1974).

pates that diplomatic necessities may soon require her to be fluent in her enemy's tongue. As Katherine mentions the names of the various parts of the body in French, Alice tells her their names in English, thus allowing Shakespeare's audience to follow along. The premise of the scene is that one language translates easily into another because two different languages simply name the things of the world differently. All that is involved in learning a new language is to find out how it names the things with which one is already familiar—what one might call in pop culture terms the "Me Tarzan, you Jane" view of language acquisition.

Shakespeare's momentary violation of one of the most fundamental linguistic conventions of drama only highlights how widespread the practice actually is. Its scope became positively intergalactic in the twentieth century, as science fiction dramas in movies and television sought to extend communication, not just between different nations on Earth, but between humans and species from other planets. Basically, despite a few acknowledgements of the difficulties of inter-species communication, we have learned from *Flash Gordon* to *Buck Rogers*, from *Star Trek* to *Star Wars*, that everyone in the cosmos speaks English, often with less of an accent than Chekov or Scotty.

Science fiction writers cannot fall back on the premise that makes French-English translation seem to work so easily in *Henry V.* Whatever their differences, the French and the English share the same human body, and as long as their languages refer to a single underlying reality, one can move between them smoothly. But when it comes to alien species, we would not need such skilled make-up departments if their bodies were indistinguishable from the human form. As the chameloid Martia says in *Star Trek VI: The Undiscovered Country,* "Not everybody keeps their genitals in the same place," and one would think that science fiction scripts would occasionally reflect this sense of fundamental biological difference in some sort of fundamental linguistic difference. Would a truly alien species be able to understand our language? Would a truly alien language simply give different names to the same things in the world? Or would such a language divide the world into things differently in the first place? Might it perhaps not even work with the category of *things* at all? A race of disembodied, shape-shifting beings might have a language consisting of all verbs and no nouns.

Wittgenstein and the Talking Lion

These speculations are summed up brilliantly in one of Wittgenstein's typically gnomic utterances: "If a lion could talk, we could not understand him."[3] Ludwig Wittgenstein (1889–1951) was an Austrian philosopher and one of the most influential thinkers on language in the twentieth century. Through his teaching at Cambridge, England and his many publications, above all *Philosophical Investigations*, Wittgenstein reoriented the way many philosophers speak about language and indeed the very way they do philosophy. Wittgenstein felt that the problems that have traditionally troubled philosophers are at bottom problems of language. In his view, our failure to understand how language really operates generates a whole series of artificial—and unnecessary—metaphysical concerns. Wittgenstein's goal was to produce a more valid understanding of the nature of language that would lead us out of the intellectual dead-ends into which modern philosophy had in his view conducted us. As he put it, "The results of philosophy are the uncovering of one or another piece of plain nonsense and of bumps that the understanding has got by running its head up against the limits of language" (Part I, §119). Above all, Wittgenstein struggled against a conception of language that he believed vitiated all our attempts to understand ourselves and our world: "A *picture* held us captive. And we could not get outside of it, for it lay in our language and language seemed to repeat it to us inexorably" (§115).

The picture of language from which Wittgenstein hoped to escape is precisely the one that we just saw embodied in Shakespeare's *Henry V* and that we will see recur in *Star Trek*. Wittgenstein found it expressed in St. Augustine's account in his *Confessions* of how he had learned language as a child: "When they (my elders) named some object . . . I saw this and I grasped that the thing was called by the sound they uttered when they meant to point it out . . . I gradually learnt to understand what objects they signified." Wittgenstein articulates the conception of language implicit in Augustine: "These words . . . give us a particular picture of the essence of human language. It is this: the

---

[3] Ludwig Wittgenstein, *Philosophical Investigations* (New York: Macmillan, 1953), Part II, p. 223.

individual words in language name objects—sentences are combinations of such names.—In this picture of language we find the roots of the following idea: Every word has a meaning. This meaning is correlated with the word. It is the object for which the word stands" (§1).

Wittgenstein argues that this understanding of language takes for granted the very phenomenon it ought to be investigating, the articulation of the world into things in the first place. In Augustine's account, the world of the child is already divided up naturally into things, and learning a language is merely a matter of finding out what they are called in the conventions of his society. As Wittgenstein puts it, this account may successfully characterize how we learn a *second* language, but it ignores what must be involved in learning a *first*: "Augustine describes the learning of human language as if the child came into a strange country and did not understand the language of the country; that is, as if it already had a language, only not this one" (§32).

For Wittgenstein the fundamental question is not how words correspond to things but how words are used to articulate the world into things in the first place. In the crucial move in his later philosophy, Wittgenstein sought to get away from the common notion that the meaning of a word is the thing it corresponds to,[4] and turned to the idea that a word's meaning is to be found in the way it functions in making the world intelligible to us. In Wittgenstein's famous formulation: "For a *large* class of cases—though not for all—in which we employ the word 'meaning' it can be defined thus: the meaning of a word is its use in the language" (§43). Wittgenstein rejects an atomistic approach to language, in which one focuses on individual words as individual units of meaning that are only gradually built up into larger units of meaning like sentences. Noting that it is sometimes difficult to tell if a given utterance is a word or a sentence (§19), Wittgenstein opts for a more holistic approach to language, in which one would begin with the larger units of significance out of which separate words are only gradually articulated.

---

[4] Wittgenstein himself had been a powerful advocate for this understanding of language in his earlier work, especially his *Tractatus Logico-Philosophicus.*

These larger units take their meaning only in the larger context of human life and human action. In Wittgenstein's view, only because we use language as human beings does it have any meaning at all. Wittgenstein builds the idea of use into his criterion for recognizing something as a language to begin with, as we can see in his description of a situation that sounds like a typical *Star Trek* episode:

> Suppose you came as an explorer into an unknown country with a language quite strange to you. In what circumstances would you say that the people there gave orders, understood them, obeyed them, rebelled against them, and so on? The common behavior of mankind is the system of reference by means of which we interpret an unknown language (§206).

Thus, in Wittgenstein's view, our problems in understanding language arise from trying to abstract it from its larger human contexts, for example, to isolate individual words from the way they are in fact embedded in concrete utterances where they perform real functions. For Wittgenstein, language and life are inseparable: "to imagine a language means to imagine a form of life" (§19). To highlight the way words are to be understood in terms of the rules for using them, Wittgenstein speaks of "language-games": "Here the term 'language-*game*' is meant to bring into prominence the fact that the *speaking* of language is part of an activity, or of a form of life" (§22). Wittgenstein thus makes a connection between being human and using language:

> It is sometimes said that animals do not talk because they lack the mental capacity. And this means: "they do not think, and that is why they do not talk." But—they simply do not talk . . . Or to put it better: they do not use language—if we except the most primitive forms of language.—Commanding, questioning, recounting, chatting, are as much a part of our natural history as walking, eating, drinking, playing (§25).

Here Wittgenstein argues that speaking a language is bound up with the distinctively human form of life, as shown by all the characteristic ways in which human beings use language in their everyday lives.

It is in this context that we must understand Wittgenstein's seemingly enigmatic claim: "If a lion could talk, we could not understand him." Humans and lions represent different forms of life, and thus if lions did use language, it would be for purposes other than those of human beings. Lions would not simply name things differently; if they did formulate concepts, they would divide up the world differently, in accordance with their different forms of life. For example, with a predator's heightened sense of smell, lions might have a far richer olfactory vocabulary than human beings do. Thus, for Wittgenstein, moving between two languages may not be a simple matter of finding the equivalences between two sets of names. Rather, it may involve complex negotiations between two different forms of life.

Philosophical Investigations in Outer Space

Wittgenstein's talk of different forms of life—what one might call alien life-forms—points us in the direction of science fiction. When he writes of talking animals and explorers entering strange lands, he makes us think of some of the archetypal sci-fi scenes. But science fiction writers have been reluctant to take up the challenge Wittgenstein poses to the idea of easy translation between alien languages. In its first incarnation on television, *Star Trek* was one of the worst offenders in this regard. The writers of the show conveniently conjured up a Universal Translator for the crew of the starship *Enterprise*, which made exploring strange planets easier for them, and, more importantly, made producing scripts much easier for the show's writers. It is no wonder that the alien life-forms Captain Kirk encountered often turned out to be disappointingly familiar. In "A Piece of the Action" a whole planet operates by the rules of Chicago gangsters from the 1920s—indeed its inhabitants seem to have watched too many re-runs of *The Untouchables.*

In this, as in many other respects, *Star Trek: The Next Generation* marked an advance beyond its predecessor, and several of its episodes raise issues of translation—for example "The Ensigns of Command" in the third season and "Masks" in the seventh. Above all, in a fifth season episode called "Darmok," the show explored the issue of alien language with a depth and a seriousness rarely seen in television or any other sci-fi medium.[5] The episode is in fact wholly devoted to the problems

---

[5] "Darmok" was chosen as *the* "classic episode" of *Star Trek: The Next*

of communication between two different species. As the episode opens, Captain Picard and his crew are on a mission to establish communication and perhaps trade relations with what is described as an "enigmatic race," the Children of Tama. During previous encounters, their language had been "called incomprehensible," and it still is—as we soon discover when the captain of the Tamarian starship offers a strange greeting to the *Enterprise*: "Rai and Jiri at Lungha. Rai of Lowani. Lowani under two moons. Jiri of Ubaya. Ubaya of crossed roads at Lungha. Lungha, her sky gray." Like Picard, we are completely baffled by this sequence, and we look in vain for the customary subtitles that might enlighten us, the normally privileged audience, as to what this attempt at communication means.

Note that the problem here is not the usual one with foreign languages. The Universal Translator has not failed completely; we are hearing English words from the Tamarian captain—his name turns out to be Dathon—but they are still incomprehensible to us in the way they are combined. This is then the sort of language-game Wittgenstein loved to imagine—a situation where we can understand individual words, but not whole sentences, where recognizable words do not appear to be functioning in the way we normally expect. In short, the lion of Tama is speaking, but, just as Wittgenstein predicted, we cannot understand him. Picard nevertheless persists in his efforts to comprehend the alien's words. Ever the optimist about intergalactic harmony, the captain reassures his crew: "But are they truly incomprehensible? In my experience, communication is a matter of patience, imagination." Picard's patience and imagination are indeed about to be tested. With the enigmatic words: "Darmok and Jalad at Tanagra"—which will be repeated many times throughout the episode and give it its name—Captain Dathon has Picard transported to the surface of the planet they are both orbiting, El-Adrel IV.

For the rest of the episode, Picard, the remaining crew of the *Enterprise*, and we as audience only gradually figure out how the Tamarian language functions. At considerable risk to himself, Captain Dathon has created a situation which he hopes will teach Picard how to speak Tamarian. After several frustrating

---

Generation in *TV Guide: Guide to TV* (New York: Barnes and Noble, 2004), p. 599.

failures at communication, Dathon achieves his first success when he offers to share his fire using the words: "Temba. His arms wide." Evidently a good Augustinian, Picard begins with the view of language Wittgenstein rejected. He wants to know the objects Dathon is referring to with his words. Hence Picard's initial reaction: "Temba? What does that mean? Fire? Does Temba mean 'fire'?" Picard is at first a captive of the "one word–one thing" model of language. But Dathon's frustration with this conclusion leads Picard to start thinking on the level not of the individual word but of the whole utterance and thus to reconsider how *Temba* functions in their concrete situation: "Temba is a person? His arms wide. Because he's . . . he's holding them apart in . . . in . . . generosity? In giving? In taking?" Picard can do a better job of deciphering Tamarian than the ship's computer because he is placed in the same circumstances as Dathon and can recognize what the alien captain is trying to accomplish with his words. In true Wittgensteinian fashion, the meaning of "Temba. His arms wide" is not the set of objects the words refer to but their use.

Picard's understanding of the Tamarian language deepens when he grasps why Dathon has been using the words: "Shaka. When the walls fell" every time their attempts to communicate go awry. Picard speculates: "Shaka . . . Is that a failure? An inability to do something?" His ultimate realization of how Tamarian works as a language comes in a flash of insight as he tries to follow Dathon's instructions about fighting the beast that is about to attack them: "That's how you communicate, isn't it—by citing example. By metaphor!" Picard's insight elicits from Dathon what is evidently the Tamarian equivalent of "By George, I think he's got it!", namely: "Sokath. His eyes uncovered!" Mixing in Greek for good measure, the stage direction in the script at this point reads: "(eureka!)."

The mysterious words in Dathon's utterances were not the names of objects, but rather proper nouns—the names of persons and places out of Tamarian myth and history. Darmok and Jalad, for example, were two heroes who fought side-by-side on the island of Tanagra, and forged a friendship by facing a common foe. Dathon hoped that a similar bond would develop between him and Picard as they fought together against a beast on El-Adrel IV. This episode thus shows how deeply cultural a phenomenon language is. Words are not rooted in a world of self-subsistent objects in nature that might make them equally intelligible to all rational beings. Rather words are rooted in a people's distinctive culture, their specific history and mythology, which shape the categories with which they understand their world. In "Darmok" a language is embedded in a form of life.

The simultaneous and parallel investigation into Tamarian conducted in Picard's absence by the *Enterprise* crew comes up with similar results and fills in our understanding of how the language operates. After searching linguistic databases on the ship's computer, Lieutenant Commander Data and Counselor Troi are ready to give an erudite lecture on Tamarian to Commander Riker. Somehow Data has already been able to conclude: "The Tamarian ego structure does not seem to allow what we normally think of as self-identity"—another attempt to relate a language to a form of life. In a particularly Wittgensteinian moment, Data says: "The situation is analogous to understanding the grammar of a language but none of the vocabulary."

What Every Tamarian Needs to Know

The mention of vocabulary here links "Darmok" to another intellectual issue, one which had a good deal more currency than Wittgenstein's later philosophy at the time the episode aired. In 1987 E.D. Hirsch Jr. published a book called *Cultural Literacy: What Every American Needs to Know*, which quickly became a bestseller and sparked a heated controversy throughout the United States (Hirsch appeared on national television several times to discuss the book, even on the *Phil Donahue Show*, which is more than Wittgenstein ever did). Hirsch made a powerful argument against the widespread belief that education can be "content-free," that our duty is to teach children modes of learning and knowing but not any specific items of knowledge. In his studies of reading, Hirsch uncovered a great deal of evidence that contradicts this view.

Hirsch found that reading is not simply an abstract skill, something that is fully acquired once one has learned the alphabet, rules of grammar, and other means for decoding written messages. The ability to read is contingent on developing vocabulary, and that vocabulary includes historical and cultural data that a particular society assumes as common knowledge among its members. When a newspaper refers to George Washington, for example, it does not feel obliged to gloss the name as "first President of the United States" (whereas a mention of Millard Fillmore would inevitably be joined with "Thirteenth U.S. President"). Someone reading that newspaper who knows who George Washington was will obviously be able to read it faster and with greater comprehension than someone who does not. What Hirsch calls cultural literacy thus becomes essential to understanding common discourse whether in speech or in print.

Hirsch illustrates the principle of cultural literacy with a personal anecdote:

> My father used to write business letters that alluded to Shakespeare. These allusions were effective for conveying complex messages to his associates, because, in his day, business people could make such allusions with every expectation of being understood. For instance, in my father's commodity business, the timing of sales and purchases was all-important, and he would sometimes write or say to his colleagues, "There is a tide," without further elaboration. Those four words carried not only a lot of complex information, but also the persuasive force of a proverb. In addition to the basic practical meaning, "Act now!" what came across was a lot of implicit reasons why immediate action was important.[6]

If one pictures E.D. Hirsch Sr. saying "Brutus and Cassius at Sardis" on the floor of the Memphis Cotton Exchange, one has a perfect illustration of how the Tamarian language works and why it is so effective for those who have the knowledge to make it work.

Appearing in 1991, while people from prominent educators to government officials were still arguing passionately over Hirsch's book, "Darmok" raises the issue of cultural literacy exactly in his terms. In order to understand what the Tamarians say, the *Enterprise* crew lacks, not the general rules of the Tamarian language, but the specific cultural content that supplies the context in which all Tamarian utterances become meaningful. In a display of cultural literacy itself—quite amaz-

---

[6] E.D. Hirsch Jr., *Cultural Literacy: What Every American Needs to Know* (Boston: Houghton Mifflin, 1987), p. 9. The passage in Shakespeare Hirsch refers to is from *Julius Caesar*, Act IV, scene 3, where Brutus says to Cassius: "There is a tide in the affairs of men, / Which taken at the flood, leads on to fortune."

ing for a commercial television program—"Darmok" raises the related issue of Great Books. Some of those who followed Hirsch in championing the cause of cultural literacy also advocated a Great Books curriculum on the college level, in order to make students familiar with Shakespeare and other foundational authors in our cultural tradition.[7]

As if alluding to this aspect of the controversy, "Darmok" includes several scenes that celebrate the cultural heritage of the human race. When Troi is trying to illustrate how Tamarian works, she chooses an example from Shakespeare: "Juliet on her balcony," which her colleague Beverly Crusher explains is "an image of romance." When Dathon is dying, he wants Picard to tell him one of the stories that has a meaning for his own people. Reluctantly at first, Picard is soon eloquently relating the tale of Gilgamesh, the ancient Sumerian narrative that stands at the fountainhead of the epic tradition. As a story of Gilgamesh's problematic friendship with Enkidu, this epic is particularly appropriate in the circumstances. By the time Picard is finished, the phrase "Gilgamesh and Enkidu at Uruk," with its distinctly Tamarian ring, stands ready to enter the alien vocabulary as a new way of saying "friendship in extremity."

In an even more pointed moment, at the very end of the episode, Riker finds Picard reading a book in ancient Greek. Picard explains: "The Homeric hymns—one of the root metaphors of our own culture." The lesson in multiculturalism Picard has learned from his encounter with the Tamarians has not weakened his attachment to his own culture. On the contrary, as he thinks of future encounters with the Tamarians, it only strengthens his desire to know his own roots: "More familiarity with our own mythology might help us to relate to theirs." A defender of the Great Books like Allan Bloom could not have put it better. The irony is striking: although television has often been blamed for the decline in cultural literacy, in "Darmok" we witness a television program explaining the need for cultural lit-

---

[7] The fact that Hirsch's book came out at virtually the same time as Allan Bloom's *The Closing of the American Mind* meant that the two books tended to be associated in the public's view, and Hirsch was often linked to the Great Books movement. However, he dissociated himself from this movement, for a variety of reasons, including the fact that his studies focus on curriculum for grades K–12 and not for college.

eracy and championing our heritage of Great Books. No wonder *Star Trek* in its many incarnations kept returning to Shakespeare for inspiration. As Picard counsels Data in "The Defector" when he plays Henry V: "Data . . . You're here to learn about the human condition. And there is no better way of doing that than by embracing Shakespeare."

Never Underestimate a TV Writer

With its sophisticated awareness of some of the subtlest problems in the philosophy of language, "Darmok" represents a remarkable moment in television history. I am not claiming that the writers of the episode—Joe Menosky and Philip LaZebnik—had Wittgenstein in mind, but I would not put it past them.[8] Or they might have been inspired by the writings of Benjamin Lee Whorf (no relation to the Klingon officer Mr. Worf on board the *Enterprise*—at least none that I know of). Whorf's studies of the complex tenses and other aspects of Native American languages such as Hopi raise many of the issues that Wittgenstein highlights, above all the way a language embodies a distinct worldview and system of categorizing reality.[9]

But whatever theorists of language guided Menosky and LaZebnik, the main point is that—contrary to our stereotype of television writers as ignorant hacks—they are both highly educated, Menosky with a degree from Pomona College and LaZebnik from Harvard. Menosky began his career as a journalist. He was a science editor and reporter with *Morning Edition* and *All Things Considered* on National Public Radio and wrote extensively on scientific and technological issues for such journals as MIT's *Technology Review*. LaZebnik's credentials are

---

[8] Menosky and LaZebnik are credited with writing the story; Menosky alone gets teleplay credit. Michael Piller, the head of the writing staff, said that "Darmok" "had the longest gestation period of any episode during his tenure. The inability to communicate had been the central theme of a story by Philip LaZebnik, but it was Menosky who worked out the Tamarians' language of allusion and metaphor. He also changed the story's focus from a complex and confusing 'ant farm' visit to an exploration of the two strong commanders, Picard and Dathon." See Larry Nemecek, *Star Trek: The Next Generation Companion* (New York: Simon and Schuster, 2003), p. 177.

[9] See Benjamin Lee Whorf, *Language, Thought, and Reality* (Cambridge, Massachusetts: MIT Press, 1956).

even more relevant to the linguistic aspects of "Darmok" and perhaps explain how an ancient work like the *Epic of Gilgamesh* made a rare appearance on a weekly television show. LaZebnik's field at Harvard was Classics, and his senior honors thesis was on the highly arcane subject of Homer's music. Since the music to Homer's epics does not in fact exist anymore, LaZebnik's exploration of the topic was in a way an early exercise in fantasy and science fiction for him.

Despite the evident erudition that goes into writing *Star Trek*, or perhaps precisely because of it, fans love to find errors in the scripts. The Net is filled with various forms of nitpicking about "Darmok," such as the question: How could a civilization with such a poetic—and seemingly unscientific—language ever have succeeded in building a starship?[10] If one really wanted to nitpick, one might ask: Why would Picard think even for a moment that "Temba" means "knife," when the Universal Translator would have rendered it as such if it did? One cannot expect thoroughgoing logical consistency from a television episode, and, despite a few questionable aspects of the script, the writers of "Darmok" are to be applauded for operating well above the normal level of television fare. If, upon repeated viewing, the episode may seem heavy-handed in its exposition, we must remember that it was, like all weekly television, essentially designed for first-time viewing. And I recall being bowled over when I saw its first-run broadcast. With no preparation, I, like most viewers I'm sure, found the dialogue astonishingly opaque. I remember thinking to myself: "Can they really be doing this on television? It's like broadcasting *Finnegans Wake*."

What most struck me after first viewing the episode was the respect the show displayed for its audience. It relied on them to stick with the episode despite their bewilderment and to await as

---

[10] The commentary on "Darmok" on the Web is interesting but so vast that I cannot possibly summarize it. When I googled 'Darmok,' I got roughly 7,200 entries. Googling 'Darmok and Wittgenstein' yields mostly phantom connections, but I did find relevant remarks from Patricia Burton, President of the Delta chapter of Phi Beta Kappa of Missouri. At an initiation ceremony on April 13, 2003, she explicitly links "Darmok" with Wittgenstein's talking lion. Googling 'Darmok and Cultural Literacy' yields several genuinely pertinent results. Many teachers at both the high school and the college level are using "Darmok" in class to illustrate points about language and cultural literacy. Perhaps "Darmok" itself is becoming part of our cultural literacy.

patiently as Picard the elucidation of what was going on. By the end of the episode, the writers trusted the audience to follow Picard's parting dialogue with the crew remaining on Dathon's ship—with no glosses from Data or any other nearby know-it-all. For first-time viewers, only the earlier careful explanation of the principles of the Tamarian language made this possible.

To be sure, "Darmok" does not explore the issues it raises as fully as it might have, and Wittgenstein no doubt would have torn its logic to pieces. How alien is the Tamarian life form after all? Although their mode of expression may at first seem peculiar, their words in the end express concepts familiar to a human being like Picard. It takes him a while to figure out that "Shaka. When the walls fell" means "failure," but at least he knows what failure is. If one really wanted cultural difference, one could imagine a race of superhuman, perhaps omnipotent beings who literally do not know the meaning of the word *failure*.

Moreover, the world of the Tamarians bears a striking resemblance to the world of classical epic on earth, and Dathon and Picard share the concept of epic friendship. Wittgenstein might point out that we could imagine a form of life for whom the concept of friendship is completely unknown—perhaps a world so devoted to cutthroat competition that friendship becomes literally unthinkable—the Planet of the Trumps. In the end, I have to admit that "Darmok" does not explore the full range of alien forms of life, but the fact that it can lead us to come up with even more bizarre possibilities is one more measure of how genuinely philosophic this television episode is.

2

Death and Rebirth of a Vulcan Mind

RITOKU, PROFESSOR OF VULCAN
PHILOSOPHY, STARFLEET ACADEMY[1]

I was not born a Vulcan. I was taught to be one. I am writing as a Vulcan philosopher and a student of Spock, who is my mentor and will serve as a case study of Vulcan philosophy as it is lived. To understand Vulcan philosophy and the teachings of Spock you have to understand Vulcan civilization, which begins with the philosophy of Surak who lived in the fourth century A.D. (old Earth calendar).

Surak established logic as the soul of Vulcan. Before him, Vulcan was violent and at war. Surak ushered in the reformation known as the "Awakening," which is the beginning of Vulcan's history as a peaceful society. He did not invent or discover logic, for the use of logic pre-dated his life—what he did was to put forth a *philosophy* of logic that would become fundamental to Vulcan civilization. While the word "logic" is from an Earth language with roots in Greek, and carries with it a meaning developed throughout human history, Vulcan is a world apart, and the Vulcan understanding of logic must be understood in the context of Vulcan culture and history.

"Logic Is the Soul of a Vulcan"

Before the Awakening, the people of Vulcan were violent and war-like, driven by dark and destructive passions. The Romulans, labeled as "warlike, cruel, treacherous" by humans who fought a war with them two centuries ago, share a common ancestry with

---

[1] Transmitted to Walter Robinson, a twenty-first-century Zen Buddhist priest.

Vulcans; but they separated from Vulcan after the Awakening and retained the warrior philosophy with all its violent passions ("Balance of Terror," *TOS*).[2] As evidence of Vulcan's violent history the "Stone of Gol" was developed, a powerful psionic resonator that amplified an enemy's violent aggressive emotions to create a destructive force of energy. The Stone of Gol became useless, however, after the Awakening; for if one's enemy has no violent emotions, the weapon can do no harm ("Gambit, Part II," *TNG*). As Surak's teaching spread, the tools of war became useless; and time, resources, and energy were employed in building a peaceful society.

Throughout the twentieth and well into the twenty-first centuries of Earth history, humans were confronted with much of the same problems as Vulcans before the Awakening. Humans had developed sophisticated technologies of killing, and invented ideologies in order to rationalize killing. But the real motivation comes down to irrational desires for power and control driven in large part by fear and greed. Just like on Vulcan, these irrational passions threatened the very survival of the human species. This violent tendency of humans remained in play well after official first contact with Vulcans in 2063.

The great Vulcan philosopher T'Plana-Hath said, "Logic is the cement of our civilization with which we ascend from chaos using reason as our guide" (*Star Trek IV: The Voyage Home*). There are three modes of logic in Vulcan philosophy, each interrelated to create a synergistic whole. One of these modes is *formal logic* akin to classical Earth systems, such as Aristotle's, as well as modern forms of symbolic logic. This mode forms the basis of Vulcan metaphysics, the first law of which, as stated by Vulcan philosopher Kiri-kin-tha, is that "nothing unreal exists" (*Star Trek IV: The Voyage Home*). This axiom parallels a similar claim made by Earth philosopher Parmenides, who asserted that you cannot get something out of nothing—if it does not exist, it is not. This teaching is also fundamental to the Yogic philosophy of the Earth religion of Hinduism. In one of Hinduism's most important holy books, the *Bhagavad-Gita,* we read, "That

---

[2] These parenthetical references are to the chronicles of the *U.S.S. Enterprise* and other famous Federation starships that were transmitted to the twentieth-century writer, Gene Roddenberry, who used this historical information to develop a television series he titled "*Star Trek.*"

which is unreal has no existence, and to be without existence is to be unreal."[3] A related axiom that is foundational to Earth-based logic is known as the "principle of non-contradiction": The same thing cannot both be and not be at the same time, at the same place, in the same respect.

Another mode is *ethical logic,* a variation of which Surak developed. Before Surak, Vulcans used formal logic without ethical concerns. Pure formal logic has no particular ethical content, and thus can be adapted to most any agenda. Vulcan ethical logic evolved out of a crisis of survival. Those who used their intelligence to reflect on the circumstances of their species realized that its survival required a significant change in behavior. What was needed was a change in the way individuals relate to their social environment. When individuals pursue their own self-centered interests without concern for the social good, chaos follows. The same is true when groups pursue their interests apart from consideration of the overall good of those affected. The maxim, "The needs of the many outweigh the needs of the few, or the one," is axiomatic in Vulcan ethics since it concerns the relation of individuals to their social environment (*Star Trek II: The Wrath of Khan*). No society can exist without ethical principles. This axiom implies that it is ethically necessary that the behaviors of individuals be regulated by social consideration, and to do otherwise results in disadvantage to all. Indeed, one cannot separate the good of individuals from the society in which they participate. Ethics must go beyond self-centered concerns, and at the same time include them. For Vulcans, this requires a social psychology of self-control. Vulcan ethics has a psychological dimension of mental discipline in which discordant passions and irrational emotions are subdued and repressed. This involves the third mode of logic, which is the mental discipline of *meditation.*

Meditation entails concentration. To concentrate means to center one's consciousness on one-pointedness. The undisciplined mind is usually drifting from one thought or feeling to another with little or no control, and is dominated by emotions and passions. Logical thinking is more controlled, more one-pointed. The first stage in the practice of meditation is to bring

---

[3] *The Bhagavad-Gita*, Chapter 2, verse 16.

consciousness into a calm so as to quiet down the mind's activity. Once this calm has been entered into, one may concentrate on an object of meditation, such as a geometric pattern. This technique is much like the use of a mandala (a circular geometric configuration as seen in the practice of Tantra widely employed in Tibetan Buddhism). The use of a mantra as an object of meditation is also common among Vulcans, such as the following used by Tuvok, chief of security on the *U.S.S. Voyager*: "A structure cannot stand without a foundation; logic is the foundation of function; function is the essence of control. I am in control." While reciting this mantra, Tuvok blindly assembles a geometric apparatus called a "*keethara*," translated as "structure of harmony" that helps "to focus thought and refine mental control." The final form of the *keethara* "is a reflection of the builder's state of mind; thus it is different each time" ("Flashback," *VGR*).

Much of Vulcan culture is devoted to meditation. It is the core of the education by which Spock and I, indeed all Vulcans, have been trained. Monasteries are common, and Vulcans will often go on monastic retreats to deepen their meditative practice. The most important monastery is the T'Karath Sanctuary founded by Surak himself and is where his *katra* (the essence of his consciousness) is kept. Some Vulcans devote a lifetime to meditative practice and the study of the Kir'Shara—Surak's original teachings ("Kir'Shara," *ENT*).

"It Is Not Logical, But It Is Often True"

The cultures of East Asia on Earth have placed a priority on developing meditative disciplines. Yoga is the most systematic science of meditation that humans have developed. The ancient Indian philosopher and teacher of Yoga, Patanjali, defines it as "the restraint of the activity of the mind."[4] He asserts that only with a quiet mind that is at peace with oneself is true knowledge possible.

Much of what we assume we know is a projection of our biases, prejudices, and social imprinting. Right knowledge, according to Yogic epistemology, comes from three sources: direct pure experience, logical inference, and authoritative testi-

---

[4] Patanjali, *Yoga Sutras*, Sutra Two.

mony. The first of these is by far the most important and is the basis of all true science. This is because logical inference is only as good as the data on which it is based; experience trumps logic. Vulcans long ago discovered that something can be true yet not logically valid, or valid but not true. The practical side of Vulcan philosophy teaches that logic must orient itself with experience as its guide. Of course we cannot always go on what we personally know from direct experience, for the scope of what is in experience is greater than any one mind can contain. So we often rely on the testimony of others; but to the extent that such testimony is authoritative, it must relate back to logically articulated and verifiable experience. To give logical articulation to direct experience requires a psychological discipline that frees the mind of bias and prejudice, or as a Vulcan would say, free of emotionalism.

The prime concern of Yogic philosophy is *moksa*. This Sanskrit word more or less means liberation, or being free of all which inhibits one from the fullness of peace and truth. Hinduism and Buddhism share this prime concern with Yoga. The Hindu philosophy of logic, known as *Nyaya* asserts that through clear and logical thinking the mind can free itself from ignorance, which is the cause of distractive emotions. Buddhism teaches that the cause of suffering is desires generated from ignorance. The nature of this ignorance is a false identity of one's self as a fixed and isolated entity.

The Vulcan sense of self is very different from human egoism. Vulcan self-consciousness is rooted in cultural orientation and grounded in a meditative cosmic experience. Vulcans have "seven senses." These include the five senses known to humans and a sixth animal sense which is "the ability to sense the presence of disturbance in magnetic fields." The seventh sense is "the sense of oneness with All, i.e., the universe, the creative force, or what some humans might call God. Vulcans do not, however, see this as a belief, either religious or philosophical. They treat it as a simple fact which they insist is no more unusual or difficult to understand than the ability to hear or see."[5] Vulcans call this the philosophy of "Nome," meaning "the

---

[5] Gene Roddenberry, *Star Trek: The Motion Picture* (New York: Pocket Books, 1979), pp. 126–27.

combination of a number of things to make existence worth-while" ("The Savage Curtain," *TOS*).

This sense of oneness fundamental to the Vulcan experience is known in Yogic practice as *samadhi*. This word refers to the culmination of meditative practice into the experience of cosmic oneness. Hindus and mystics call this God; Buddhists call it Buddha-nature. Patanjali outlines eight stages of practice leading up to the realization of *samadhi*. The first two are ethical in nature, and consist of five restraints and five observations. The five restraints are: non-harming, non-lying, non-stealing, sensory control, and non-possessiveness. These restraints fully agree with Vulcan ethics.

Like most practicing Hindus and many Buddhists, Vulcans are vegetarians, and are pacifists except for self-defense. This first restraint, translated from the word *ahimsa*, was central to the ethics of Gandhi, who influenced Martin Luther King, Jr., and is fully congruent with the teaching of Surak. Gandhi, King, and Surak all believed in non-violence as a means to reform society. Non-lying is also well known as a central tenet of Vulcan ethics.

It is often said that a Vulcan is actually incapable of lying, although Vulcans have been known to exaggerate. Sensory control may and often does include abstaining from lust, or any other sensory indulgence that leads to heedlessness or loss of rational control. Adult Vulcan males lose this ability for a short time every seven years with the experience of *pon farr*, but otherwise they maintain sensory control ("Amok Time," *TOS*). Non-possessiveness is also characteristic of the Vulcan ethos. It is illogical to own more than one can use, so Vulcans tend not to own a great deal. And for those things rarely used, it is more logical to hold them in common with the community, so they can be used as needed and then made available for someone else to use.

Pantanjali's five observances are: purity, contentment, auster-ity, intellectual cultivation, and surrender to ultimate reality. The notion of purity entails refraining from physical and psycholog-ical pollution. No Vulcan would smoke cigarettes, get drunk, use recreational drugs, or consume sugar-saturated synthetic sub-stances devoid of nutritional value. A Vulcan also would not read for mere entertainment, or do anything that failed to serve the need for self-improvement. Like Yogis, Vulcans maintain contentment with life. Life is what it is, and although it may in some ways be improved upon, for the most part it is illogical to make oneself unhappy because things are not as one may wish them. Austerity teaches non-attachment to conditions of pleasure or pain. This is the goal and reason for intellectual cultivation in Vulcan culture. Vulcans are focused on gaining knowledge, not for its own sake, but for developing mental discipline, expanding understanding, and fostering wisdom. As Spock says, "Logic is the beginning of wisdom . . . not the end" (*Star Trek VI: The Undiscovered Country*). To this end one lets go of his or her own ego to surrender to ultimate reality—the Oneness with all as known by way of the seventh sense. The "needs of the many" is part of this Reality, and when one is enlightened to the oneness of life, then one lives to serve life.

The third stage of Yogic practice leading to *samadhi* is called Asanas, which includes the physical exercises commonly associated with Yoga. Asanas, moreover, includes designing one's lifestyle to accommodate ethical and meditative practice—involving lifestyle changes to implement the ethical precepts of stages one and two, and to accommodate time and space to regular daily meditation. The fourth stage is known as Pranayama, which is the cultivation of the life force energy. This naturally comes about through the Yogic exercises and is magnified when meditation is practiced alongside it. On Earth, in China, this energy is called "ch'i," also known in Japanese as "ki," and is basic to the martial arts of Asia. A Vulcan's strength is based on this energy.

The fifth stage is the gateway into meditation, which is to withdraw consciousness from exclusive dependence on the physical senses. This is where ability is not dependent on Vulcan biology. Romulans are just like Vulcans biologically, but apparently cannot perform mind melds. Vulcans who have not been trained also cannot.

During the period when Vulcan government was under the "High Command" and Vulcan society was losing the ways of the Awakening, mind melding was forbidden, and most Vulcans of that time could not do it and ran the risk of developing a stigmatized illness if they did ("Fusion," "Stigma," *ENT*). In the mid-twenty-second century, a Vulcan named Syran came to posses the *katra* of Surak, and based on the knowledge gained founded the Syrannite movement that re-established Surak's true teachings ("The Forge," "Awakening," "Kir'Shara," *ENT*). After the downfall of the High Command, Vulcan society was reformed, as was Vulcan education to include the training that enables mind melding. Some humans who are advanced in Yoga can do the same. The Yogis call such paranormal phenomena "siddha," but discourage the development of them, as they may become distractions to the main intention of Yoga, which is spiritual enlightenment.

"Here on These Sands, Our Forebears Cast Out Their Animal Passions"

The last three stages of Yogic practice are: concentration, meditation, and *samadhi*. The three are interwoven such that *samadhi* is deep meditation, and meditation is prolonged concentration. When *samadhi* become an ongoing presence within consciousness, the mind becomes free of discordant passion and emotionalism. When this becomes a fixed part of a person's character, they have achieved what Vulcans call "Kolinahr." After years of intense meditative practice using logic to purge all traces of emotion, one enters "those consciousness levels that are beyond the reach of confusion, fatigue, and pain" (p. 21). The ancient Vulcans, by attaining Kolinahr, made the Stone of Gol an obsolete weapon—for if one has not a trace of violent thought or emotion, such a weapon is harmless. Upon the Stone are the symbols for War and Death, to which was added, at the time of Awakening, the symbol of Peace placed between and thereby separating the other two—thus meaning that Peace neutralizes War and Death ("Gambit, Part II," *TNG*). This is a metaphor for the peace attained on the high plateau of Gol, where Vulcans go to achieve Kolinahr.

After serving in Starfleet for several years, Spock went to Gol in 2270 to attain Kolinahr under the guidance of the monastic Vulcan masters. He hoped that in this way "he could once and for all time unburden himself of his human half, which he believed responsible for his pain" (p. 20). At the same time there was a "powerful entity" that was "searching the galaxy for some long-needed answers" (pp. 22–23). Spock was able to telepathically sense the entity, and the entity was also able to sense him. This entity was V'Ger, whose existence began as the Earth probe Voyager VI, but whose programming was upgraded by an advanced extraterrestrial machine intelligence to empower it to fulfill its mission to "learn all that is learnable." On its journey home to Earth it grows in knowledge, power, and consciousness.

Both Spock and V'Ger suffered from an existential crisis, which emerged out of extreme rationalism: for both, logic failed to give their consciousness a sense of purpose. V'Ger was the ultimate thinking being, purely logical and in possession of everything knowable, or so V'Ger believed, but this was not enough. Spock sensed V'Ger's feeling of profound emptiness, as if the entity were asking, "Is this all that I am? Is there nothing more?" in the fear that there would be no answer. This sense of the absurd that afflicted V'Ger's consciousness was akin to what Spock was experiencing. To the philosophical question, "What is the meaning of life?" logic can't provide an answer.

Spock himself has had a difficult time answering this question. He was born of a Vulcan father and a human mother. He grew up and was educated on Vulcan, and identified himself as Vulcan; but most of his adult life was lived working with humans, all the time denying his human half. It was the cold and unfeeling childhood he experienced on Vulcan that drove him to join Starfleet, and thus get away from his father, with whom he had a problematic relationship ("Journey to Babel," *TOS*). It is illogical to deny one's nature, even if that nature is irrational. And this was the contradiction that Spock was living. His human side could be repressed for only so long before it asserted itself—the more powerful the denial, the more forceful the assertion. The pain that Spock experienced was a consequence of the self-estrangement resulting from his denial of his humanity.

"The fact that you had sensed patterns of perfect logic," Kirk asked Spock during the V'Ger mission, "does that have something to do with your being here?" Spock answered, "It is my only hope of accomplishing what the Masters [of Gol] could not" (p. 136). The cosmic sense of oneness that Vulcans have poses a metaphysical issue, which they could not logically resolve: "This relationship of consciousness and the universe was the only reality which actually existed. The Masters at Gol, of course, spent much of their lives seeking to unravel the puzzle of how a living consciousness could at every moment be both part and all" (p. 127).

Spock was motivated to enter into direct contact with V'Ger and mind meld with it. As his mind merged with V'Ger, he discovered "more knowledge than filled the worlds' libraries. He become cognitive of reality at some level that his own limited mind could not comprehend ... layer after layer of information . . . How could the unimaginable immensity of this universe around them be only a brief spark in a still greater reality? It had all seemed so clear and logical to Spock when he had been part of [V'Ger's] thoughts. Spock had also seen that [V'Ger] was almost capable of traveling into these higher dimensions" (pp. 206–217).

The mind meld was so overwhelming to Spock's brain that he lost consciousness, which may have saved his life. This experience was so intense that it resulted in a psychological death and rebirth. He would later in his life undergo a physical death and rebirth, but it was here, with V'Ger, that his spiritual rebirth happened that would be a precursor to his later material rebirth (*Star Trek III: The Search for Spock*). It was through his experience with V'Ger that he discovered within himself the value of humanity.

"Logic Without Need Is Sterile"

SPOCK: V'Ger has knowledge that spans this universe. And yet . . . with all its pure logic . . . V'Ger is barren . . . cold. No mystery. No beauty . . . Jim . . . this [Spock takes hold of Kirk's hand] . . . simple feeling . . . is beyond V'Ger's comprehension. No meaning, no hope. Jim . . . no answers. It's asking questions. "Is this . . . all that I am? Is there nothing more?"

—*Star Trek: The Motion Picture*

V'Ger was reaching out to its creator for answers. It was returning to its place of origin to become one with the creator, not knowing that humanity was the creator, not realizing that the only way to fulfill its needs was to become one with humanity. V'Ger knew that the *Enterprise* was from the planet of its origin, and thus studied it in detail. To this end it created a probe out of the form of the *Enterprise's* navigator, Ilia, replicating her biological form in all details. Ilia was Deltan, a species highly evolved in sexuality and empathic sensitivity. As V'Ger merged its consciousness with Ilia's Deltan sensitivity, it became aware of feelings and of the needs that feelings involve. It became intimately aware of its need to merge with the creator, the source of its self. Since the source of its self is humanity, V'Ger chose to physically join with a human. This union is *tantric* in nature.

Tantra is a form of Yoga based on the practice of integration with, and through the use of, sexual energy. Classical Yoga has its origins in a *dualistic*, or two-tiered, philosophy known as Samkhya. It is very much like Plato's views in its rejection of the world of sensation. Both Samkhya and Platonism assert that what is real is eternal existence beyond the body, and in order to come into knowledge of eternal truth, one must overcome the body. For Plato, this means overcoming the sensations and feelings of the lower world of the physical, and instead dwelling in the upper world of pure reason. These ideas are not alien to Vulcan philosophy, the pressures of which led to Spock's existential dilemma. Not only Spock, but also his half-brother, Sybok, as well as other Vulcans have turned to feeling and other non-rational ways of being to overcome the limits of reason (*Star Trek V: The Final Frontier*, "Fusion," *ENT*). Among the Yogic philosophers, this was never the main problem. The Yogis of Earth understood that truth is beyond thinking—that reality is more than what reason can know. For them, the problem was duality. In deep mediation, the oneness of being is experience, and the one is non-dual—it is all-inclusive. In Tantric yoga, body and spirit are equally one with the ultimate energy of the universe. The modes of consciousness are fully integrated into one another to yield a synergistic whole, which transcends all limits and is in harmony with the universal and unified field intelligence of the cosmos.

V'Ger transcends its original programming and merges with higher dimensions of consciousness. For his part, Spock is transformed, receiving a new openness that resolves the conflict and contradiction that had dominated his life. Henceforth, he is at home with both his Vulcan mind and his humanity. He gave up on Kolinahr, as it was no longer relevant to his needs, but he did not give up on Vulcan philosophy. Logic has its place and proper field of application, but as he said to one of his Vulcan students, Valeris, "Logic is the beginning of wisdom . . . not the end" (*Star Trek VI: The Undiscovered Country*). Of the three modes of Vulcan logic—formal, ethical, and meditative—Spock learned the limits and the proper application of each. Formal logic cannot function apart from the principle of non-contradiction, but experience includes much that seems contradictory. Quantum physics is full of examples such as the principle of uncertainty, the wave-particle paradox, the problem of non-locality in particle interaction, and so forth. Even at the level of pure logic there is inherent uncertainty as entailed by the "Principle of Incompleteness," known on Earth as Gödel's Theorem, which states that given any formal system of logic sufficiently complicated to be descriptive of experience, if it explicitly states all functional axioms, theorems, and postulates, it will contain contradictions.[6] The Principle of Incompleteness demonstrates that in order to maintain non-contradiction in formal reasoning, it is necessary to have open-endedness.

This open-endedness is equally true in ethical concerns, for understanding is always limited. One often does what seems to be good only to find that it has unforeseen consequences which are not good. Spock discovered this for himself after battling Kirk for T'Pring. After giving her to Stonn, Spock exhorts him, "After a while, you may find that having is not so pleasing a thing after all as wanting. It is not logical, but it is often true" ("Amok Time," *TOS*). Often, there is no clearly rational solution to an ethical dilemma. Sometimes, we must simply trust our feelings. Spock came to this realization when he committed an act of desperation in jettisoning the shuttlecraft *Galileo*'s fuel in the seemingly vain hope of gaining the *Enterprise*'s attention; although he attempted to convince his crewmates that logic informed him that an act of desperation was called for in that situation ("The *Galileo* Seven," *TOS*).

In order to have this deeper intuitive sense of the moral good, it is necessary to have a disciplined mind that is sufficiently quiet and centered. When Captain Archer feels the unleashed force of a Vulcan's temper, he tells T'Pol that he now understands why she meditates each night ("Fusion," *ENT*). The three mode of logic must therefore work together, and within the limits of proper application and adaptation.

After Spock's physical rebirth, he re-educated his mind in the ways of Vulcan logic. His mother asks him how he feels, which Spock is unable to answer and deems an "irrelevant" question. It is upon his return trip to Earth and into its past, to merge with

---

[6] For further discussion of Gödel's Theorem, see Chapter 18 in this volume.

the deep ecology of the planet and the future survival of life thereon, that Spock finally integrated his humanity with his Vulcan heritage. The feeling side of Spock appeals to Kirk not to leave an injured Chekov behind on twentieth-century Earth. Hearing this appeal from his reborn Vulcan friend, Kirk asks, "Is that the logical thing to do, Spock?" He replies, "No, but it is the human thing to do" (*Star Trek IV: The Voyage Home*). And whereas before his transformation he was unable to answer his mother's question, "How do you feel?" Spock, in his new openness, is able to relay a message through his quizzical father: "Tell her . . . I feel fine."[7]

---

[7] I am grateful to Jason Eberl for his work in translating this from Vulcan to English.

3

"Humans Smile with So Little Provocation"

HARALD THORSRUD

Data's desire to be more human leads him to think that life is better with emotion. This is a problem since he's dispassionate by design. Spock has the opposite problem. He's dispassionate by choice, so he constantly struggles to rid himself of emotion. The two fundamentally disagree—Data thinks life is better with emotion, Spock that it's better without. Consider the following exchange from "Unification, Part II" (*TNG*):

SPOCK: He intrigues me—this Picard.

DATA: In what manner, sir?

SPOCK: He's remarkably analytical and dispassionate, for a human. I understand why my father chose to mind meld with him. There's an almost Vulcan quality to the man.

DATA: Interesting. I had not considered that, and Captain Picard has been a role model in my quest to be more human.

SPOCK: More human?

DATA: Yes, Ambassador.

SPOCK: Fascinating. You have an efficient intellect, superior physical skills, no emotional impediments. There are Vulcans who aspire all their lives to achieve what you've been given by design.

DATA: Hmm. You are half-human.

SPOCK: Yes.

DATA: Yet you have chosen a Vulcan way of life.

SPOCK: I have.

DATA: In effect, you have abandoned what I have sought all my life.

We might say that they're only expressing personal preferences, and so they can both be right. A rich emotional life would be better for Data and the dispassionate life would be better for Spock.

But this won't do. Although it's not immediately obvious, what they disagree about is the nature of emotion itself. Spock believes that emotion interferes with the proper functioning of reason and that we're better off when reason is in charge since logic is the most reliable way to achieve our desired goals ("The *Galileo* Seven," *TOS*). So everyone should seek to eliminate emotion from their lives—even the positive feelings we have towards our friends are bad if they're irrational. This is why he's surprised that Data actually wishes to experience emotion. According to Spock, Data's better off as he is, and we'd all be better off without emotion.

Data, on the other hand, believes that emotions are a natural and necessary part of a good life. He's reluctantly dispassionate and thinks he's missing out on something really important. Experiments with his emotion chip, however, reveal the danger of being carried away against his better judgment—or at least his ethical subroutines ("Descent," *TNG*; *Star Trek: Generations*). Emotions are powerful forces that can drive us to commit terrible acts: they only become part of a good life when they're moderated in accordance with reason.

So should we seek to *eliminate* or merely *moderate* our emotions? Spock and Data's disagreement isn't new. In the third century B.C.E., a similar debate arose between two schools of ancient Greek philosophy: the Stoics and the Peripatetics, or followers of Aristotle. What Spock maintains about Vulcans, the Stoics claim for humans as well: emotion is an impediment to our flourishing as rational beings. And Data's worry that his lack of emotion makes him deficient is echoed by the Peripatetics: properly moderated, emotion enriches our lives, and motivates us to do the right thing.[1]

---

[1] The most extensive report of the debate can be found in Cicero, *Tusculan Disputations* (Chicago: University of Chicago Press, 2002). Interest in this topic has grown enormously over the past thirty years; see Chesire Calhoun and

"The Emotional Bonds that Make Us Who We Are"

Let's start with Deanna Troi's observation in "Descent, Part I" that emotions themselves are neither positive nor negative, but only with regard to what one does with them. Data's concerned about this because he unexpectedly feels an intense and pleasurable anger while fighting, and then killing, a Borg. What he doesn't realize is that his brother Lore is actually manipulating him from a distance using the emotion chip their father, Dr. Noonien Soong, had created for Data ("Brothers," *TNG*). So Data isn't really responsible for his violent emotions. Nonetheless, his emotional experience was real.

On Aristotle's view, emotions are always accompanied by pleasure or pain.[2] When we have the impression that something good or bad is happening or about to happen, we feel accordingly. Data has the complex impression both that the Borg are evil, and that it's good to kill one. So he's in the presence of something both good—killing the Borg—and bad—the Borg itself. Data feels a confusing mixture of painful rage and pleasure. Afterwards, Deanna tells him that becoming angry at an injustice can help motivate you to do something about it. A bit of righteous anger can also keep you from becoming a doormat. But on the other extreme, we can feel too much anger and be paralyzed by it, or moved to commit an injustice in turn.

It's not easy to determine how much emotion one should feel in any given situation. The crucial point is that there *is* a right amount to feel, though this will differ from person to person and situation to situation. The same is true for many other emotions. Too much fear, for example, can cause one to behave in a cowardly way, while too little can cause recklessness.

But we shouldn't try to moderate every emotion. Some of them are worthless, morally speaking. You're not much better off being only moderately spiteful for example. Similarly, it's absurd to try to be only moderately joyful at the murder of your friendly rival—you shouldn't be joyful at all in this case. Neither

---

Robert Solomon, eds., *What Is an Emotion?* (Oxford: Oxford University Press, 1984).

[2] See Aristotle, *On Rhetoric* (Oxford: Oxford University Press, 1991), Book II, lines 1378a20–23.

should you be moderately hopeful about the prospects of stealing from an orphanage. The only acceptable emotions are those that contribute to a good life. For Aristotle, such emotions must be consistent with being a morally good person. So his general idea is that we'll live better lives if we learn to feel the right way in any given situation.[3]

And this seems to be what Data wants. As he sees it, to be human is to be vulnerable. At least on one occasion he says that he would be willing to feel bad if he could also feel good ("Hero Worship," *TNG*). But Data is incapable of being emotionally moved by his friends' actions. We see this played out in "Legacy" (*TNG*), when the crew of the *Enterprise* enlists the help of Ishara Yar, the sister of their deceased colleague Tasha. The respect and love the crew felt for Tasha leads them to trust her sister, especially Data who has shared his "full functionality" with Tasha ("The Naked Now," *TNG*). But it turns out that Ishara is only using Starfleet to pursue her own political ends and isn't the least bit interested in helping them. After her betrayal is revealed, Data has the following exchange with Commander Riker:

> **DATA:** Recent events have left me puzzled, sir. It has been days since Ishara left, and yet, my thoughts seem to dwell on her, almost as if I were experiencing a feedback loop in my mnemonic network . . . It is curious that I was so easily misled.
>
> **RIKER:** Make that "we" . . . In all trust, there is the possibility of betrayal. I'm not sure you were prepared for that.
>
> **DATA:** Were you prepared, sir?
>
> **RIKER:** I don't think anybody ever is.
>
> **DATA:** Hmm. Then it is better not to trust.
>
> **RIKER:** Without trust, there's no friendship, no closeness. None of the emotional bonds that make us who we are.
>
> **DATA:** And yet you put yourself at risk.
>
> **RIKER:** Every single time.
>
> **DATA:** Perhaps I am fortunate, sir, to be spared the emotional consequences.
>
> **RIKER:** Perhaps.

---

[3] See Aristotle, *Nicomachean Ethics* (Indianapolis: Hackett, 1999), Book II, Chapters 5–7.

Riker is uncertain whether Data is better off as he is. But he does think we humans are better off for our vulnerability and "the emotional bonds that make us who we are."

Data's connection with Ishara should have made the betrayal even more painful, but he feels only puzzlement. He can't be disappointed in the way we can, so trusting others doesn't make him vulnerable. Consequently, he's only able to achieve a very convincing simulation of friendship:

> **DATA:** . . . even among humans, friendship is sometimes less an emotional response and more a sense of familiarity.
> **ISHARA:** So, you can become used to someone.
> **DATA:** Exactly. As I experience certain sensory input patterns, my mental pathways become accustomed to them. The input is eventually anticipated, and even missed when absent.

The sense in which Data "misses" familiar sensory input patterns doesn't cause him to feel sadness. But if we think friendship requires the possibility of being emotionally moved by our friend's actions, then becoming "used to someone" will only be a simulated form of friendship.

This is especially clear when Data has a go at romantic love ("In Theory," *TNG*). Despite the fact that he does all the right things, his newfound love, Jenna, eventually grows dissatisfied: "as close as we are, I . . . I don't really matter to you. Not really. Nothing I can say or do will ever make you happy or sad, or touch you in any way." Without a hint of regret, Data replies, "That is a valid projection." The fact that Data feels nothing as a result of being dumped by Jenna is cold comfort—in fact, Data doesn't need to be comforted in the first place. He just doesn't feel bad, despite the fact that he might miss her familiar sensory input patterns. And yet having lost something really valuable, he should feel bad. The resulting sadness would need to be moderated—there will be an appropriate duration and intensity of grief—but it still needs to be felt.

For us humans, the alternative may be to suppress the painful emotions we aren't able or willing to face. There's an excellent example of this in "Hero Worship." Data manages to save a young boy, Timothy, from the wreckage of a ship drifting through space. Everyone else onboard had been killed, including Timothy's parents. To make things worse, Timothy believes he was responsible for the disaster. Rather than allow himself to feel the full weight of his grief and regret, he begins to imitate Data: as Deanna observes, it's much easier for Timothy to feel nothing.

It's true that most people would prefer *not* to experience crushing grief, anxiety, or fear. If it were possible, they might choose to experience only positive emotions. But it seems to be a package deal. And it seems preferable to take the good with the bad if the only alternative is to become invulnerable and *dead* inside. This is the criticism that the Peripatetics level against the Stoics and that Dr. McCoy levels against Spock:

> Do you know why you're not afraid to die, Spock? You're more afraid of living. Each day you stay alive is just one more day you might slip, and let your human half peek out. That's it, isn't it? Insecurity. Why, you wouldn't know what to do with a genuine, warm, decent feeling. ("Bread and Circuses," *TOS*)

As far as McCoy is concerned, Spock's willingness to face death is actually a kind of cowardice—it's a pre-emptive strike against all the sadness and misery he might confront.

So, there are two good reasons to let emotions play a moderate role in our lives. First, emotions seem to be unavoidable for organic, rational beings, even if they can be suppressed for a time. So they should be incorporated in our lives to our advantage because, properly moderated by reason, they help us to do the right thing. Second, such emotion enriches our experience. Even if we could eliminate it, the result would be a disaster. We may achieve invulnerability only at the cost of indifference. But both the Vulcan and the Stoic would dispute these claims, as we'll see next.

"Insults Are Effective Only Where Emotion Is Present"

The Stoics believe that invulnerability *can* be achieved without becoming indifferent—we can see an approximation to this ideal in Spock's imperturbability.[4] But first we must confront the supposed necessity of emotions. If we can't eliminate them, it'll be pointless to claim that we should.

Initially, it seems implausible that we *choose* to feel the way we do. Surely Captain Picard doesn't choose to feel fear as he, Data, and others search through darkened passageways for the Borg in *First Contact*. Picard even expresses his envy at Data's ability to turn off his emotion chip. There are many times we would "turn off" our emotions if we could. So it seems that they're not within our control. But according to the Stoics, Picard's emotion of fear is not the same thing as physical reactions within his body. Epictetus puts it this way:

> When some terrifying sound . . . or anything else of that kind occurs, even a [Stoic] wise man's mind must be slightly moved . . . by certain rapid and involuntary movements which forestall the proper function of mind and reason . . . however, the wise man does not assent to such impressions nor does he add an opinion to them, but he rejects and belittles them and finds nothing in them that should be feared.[5]

Had a well-trained Vulcan been walking alongside Picard, he would have received the same impressions of darkened passageways and imminent danger. And these impressions would produce the same physical reactions. We can't control the release of adrenaline, the sweaty palms and queasy stomach, but we don't have to judge that something bad is the cause. By refusing to make that judgment, the Vulcan would feel no fear.

To see that the physical reaction is different from the judgment, just imagine that Picard has been tricked. While he thinks he's on a dangerous mission, he's in fact in the holodeck. His body responds just as it would if he were on the "Borgified" *Enterprise*, but the instant he learns that he's on the holodeck, he'll cease to feel any fear. What changes here is his judgment

---

[4] Judith Barad makes this case in *The Ethics of Star Trek* (New York: Harper Collins, 2000), pp. 154–57. But she repeats the common error that the Stoics encourage suppressing emotion, as if we should be at war with ourselves all the time.

[5] Aulus Gellius, *Attic Nights*, in *Hellenistic Philosophers,* Volume 1 (Cambridge: Cambridge University Press, 1987), p. 419.

(unless, of course, he also learns that the holodeck's mortality failsafe has been overridden, as often occurs).

Emotion always presupposes a judgment that something is good or bad. Most of the time we assent to things or circumstances as good or bad without reflecting on what we are doing. The situation seems dreadful. Having accepted this impression we begin to feel fear. Picard doesn't need to actually think or say to himself, "Something dreadful is afoot." It's enough that the situation seems dreadful and that he assents, consciously or otherwise. But while he has no immediate control over how things seem at that moment, he's not forced to assent to his impression, and thus believe the situation is in fact dreadful. Rather than being swept along by our impressions, Epictetus advises us to test them in order to find out what we are really assenting to, and rationally decide whether we should accept that the situation is at it initially appears.[6] We develop the habit of fear by unreflectively assenting to apparently frightful impressions without testing them first.

Of course Picard's no coward. He's well aware of the danger and risk involved in his mission, but he also believes that it's for the best to carry on. So he proceeds cautiously. Picard moderates his fear and turns it to his advantage. But the fact that he envies Data on this occasion is a point for the Stoics: he would rather eliminate than moderate his fear. He may diminish it right away by refusing to believe the threat of physical harm is bad. Of course, that's easier said than done. Picard would need to habituate himself to seeing the world as a Vulcan or a Stoic does. Eventually, he would find it easy to believe that physical harm is not genuinely bad, despite the fact that it's still painful.

Stoics believe that nothing is genuinely good or bad except what's within our control. If I am physically harmed, I haven't suffered anything really bad, as Epictetus explains:

> Being tied to many things, we are weighed down and dragged along with them . . . "Must I be beheaded now, and alone?" Well, would you like everyone to be beheaded so that you can feel better? . . . What should we have ready at hand in such circumstances? What else but knowledge of what is mine and what is not mine,

---

[6] See Epictetus, *Discourses* (Oxford: Clarendon, 1998), Book II, §18.

what I can do and what I cannot do? I must die. But must I die groaning? I must be fettered. And crying too? I must be exiled; but does anyone keep me from going with a smile, cheerful and serene? "Reveal your secrets." I refuse, for this is in my power. "But I will fetter you." What do you mean, man? My leg you will fetter, but not even Zeus can conquer my moral choice. "I will throw you into prison." My body, you will . . . What constrains you is not the threat [of death] but your decision to do something else rather than die. (Book I, §1.15–24, §17.25)

Neither death nor physical harm nor anything else that happens *to* us is really bad. All that counts is what we do, and how we respond, and this is entirely up to us.

The Stoic takes aim at the things we normally think of as good as if he were an archer. He aims at friendship, health, wealth, good reputation, and the like. Once he lets the arrow fly he's done all he can to secure those things. If a gust of wind comes up, he's undisturbed, knowing that he's done all he can. Besides, becoming disturbed at the gust of wind changes nothing and is really pretty ridiculous—like taking revenge on the stone that stubbed your toe by kicking it back. For the Stoics, the most important challenge is to learn how to engage in life, pursuing some things and avoiding others, while not letting the inevitable victories and defeats get the better of us. Emotion arises only when we mistakenly think these victories and defeats are really good or bad. Cicero makes use of this idea in his objection to even moderate emotions:

When one fails to obey reason, is that not a fault? Does not reason insist quite strongly that the thing for which you burn with desire, or which you are inordinately excited to possess, is not a good, and that the thing under which you lie crushed, or are beside yourself with fear lest it crush you, is not an evil? And that it is only through error that these objects become so very awful or delightful? . . . Therefore it makes no difference whether they give approval to moderate emotions or to moderate injustice, moderate cowardice, moderate intemperance. He who sets a limit for our faults takes the part of fault. (Book IV, §39, §41)

Just as it makes no sense to try to moderate rather than eliminate the flu, it makes no sense to try to feel just the right amount of emotion.

Not only do emotions result from mistaken judgments, they also cause mistaken judgments. In general, emotions interfere with the proper use of reason. They cloud our judgment and often lead us to do things we shouldn't. Spock puts it well: "Insults are effective only where emotion is present" ("Who Mourns for Adonais?" *TOS*), and "Where there's no emotion there's no motive for violence" ("Dagger of the Mind," *TOS*). If we never allow ourselves to become angry or afraid, we'll never seek to harm someone without a good, rational justification.

Spock is true to his word. In "Balance of Terror" (*TOS*), the crew gets a first glimpse of the Romulans and find that they're strikingly similar to Vulcans. Lieutenant Stiles develops a hostile suspicion of Spock. Kirk has to warn him to leave his bigotry in his quarters, but Spock is unmoved by Stiles's unfounded hatred. Later, Spock even risks his own life to save Stiles. Rather than becoming angry at the injustice, Spock continues to follow the dictates of reason: "I saved a trained navigator so that he could return to duty. I am capable of no other feelings in such matters." "Anger has this great fault," says Seneca, "it refuses to be ruled." Further, "it is enraged against truth itself if this is shown to be contrary to its desire."[7] Anger and fear have a way of distorting the world so that we see only what will justify our rage. These emotions are contrary to the spirit of calm deliberation that we need to arrive at the best course of action.

The same is true for positive, pleasurable emotions. Spock's experiences with romantic love testify to this, even though they're all inspired by factors outside his control. For example, in "This Side of Paradise" (*TOS*), the *Enterprise* visits an agricultural outpost on Omicron Ceti III expecting to find the colonists all dead due to dangerous radiation bombarding the planet. Instead they find a group of people who have been infected by spores and are now more interested in free love than agricultural research. Once infected, Spock joins right in. Dropping his scientific detachment, he looks at the colors of a rainbow as a poet and sees dragons in the clouds. Under the influence of the spores, he even falls deeply in love. Though his liberation brings him a great deal of joy, it's not stable. When Kirk confronts him

---

[7] Seneca, *On Anger*, in *Moral Essays*, Volume 1 (Cambridge, Massachusetts: Harvard University Press, 1928), Book I, §19.1.

hanging from a tree with his newfound love and orders him back to the ship, Spock's joy quickly turns to anger. Such volatility is the price of emotional highs. But Spock seems willing to pay it, even after he regains his composure. At the end of the episode, he claims that for the first time in his life he had been happy.

That's his human half talking, influenced by the memory of intensely pleasurable emotions. More often, Spock thinks he's better off without emotion. From the Vulcan perspective, the happiness he experienced on Omicron Ceti III seems artificial and unworthy of his rational nature. It's a fine thing to appreciate the colors of a rainbow and to enjoy the pleasures of romantic love—even Spock's Vulcan father, Sarek, shares romantic love with not one, but two human women during his life ("Journey to Babel," *TOS*; "Sarek," *TNG*). But Vulcans still answer to the higher calling of their rational nature. Because emotion interferes with rational thought and action, it must be eliminated. Whether positive or negative, once it's unleashed, emotion has the ability to carry us away. In the grips of powerful emotion we're not able to reassert rational control when we wish. As Cicero puts is, "To try to find a limit for [emotion] therefore, is like believing that one who hurls himself off the cliff . . . can check his fall whenever he wants. That is how impossible it is for the disturbed and agitated mind to contain itself or to stop where it wants to stop" (Book IV, §41).

A "Quite Logical Relief" and Other Tranquil Affections

The accomplished Stoic never hurls himself off cliffs. He's never moved to act because of the way he feels. But he does feel something: unlike the turbulent and manipulative emotions that most of us experience, the Stoic experiences "tranquil affections." These arise when he correctly judges, for example, that bars of gold-pressed latinum are merely *targets to be aimed at.* Whether or not we acquire the latinum is ultimately irrelevant. Assuming the Stoic succeeds in getting the money, and then faces the prospect of losing it, he'll feel cautious and attentive, but not afraid. His concern isn't with the money, which is ultimately out of his control, but rather with maintaining the proper attitude, which is within his control. A Ferengi in the same circumstances will be terrified at the thought of losing his precious latinum. The Ferengi's fear will move him to every imaginable extreme whereas the Stoic's caution doesn't cause him to do anything; it's merely a byproduct of his correct assessment of the situation.

The Stoics allow for such tranquil feelings since they don't interfere with the exercise of reason. Spock allows himself these feelings as well. At the end of "Amok Time" (*TOS*), when he discovers that he hadn't killed Kirk in the battle required by the Vulcan mating ritual, he is, for just a moment, ecstatic. "Jim!" he says, grabbing his friend by both arms. Then, more coolly, "I am . . . pleased to see you, Captain. You seem . . . uninjured. I am at something of a loss to understand it, however." McCoy explains that he had injected Kirk with a drug that mimicked the effects of death. He then remarks, "There's just one thing, Mr. Spock. You can't tell me that when you first saw Jim alive that you weren't on the verge of giving us an emotional scene that would've brought the house down." Spock replies, "Merely my quite logical relief that Starfleet had not lost a highly proficient Captain." McCoy is incredulous: "Of course, Mr. Spock. Your reaction was quite logical . . . In a pig's eye."

McCoy's right. But Spock's purely "logical relief" is an excellent description of the kind of affection the Stoics would allow. We shouldn't believe that the continuation of Kirk's life is in and of itself good. A long life, like stacks of latinum, may be good or bad, beneficial or harmful, depending on how it's used. Spock doesn't want to give the impression that he has any irrational attachment to Kirk. He is "pleased" that Kirk is alive because this enables Kirk to continue his stellar performance as a Starfleet captain and as Spock's friend.

There's a similar scene in "The *Galileo* Seven" (*TOS*). While trying to flee Taurus II, Spock and the surviving members of a landing party are physically restrained by the giant inhabitants. They manage to break free by firing the shuttle's boosters but waste vital fuel in the process. Once in orbit, there's only enough fuel to maintain it for forty-five minutes. After that the shuttle will re-enter the atmosphere and burn up unless they're rescued. Spock makes a bold move. He jettisons the remaining fuel and ignites it, hoping the *Enterprise* will see the flare. Once back on board the ship, Kirk presses him on this strategy:

KIRK: There's really something I don't understand about all this, and maybe you can explain to me—logically, of course. When you jettisoned the fuel and you ignited it, you knew that there was virtually no chance of it being seen, and yet you did it, anyhow. Now, that would seem to me to be an act of desperation.

SPOCK: Quite correct, Captain.

KIRK: Now, we all know, and I'm sure the doctor will agree with me, that desperation is a highly emotional state of mind. How does your well-known logic explain that?

SPOCK: Quite simply, Captain. I examined the problem from all angles, and it was plainly hopeless. Logic informed me that under the circumstances, the only possible action would have to be one of desperation. Logical decision, logically arrived at.

KIRK: Aha-ha-ha; I see. You mean, you reasoned that it was time for an emotional outburst.

SPOCK: Well, I wouldn't put it in exactly those terms, Captain, but those are essentially the facts.

KIRK: You're not going to admit that for the first time in your life, you committed a purely human, emotional act?

SPOCK: No, sir.

KIRK: Mr. Spock, you're a stubborn man.

SPOCK: Yes, sir.

Spock is right this time. His desperation didn't cause him to jettison the fuel and ignite it—reason did. Desperation didn't even enter into it, for at no time did Spock mistake *what was not up to him* for *what was*.

"All Good Things Must Come to an End"

The root of the disagreement between Spock and Data is not only their views of emotion, but also their differing assessments of the goods of fortune. According to the Stoics, the conditions of our birth, the wealth and social status of our family, or our physical features, simply don't matter in the pursuit of happiness. All of these things, like material goods, can be used well or badly. Stoicism aims to show us how to use everything well. Once you learn this, you can be injured and insulted, but you can't be truly harmed, because what's ultimately valuable is what is up to you. You can even be imprisoned on Rura Penthe and deprived of everything that most people believe to be good, but you can still be happy—cold, tired, and hungry no doubt, but happy.[8]

Spock's remark in "Journey to Babel" that "humans smile with so little provocation" suggests that we're too often moved by circumstances. This isn't necessarily to say that we smile too much—thereby provoking Klingon Commander Kor's distrust— but that we're not masters of our pleasure, and conversely we're not masters of our pain. Circumstances move us like specks of foam on the waves. Vulcans prefer to see themselves as the wave and not the speck. That's what we find admirable about Spock: he refuses to be the plaything of fortune. Like the Stoic he shows us that there's something unconquerable and noble about our rational nature.

On the other hand, the ease with which we smile needn't be objectionable. We might take it as an acknowledgement of just how fragile human existence is, even at its most rational. The Peripatetics defend the commonsensical view that while happiness is mostly up to us, extreme misfortune can tear it away. You might be able to endure life on Rura Penthe, but it's not a good one, and you can't really be happy there. In such a case you'd be right to grieve the loss of your former life, your loved ones, and your possessions. From this point of view, we may still admire Spock's aspiration, even if we find it unrealistic. If human life is a vulnerable and sometimes tragic affair, the best we can do is to smile with little provocation, knowing that the value of life is caught up in its fragility.[9]

---

[8] See the writings of Admiral James Stockdale for vivid accounts of how he endured torture and imprisonment by relying on the teaching of the Stoics. An excellent fictional account of Stoic ethics in action can be found in Tom Wolfe, *A Man in Full* (New York: Farrar, Straus, 1998).

[9] I would like to thank the editors, Jason Eberl and Kevin Decker, along with my friends, Ralph Anske, Wilhelm Nightingale, and Andy Glasser for their many insightful suggestions and comments.

4

The Wrath of Nietzsche

SHAI BIDERMAN and WILLIAM J. DEVLIN

> **JOACHIM:** Sir, may I speak? We're all with you, sir. But consider this—We are free. We have a ship and the means to go where we will. We have escaped permanent exile on Ceti Alpha V. You have proved your superior intellect and defeated the plans of Admiral Kirk. You do not need to defeat him again.
>
> **KHAN:** He tasks me. He tasks me, and I shall have him. I'll chase him 'round the moons of Nibia and 'round the Antares maelstrom and 'round perdition's flames before I give him up.
>
> —*Star Trek II: The Wrath of Khan*

> The magnanimous person . . . appears to me as an extremely vengeful person who beholds satisfaction so close at hand and who drains it so fully and thoroughly to the last drop, in anticipation, that a tremendous and quick nausea follows this quick orgy, and he now rises "above himself," as they say, and forgives his enemy, and even blesses and honors him.
>
> —Friedrich Nietzsche, *The Gay Science*

Socrates tells us that "the unexamined life is not worth living." But this famous claim tells us more about what a worthwhile life isn't, than about what it actually is. And so we're left with further questions, each more vexing than the other: What does it take to create a meaningful life? Is there a universal answer, or is it a matter of personal decision? Where does one begin when attempting to seriously answer the question concerning the meaning of life? And what sort of answers can we find?

In the *Star Trek* series and movies, the meaningful life is generally presented in terms of the quest. The voyages of the starship *Enterprise* are quests of space exploration—voyages aimed at exploring the universe, searching for truth and knowledge in the final frontier, discovering strange new worlds, seeking out new life and new civilizations, and boldly going where no one has gone before. Space exploration becomes a metaphor for a meaningful life, insofar as the crew of the *Enterprise* lives meaningful lives investigating the universe.

Within this exploration-based context for understanding what makes a life meaningful, *Star Trek* also explores more specific philosophical questions that pertain to the topic of a meaningful life. We find that the series raises such questions as "How do I personally determine the meaning of my own life?"; "How should we ethically treat other life forms?"; "What is the right thing for me to do when others are in danger?" In *Star Trek II: The Wrath of Khan* (*TWOK*), the question is one of revenge. Does revenge help to construct a meaningful life, a life that is worth living, or does revenge obstruct an individual's pursuit of a meaningful life, an obstruction that may even eventually lead to the destruction of life itself?

"Galloping Around the Cosmos Is a Game for the Young, Doctor"

In *The Wrath of Khan*, the quest as metaphor for the search for a meaningful life reveals itself clearly at two levels. At the first, personal level, there's Admiral Kirk as "a fish out of water": Since his five-year mission has ended, his life has become less meaningful, despite his accomplishments and honors. Once the youngest captain in Starfleet history, Kirk now reflects on the meaning and purpose of his own life from the perspective of middle age. He's been promoted to admiral, but this promotion doesn't make him feel more fulfilled in his career. He's a father, but has no relationship with his son (who doesn't even know Kirk *is* his father). As McCoy puts it, Kirk treats his birthday "like a funeral," since he'd rather explore strange new worlds than waste his remaining years "flying a goddamn computer console." As an admiral, he currently feels he has lost an understanding of who he is, and thus control of his life. He longs to be back in *his* water, the waters of space exploration, so that he can achieve what he sees as his personally meaningful life.

At the second, "global" level, there is Project Genesis, the scientific experiment which creates "life from lifelessness" on a planetary scale. Here the quest for meaning through science suggests that a meaningful life involves creativity. Science no longer confines itself to simply explaining life as it is, but now also aims to give human beings the "power of creation." The project's name derives from one of the hundreds of creation accounts in world religions; particularly, the account found in the Biblical book of *Genesis*, in which God creates the world and all life in six days. But now, to McCoy's chagrin, God the creator is no longer necessary to scientists. "Genesis" now has only scientific (and human) connotations: *we* are the ones who have the ability to create "life from lifelessness" in nearly "*six minutes.*"

These themes of creating a meaningful life without appealing to God (through Kirk's endeavor to find meaning in his personal life or the scientist's quest to create new life) have much in common with Nietzsche's philosophy. For Nietzsche, God is irrelevant to the construction of a meaningful life. But this is not because Nietzsche simply ignores God; rather, Nietzsche famously maintains that "God is dead": God never existed aside from existing in creation myths such as the Bible (*The Gay Science*, aphorism 125). God is no more than a myth, according to Nietzsche, created by humans to comfort us in an uncertain world. The myth of God comforted us insofar as God's plan provided us with the universal meaning of life. But with the death of God, Nietzsche maintains, we collapse into nihilism and lose this solid ground for determining a meaningful life. We find "that becoming has no goal and that underneath all becoming there is no grand unity in which the individual could immerse himself completely as an element of supreme value."[1] For Nietzsche, we've lost the goal of human existence that God provided in the western tradition. We are thus challenged to create a meaningful life without appealing to God as the foundation. And while Nietzsche found humans of the late nineteenth century unpre-

---

[1] Friedrich Nietzsche, *The Will to Power* (New York: Vintage Books, 1967), p. 13.

pared for this challenge—as he maintains that he has "come too early" to announce the death of God (*The Gay Science*, aphorism 125)—we find that the humans of the twenty-third century in the relentlessly secular *Star Trek* universe seem quite ready for the challenge.

The third member of *The Wrath of Khan*'s fatal triangle is Khan Noonien Singh, "a product of late twentieth-century genetic engineering." He first appeared in "Space Seed" (*TOS*) as the rebellious and unwanted heir of positive achievements.[2] After his attempt to murder Kirk and commandeer the *Enterprise*, Khan and his followers are sentenced to a lifetime of exile on Ceti Alpha V. Once a habitable environment, the planet becomes a wasteland after its sister planet explodes, and Khan loses many of his people in the ensuing years, including his "beloved wife," former *Enterprise* crewmember Marla McGivers.[3] In *The Wrath of Khan*, Khan and his remaining crew are able to escape by hijacking the starship *Reliant* and he learns of Project Genesis. Now in control of his own starship, Khan has two goals: to steal Genesis and, perhaps more importantly, to exact revenge on *Admiral* Kirk. Khan blames Kirk, who "never bothered to check on our progress," for sending "seventy of us into exile on this barren sand heap."

Khan thus faces a dilemma: having already defeated Kirk by escaping from exile, should he now pursue freedom by creating a new life for himself and his people, or lead his people towards pursuing his personal revenge against Kirk? More importantly, as far as the question of a meaningful life is concerned: Can we say that Khan is faced with two equally meaningful projects—that of creation and rehabilitation, or that of revenge? Can revenge be a meaningful project?

---

[2] *The Wrath of Khan* takes place fifteen years after the exile imposed by Kirk began. Michael Okuda points out in his text commentary on the *Wrath of Khan* DVD release that Khan didn't feel any malice towards Kirk for this punishment during the episode; in fact, Khan alluded to Milton's words for Lucifer in *Paradise Lost*: "It is better to rule in hell than serve in heaven." Khan's revenge grows over the fifteen years in exile and the losses he had to deal with during his struggle for survival.

[3] The trials Khan and his people endure during their fifteen-year exile are chronicled in Greg Cox's novel, *To Reign in Hell: The Exile of Khan Noonien Singh* (New York: Pocket Books, 2005).

"Revenge Is a Dish that Is Best Served Cold"

We begin by laying down a definition of revenge in order to answer this question. Francis Bacon describes revenge as a "kind of wild justice, which the more man's nature runs to, the more ought law to weed it out."[4] Contemporary philosopher Robert Nozick agrees with Bacon: revenge is considered *personal* (I seek vengeance because you did something harmful to me), and so involves the goal of producing "a psychological effect in the person who seeks revenge."[5] That is, the purpose of revenge, according to Nozick, is to achieve the personal and particular emotional state of finding pleasure and satisfaction in the suffering of others. Nozick maintains that one should always choose *retribution* over revenge, since retribution is the non-emotional and universal pursuit of justice. Retribution is more "tame" and localized than revenge, since it limits its aim to the achievement of justice. Revenge, as a kind of "wild justice" that seeks out the suffering of others, is morally bad and so should be avoided and even outlawed by society.

On the one hand, this picture of revenge suggests that it's not a meaningful project. Khan's yearning to avenge himself upon Kirk is just a subjective emotional state that we, as a society, cannot tolerate in its consequences. Though we can perhaps sympathize with Khan, in order for it to become a project that we can accept as meaningful, the wild justice has to become tamed so that it takes the form of *retributive justice*. Khan shouldn't seek vengeance; rather, he should bring Kirk to a Federation court to be put on trial for negligence.[6]

On the other hand, we can't ignore the fact that despite being condemned by the social order, revenge could nevertheless yield a result which will satisfy the avenger and make his life meaningful. Since we may sympathize with Khan's anger

---

[4] Francis Bacon, *The Essays* (Harmondsworth: Penguin, 1985), p. 72.

[5] Robert Nozick, *Philosophical Explanations* (Cambridge: Harvard University Press, 1981), p. 368.

[6] Khan might have a good chance of showing that Kirk is guilty of negligence, and even abuse of power. In "Space Seed," Kirk first *drops* all the "charges and specifications" against Khan, which McCoy agrees he has the authority to do as vested by Starfleet Command. However, having dropped all the charges against Khan, it appears that Kirk exceeds his authority in then *sentencing* Khan and his people to exile.

and with his desire to destroy the arrogant and self-centered Kirk, it doesn't take a stretch of the imagination to see Khan as the protagonist of the film (much like Beatrix Kiddo in *Kill Bill* or Paul Kearsey in *Death Wish*). But in order for this to work, we have to be convinced that the feelings of vengeance are not only genuine, but also *productive*. Revenge must be seen as an obstacle that has to be overcome—it's something that must be addressed, dealt with, and then moved beyond, as one creates a meaningful life. For revenge to be part of a meaningful project, the hero seeking revenge must be able to move beyond their vengeful feelings and lead a fruitful and meaningful life afterwards. Khan can follow Joachim's advice, suggested in this chapter's opening quote: by defeating Kirk's plans to keep him in exile, Khan can simply acknowledge that he has demonstrated "his superior intellect" and then move beyond his feelings of vengeance by leading his people to a new place to begin a new and meaningful life. Unfortunately, this isn't his plan. Khan becomes so blinded by revenge that he has no concern for moving beyond revenge, or for creating a meaningful life. Eventually his wrath leads to his demise, and to that of his followers.

Friedrich Nietzsche (1844–1900) has some things to say about the empty and meaningless pit of revenge into which Khan falls. Nietzsche analyzes the appetite for revenge within the context of morality. Nietzsche, as we've seen, was critical of morality traditionally grounded by reference to God. The Biblical account of God portrays Him as all knowing, all powerful, and absolutely good, and so He serves as the moral lawmaker and judge. We human beings have as an example the universal and absolute moral code given to us by God, the truth of which is guaranteed by God's authority. But remember that, for Nietzsche, God is "dead." Thus, the mere supposition of God's existence isn't a guarantee that our moral code is absolutely true. On the contrary, for Nietzsche, once we remove God, our morality becomes so open to debate that there are no moral "facts . . . only interpretations" (*The Will to Power*, p. 267). Morality becomes one of the tools used in the world, a world that, without God, is seen as a battleground of contradicting *wills to power*. For Nietzsche, the "will to power" is the dominant force maintaining life: each living thing possesses a will and attempts to force its own rule and interpretation over others.

As a tool in this battle of wills, then, morality has the function of enslaving some, and empowering others—Nietzsche's infamous master-slave relationship. For Nietzsche, those who see morality as a source of empowerment, which is used to distinguish between things that are good and bad for them, belong to the *master morality.* This moral view endorses such values as individual strength, aristocratic power, and honor. Meanwhile, those who cling to the absoluteness of moral truths are made weak, enslaved—they're part of a *slave morality.* They follow what Nietzsche calls the *herd*—a moral conformity that keeps its members from creating a meaningful life. This moral view endorses such values as weakness, humble poverty, and meekness. Through such values, the weak "slaves" thus cling to morality for the comforting, but false, safety it offers, enslaving themselves to a thoughtless and uncreative life, while the strong "masters" dominate it.[7]

The world as will to power is thus a battleground of opposing groups, the master morality and slave morality, where each group vies for power over the other, and more importantly for our case, each individual vies for power over their own self, in the sense of maintaining their autonomy and self-legislation. This struggle for power brings us to the notion of revenge. For Nietzsche, revenge is an indication of weakness and enslavement, insofar as one becomes chained to their feelings of vengeance. Nietzsche describes this feeling as one of *ressentiment,* or the resentful use of revenge, where a person is so strongly overwhelmed by revenge that it stews within him. He is consumed with vengeance, and cannot make room for any other feelings or plans in life. All of his thoughts and actions are devoted to having his day of revenge. This is true of the individuals of the slave morality who are so overwhelmed by being dominated by the master morality, that they have a deep seated hatred towards the members of the master class, and so only focus their drive on vengeance. The slave thus becomes not only a slave to the masters, but he also becomes a slave to his feeling of vengeance. He is deprived of any other "direct outlet of action" and so is compensated by "an imaginary vengeance" and treats it as an absolute value that will provide

---

[7] Friedrich Nietzsche, *The Genealogy of Morals* (New York: Doubleday, 1956).

him with satisfaction and happiness (*The Genealogy of Morals*, p. 170).

It may seem that Nietzsche takes a cynical view of a meaningless world. But while his vision may seem nihilistic and cynical, Nietzsche claims that life as the will to power is inherently valuable. Behind the struggles for power, lies the essence of the world: the desire to affirm life. Nietzsche tells us that we must face reality and accept it, as harsh as it is, so we may transcend it or *overcome* it. For him, life is "that which must always overcome itself" in the sense that we must "struggle" through its harshness so that it can ultimately be affirmed.[8] By transcending good and evil, one reaches a more advanced level of existence. Nietzsche is not talking here about a more technologically advanced state of being, but rather a transcendent attitude towards life. This is the perspective of fully valuing life itself and one's relation towards life. Nietzsche calls the person who adopts such a perspective the *Overman*.[9] The Overman represents the highest level of development and expression of intellectual, emotional, and physical strength. By overcoming traditional views and values, he creates new values for the future. Like a man reaching the top of Mount Everest who feels as if the entire world lays at his feet, so does the Overman stand at the epitome of achievement and creativity, where the entirety of human experience is revealed to him. Embracing the deep understanding that unity of creation and destruction is necessary, the Overman can accept even the most terrible and questionable qualities of life as an inseparable part of life. This allows the Overman to create his own meaning, which is expressed with an affirmation, a resounding and joyous cry of the "sacred Yes" to life as "the game of creation" (*Thus Spoke Zarathustra*, p. 139). This will to affirm life, in turn, includes the power to overcome revenge. By creating his own meaning, the Overman not only moves beyond good and evil, but also

---

[8] Nietzsche, *Thus Spoke Zarathustra*, in *The Portable Nietzsche* (New York: Viking, 1954), p. 227.

[9] In "Borderland" (*ENT*), an "Augment" like the genetically enhanced Khan refers to Nietzsche, and suggests that he and his fellow Augments embody Nietzsche's concept of the Overman insofar as humanity must be transcended, and they are the ones to do it. For further discussion of genetic enhancement as a means of transcending humanity, see Chapter 6 in this volume.

beyond feelings of vengeance, as he completes the task of saying "Yes!" to life.

"I've Hurt You . . . And I Wish to Go On Hurting You"

Khan, as you may recall, has a dilemma: Should he choose the creation of a new life, perhaps by using Genesis to create a new world for his people, or the destruction of an old one, through revenge on Kirk? This dilemma between creation and destruction can be resolved by examining Khan in terms of Nietzsche's Overman. Is Khan an Overman? Some key factors in his background may lead us to believe he's a leading contender for the role. First, Khan is a genetically enhanced human being, and so represents the highest level of intellectual, emotional, and physical strength (albeit genetically engineered strength) that characterizes the Overman. Khan's superhuman abilities are demonstrated through his actions in the film: he is able to lead his people through years of exile, free them from the barren wastelands, and devise a plan to kill Kirk and capture Genesis.

Khan further represents the Overman insofar as he has overcome the traditional views of morality, and the conceptual dichotomy between slave and master moralities. He doesn't determine the best course of action by appealing to absolute truth or the notion of what's the right way to act in terms of being absolutely good. Hence, he isn't enslaved in the herd. Khan has moved "beyond good and evil" insofar as he no longer plays the human game of moral values. Unlike Dr. McCoy, for instance, Khan doesn't have moral reservations about using Genesis. With his superhuman attributes, he leads himself and his people towards new values and new meaning in life, values and meaning determined by him alone.

But something is holding Khan back from becoming an Overman. From Khan's perspective, Kirk still holds power over his life. Considering the trials and tribulations of his fifteen-year exile, Khan believes that Kirk "tasks" him to take their battle even further. The struggle between these two wills-to-power isn't over yet. For Khan, there's one more step that needs to be taken: he's willing to chase Kirk "'round the moons of Nibia and 'round the Antares maelstrom and 'round perdition's flames" until he has his revenge.

Khan thus resolves his dilemma by seeking vengeance on Kirk. But this decision is in stark contrast to the choices of Nietzsche's Overman. By seeking revenge on Kirk, Khan is leading his life and the lives of his followers towards a destructive and nihilistic end. Although the idea of revenge provides security for him, its all-consuming nature strips him of his power, his control, and his freedom to independently create a meaningful life. The idea of revenge becomes "dearer to him than self-preservation."[10] Enchained to this one single life-destroying, and hence self-destructing desire, Khan's superior intellect becomes clouded by his superior passion. He becomes, "human, all too human" for Nietzsche, in the sense that he's so deeply a member of the herd that he can't create a positive meaning that reflects the underlying affirmation of life. Like the slave, Khan becomes driven by the false belief in the absolute value of revenge. He falsely believes that it will provide him satisfaction and happiness, and so obeys it unquestioningly, thereby annihilating the creative abilities central to his freedom.

The culmination of Khan's plummet into the slave mentality comes as he loses the freedom of the Overman to create the meaning of his life. Khan's drive for vengeance is so deep that it culminates in his choice to use Genesis, the very tool that he could use to create life, to try to destroy Kirk, the *Enterprise,* and even his own people. Forever lost from the hopes and dreams of creating meaning in one's life, reaching the Nietzschean step of the Overman, and affirming life, Khan chooses the extreme opposite. By launching Genesis to destroy all the life around him, he stamps a negation and denial upon life with a resounding "No!" in his final words: "No, you can't get away. From hell's heart, I stab at thee. For hate's sake . . . I spit my last breath . . . at thee."

Meaning: The Final Frontier

Khan serves as a test case for Nietzsche's explanation of how an individual can create a meaningful life. In Nietzsche's terms,

---

[10] Echoing the words of Thucydides, when he portrays the hubristic downfall of Athens in the Peloponnesian war. Thucydides, *History of the Peloponnesian War, Books 1–3* (New York: Leavitt, Trow, 1848), 3.82.

Khan fails to create a meaningful life precisely because his feelings of vengeance overwhelm him, subsuming his pursuit of a meaningful life to the ultimate destruction of his own life and the life of his people.

And so Khan, who at first looked promising in fulfilling Nietzsche's vision of the Overman, falls short of adopting this perspective towards life. But though Nietzsche would reject Khan's candidacy as an Overman, we wonder whether Spock, the hero of the film who sacrifices his own life to save the lives of the crew aboard the *Enterprise*, is—surprisingly—a better candidate. Spock's actions become a mirror image of Khan's: while Khan attempts to "sacrifice" himself to kill Kirk and thus negate life, Spock sacrifices himself in an act that affirms life. Spock's attitude toward his own death is more like that of an Overman. Nietzsche would probably find that logical.

5
Mind Your Ps and Qs: Power, Pleasure, and the Q Continuum

ROBERT ARP

If you could get away with doing something that you know is wrong or bad, even heinously wrong or bad, would you do it? It's no shock that some people will answer yes, while others will answer no. And it's no shock when we discover bad people doing bad things because there was no one around to catch them or prevent them from doing those things.

What comes as a shock to us, however, are those situations where we thought some person was essentially a good person, but then later find out that this good person did something incredibly bad, and would have continued to do bad things had they not been caught. This probably shocks us because we commonly think that bad people are the authors of bad deeds while good people do good deeds. This causes us to ask a further question: If an essentially good person was given the power to get away with something bad, could he be corrupted by the lure of that power to actually do it?

In the *Star Trek* stories, the Q are a race of apparently all-powerful, all-knowing, immortal, god-like beings that exist in a parallel universe known as the "Q Continuum." Most people are intrigued by the possibility of having unlimited power to go where they please and do whatever they want. What an awesome life that would be! Or, would it?

Will Power Spoil Commander Riker?

Plato (427–347 B.C.E.) explored questions like these in his famous dialogue *Republic*, especially in its story of the Ring of

Gyges. Glaucon, a student of Socrates, tells the tale of Gyges, a shepherd who happens upon a ring that gives him the power of invisibility. Gyges gets himself appointed as emissary to the king of Lydia, and using the ring's power, seduces the queen, kills the king, and becomes king himself. Glaucon then claims:

> Suppose now that there were two such magic rings, and the just [person] put on one of them and the unjust [person] the other; no man can be imagined to be of such an iron nature that he would stand fast in justice. No man would keep his hands off what was not his own when he could safely take what he liked out of the market, or go into houses and lie with any one at his pleasure, or kill or release from prison whom he would, and in all respects be like a god among men. Then the actions of the just would be as the actions of the unjust; they would both come at last to the same point. And this we may truly affirm to be of a great proof that a man is just, not willingly or because he thinks that justice is any good to him individually, but of necessity, for wherever any one thinks that he can safely be unjust, there he is unjust.[1]

This passage brings to mind *Star Trek* episodes where Q, he of the ultimate "magic ring," goes about meddling with people's lives, frustrating their desires, and, in general, menacing the crew of the *Enterprise-D*. Q's actions, in general, run the gamut from being annoying to clearly being morally unjust. For example, in the episode "Déjà Q" the crew must deal with the fact that Q has become mortal and demands asylum on board the *Enterprise*. Far more seriously, in "Encounter at Farpoint," because they are members of "grievously savage race," Q transports the crew into an obviously biased trial situation against their will. Near the end of the episode, Q also tries to goad Picard into destroying the citizens of Farpoint for their supposed treachery. In "Q Who?" Q transports the *Enterprise* into a confrontation with the Borg, and in "The Q and the Grey" he abducts Janeway with the intent of having her be the mother of his child, a child that will supposedly avert a civil war in the Q Continuum.

Because of Q's actions, communities have their way of life threatened, people are transported into psychologically, emo-

---

[1] Plato, *The Republic* (New York: Vintage, 1991), lines 360b–d.

tionally, and physically damaging situations, promises are broken, and crewmembers and other life forms are killed. If Q were likened to a human, he would be classified a tyrannical sociopath with a self-centered, insensitive, dysfunctional, and disordered personality. Consider Q's obnoxious and highly insensitive comment to the crew in "Hide and Q": "Oh, your species is always suffering and dying." The comment is made as if suffering and dying are things that humans should just "get over already." The evidence of Q's sociopathological personality causes Picard, in the episode "Déjà Q," to justifiably if mistakenly blame Q for Bre'el IV's moon falling out of orbit. Picard asks of Q: "What kind of twisted pleasure does it give you to bring terror into their lives?" In that same episode, Q claims that *torment* is a subjective term, and that "one creature's torment is another creature's delight."

In the spirit of Plato's Ring of Gyges story, we can contrast Q's "unjust" personality with that of one of the crew's "just" personalities. Was Q always a somewhat evil or self-centered being, or did he become that way as a result of his powers? We could see how an evil person would easily do evil things, if given enough power and time. On the other hand, is Glaucon correct and would a member of the *Enterprise*, whose personality seems generally just and good, eventually act the same way if that person were given enough power and time?

This theme is addressed in the aforementioned "Hide and Q." In that episode, Riker is given Q-like powers, and he uses them to save his crewmates as well as grant them what he perceives as their deepest "wishes." Picard, however, expresses concern that Riker may abuse his power and warns him that "power corrupts." In other words, Picard thinks that Riker is a good and just man *without* Q-like powers, but he fears that Riker will become a bad and unjust man *with* Q-like powers.

Interestingly enough, Riker uses his Q-like powers to help his friends, rather than help himself to the women on the ship or command of the *Enterprise*. This *Star Trek* story would seem to call into doubt Glaucon's claims about power corrupting the just person. Riker's actions would seem to be a counterexample to Glaucon's claim that "the actions of the just would be the same as the unjust" if both had the power to do what they wanted: as a just person, Riker does not become "drunk" with this power and abuse it in the way that Q seems to.

However, Glaucon could mount two responses to the Riker counterexample. First, he could say that there is a huge difference between what people do in stories and what people do in reality. Riker is just a character in a story and further, story telling with morals is about what ought to be the case, rather than what actually *is* the case. Glaucon might point to actual cases in history when good people who have been given a lot of power eventually abuse that power. Someone could further counter Glaucon by showing that the abusers actually had bad personalities or poor characters in the first place. Or, they could point to seemingly good people, in actual history, who did not let the power "go to their heads," so to speak.[2]

Second, Glaucon could say that Riker was not given enough time to experience the corrupting influence of his absolute power. At first, even though he helped his friends, eventually Riker would abuse his power just like some unjust person. In fact, Glaucon could point to Picard's cautioning Riker about the abuse of such a power as indicative of the fact that, with time, Riker would abuse the power he has been given.

In the end, someone might respond by saying that powers like that of the Q or the Ring of Gyges are impossible, so the entire debate is moot. No one has these kinds of power, so we could never offer concrete evidence to show whether Glaucon's claim is either true or false. However, Glaucon's point still seems to hold with respect to limited forms of power. In life, people sometimes have *just enough* power to get away with murder, stealing, or persecuting others. And maybe the real point of the Ring of Gyges and Q stories is to be aware of the possibility of the abuse of power. If some good person is fortunate to be given power, this awareness of its possible abuse should always be at the forefront of that person's mind. Alternatively, we

---

[2] See the accounts of the lives of the Greek tyrants Solon, Cylon, and Peisistratus in Antony Andrewes, *The Greek Tyrants* (New York: Harper and Row, 1963). Also, Leo Strauss, *On Tyranny* (Chicago: University of Chicago Press, 1961). It's been said that Jimmy Carter was a moral man who, having the power of the American presidency, did not allow this power to corrupt his moral fiber. See Douglas Brinkley, *The Unfinished Presidency: Jimmy Carter's Journey to the Nobel Peace Prize* (New York: Penguin, 1999). On the other hand, see Steven Hayward, *The Real Jimmy Carter: How Our Worst Ex-President Undermines American Foreign Policy, Coddles Dictators, and Created the Party of Clinton and Kerry* (New York: Regnery, 2004).

should be mindful not to give a bad person the kind of power that can be easily abused. Insofar as this is the case, no one person or group of persons should have powers so unwieldy that injustices occur as a result of that power.

"It's Wondrous, with Treasures to Satiate Desires both Subtle and Gross"

Over the course of the Q stories in *Star Trek*, the theme emerges that the Q are fairly miserable in their existence. This misery manifests itself in one of two ways. Either the Q are frustrated or they are bored. In other words, their existence is painfully corrupted. With respect to frustration, at the end of almost every Q story, a Q leaves the *Enterprise* (or *Voyager* as the case may be) frustrated because someone on the ship didn't do what the Q wanted, or events didn't unfold the way they anticipated. With respect to boredom, the episode "Death Wish" (*VGR*) features a Q named Quinn who is so bored with his existence that he wants to become mortal so that he can commit suicide. Perhaps this underlying misery associated with a Q's existence is *directly related* to the Q's pursuit of pleasure, with the paradoxical result that they discover pain throughout their immortal lifetimes.

This brings us to the *hedonistic paradox*.[3] The basic idea here is that, as a general rule, whenever pleasure itself is the object of our life's search, either it is not found or it is found. If pleasure is not found, the result is the pain associated with not finding the pleasure one seeks. On the other hand, if pleasure is found, especially on a consistent basis, the result is (surprisingly!) still pain. The pain results from either finding pains that we *mistake for* pleasures in the long or short term, or from the *boredom* of always getting the pleasures we want. Either way, whether pleasure is found or not found, the paradoxical result is still pain. The hedonistic paradox is "hedonistic" because of the focus on the pleasure being sought (*hedon* is Greek for pleasure); it is a "paradox" because we consistently find the exact

---

[3] The term was first introduced by Henry Sidgwick, *The Methods of Ethics* (London: Macmillan, 1874); see also Fred Feldman, "Hedonism," in *Encyclopedia of Ethics*, edited by Lawrence Becker and Charlotte Becker (London: Routledge, 2001), pp. 100–113.

opposite (pain) of what we set out to find in the beginning (pleasure).

Is there any way out of the hedonistic paradox for a Q who wants to continue pursuing pleasure for the sake of pleasure itself? Q may not fall victim to the hedonistic paradox for a couple of reasons. One of the problems with pursuing pleasure is the boredom associated with having attained pleasure, after pleasure, after pleasure. In "Death Wish," Quinn bemoans this problem, claiming that everything has already been "learned and shared." Consequently, there is nothing pleasurable to be gained, because there is nothing new out there to be discovered. But what if Quinn was wrong, and there are *innumerable* pleasures to be had? This question is important because if the possibilities for pleasure are innumerable, then boredom wouldn't be an issue, since there would always be *one more possible* pleasure out there to experience. Putting the question another way, given the number of possible activities imaginable, and the pleasures associated with those activities, is it possible to exhaust all of those activities, gain the pleasures, and become bored with the pleasures attained?

It's easier for us to conceive of people not getting bored with their pleasurable pursuits around us in the real world. Maybe multi-millionaires like David Geffen, Brad Pitt, or Hugh Hefner won't ever become bored pursuing pleasure, after pleasure, after pleasure because they could never experience all the possible forms of pleasure *to be experienced* in their limited lifetimes. In other words, they will die before they will have become bored from having experienced all possible forms of pleasure.

Now it would seem that the Q, who live through all eternity, surely would become bored after a certain amount of time. Again, think of Quinn's boredom and how it becomes so oppressive that he wants to kill himself! But this boredom would depend upon whether a particular Q had experienced each and every possible pleasure to be experienced. If there were innumerable pleasures in the universe to be enjoyed then, even for an eternal Q, it seems as though it wouldn't be possible to achieve all of those pleasures and boredom would never occur. If one is inclined to think that the amount and range of possible pleasurable experiences are limited or finite, then it's more likely that boredom would result for a Q. Apparently, this is what happened to Quinn.

"In Apprehension, How Like a God!"

A way to clear up this problem might be to distinguish between two different senses of the words "pleasure" and "pain" the way that John Stuart Mill (1806–1873) does in his terrific book, *Utilitarianism*.[4] There are those "lower" pleasures and pains that are most appropriately understood as *feelings associated with a body*. Examples would be aches, pains, and "butterflies in the stomach" as well as euphoric surges and adrenaline rushes. Think of Kirk experiencing the bodily pain of getting beaten up by the Gorn or Tom Paris being sore after his wedding night with B'Elanna. When we normally think of pleasure and pain, we think of them in this bodily way, associated with the neurophysiological processes of a living animal.

Then there are "higher" pleasures and pains understood as *qualitative experiences associated with a mind*. Examples of these would include the pleasure of discovering the solution to a bedeviling math equation, the pain of having made an immoral decision that cannot be undone, or the pleasure of knowing love from a friend. Think of Spock's experience of satisfaction in beating the ship's computer at three-dimensional chess or Quark's joy in outwitting Odo. Here, the pleasures and pains take on more mental qualities, and have names like *joy, contentment, satisfaction, regret,* and *sorrow*.

It may be the case that Q, or anyone, could avoid the hedonistic paradox by either focusing on pleasures that are associated with bodily activities not likely to bring about harm, or by focusing on the activities themselves and allowing the pleasures to "come along for the ride," so to speak. We can imagine someone pursuing bodily pleasures that are not likely to bring about harm in the short or long term, such that a person is not *mistaking* a pleasure for a pain (as Kirk did in *The Undiscovered Country* after imbibing too much Romulan ale). At the same time, we can imagine someone constantly pursuing an activity that they know will bring about pleasure, but focusing on the activity itself (rather than the pleasure). In both cases, the hedonistic paradox might be avoided. In the first case, the paradox may be avoided because the pain associated with the pursuit of pleasure never actually occurs. The second case is more of a

---

[4] John Stuart Mill, *Utilitarianism* (Indianapolis: Hackett, 2002).

total avoidance of the paradox altogether, and seems to be how some wise people live their lives. Most people don't engage in some activity for the *sole reason* of the pleasure associated with it; they engage in the activity for the sake of the activity itself and then, as added icing on the cake, for the sake of the plea-sure that comes along with the activity. Some people do learn early on in their lives that a life where only pleasure is sought ends in misery.

Is it possible, in any way, to pursue pleasure and avoid the paradox? It's probably easier to see how a life of pursuing lower, bodily pleasures leads us into the pains of either not finding what we seek, mistaking pain for pleasure, or even boredom. However, could we fall victim to the hedonistic paradox if the pursuit of pleasure pertains to the higher, mental pleasures? Here, we can introduce an important distinction from Aristotle (384–322 B.C.E.) between pleasures that result from *on-going activities* and pleasures that result from *the knowledge of being in certain completed states.* Think of the kind of pleasure that results from solving a math equation, being loved by a friend, or beating the ship's computer at chess. These kinds of situa-tions are not really on-going activities; they are completed states of being, so to speak, where one has knowledge of these states. The knowledge of these states brings with it a sustaining, almost satiating, form of mental pleasure. Aristotle had something like this in mind when he investigated various forms of pleasure in his great work in moral philosophy entitled, *Nicomachean Ethics.*[5] It may be that bodily pleasures are more the result of on-going activities, while mental pleasures are more the result of being in a certain state.

With this distinction in mind, we may be able better to understand how hard-core mathematicians or true friends achieve satisfaction, contentment, or joy associated with these states. If math equations don't do it for you, think of some tough project, assignment, or task that you completed and were happy about having completed. Or, think of the runner who, having trained all of her life, actually finished the big marathon; the father of three who finally got his Masters in Business Administration through night school; or the hero who saved the

---

[5] Aristotle, *Nicomachean Ethics* (Oxford: Clarendon, 1908), Book X.

child from drowning. Now think of these folks reflecting upon their accomplishments with joy. Such joys would seem to be of the kind that, when reflected upon, last a lifetime. Aristotle's lesson is that when we have achieved a certain completed state, it would seem that the pleasure is continuous with our knowledge of the completion.

"Condemned to Be a Member of This Lowest of Species"

The Q get us thinking about what it would be like to do whatever we want and live forever. They also get us thinking about having unlimited power and unrestrained pursuit of pleasure. Obviously, all of this sci-fi is beyond human capacity. Yet in "Déjà Q," Q is "defrocked" by being turned into a human, and it is interesting that Q should claim that he has been "condemned to be a member of this lowest of species." In the context of this episode, it's the Q-like existence, not the moral, limited one, which looks like a condemnation. During "Hide and Q," Riker tells Q that humans are "driven to grow and learn." In a somewhat uncharacteristic moment, Q claims that the human race will become very powerful in years to come, in ways the "mighty" Q cannot imagine, and he wants Riker to join the Q Continuum so that they will be able to understand this drive. Maybe the very value and meaning in human life comes from *not* doing whatever we want, *not* living forever, as well as *not* having unlimited power or pursuit of pleasure. In other words, it is the very *lacking* of these things that propels or compels us to strive for truth, justice, goodness, and love. This "striving" probably accounts for at least part of the reason why Q is so intrigued by the human race, and why he makes his regular appearances in the *Star Trek* universe.

Starfleet Directive
TWO

*Go Boldly,
Yet Morally:
Federation Ethics*

6

"Killing Your Own Clone Is Still Murder": Genetics, Ethics, and Khaaaaan!

JASON T. EBERL

Stardate: 45470.1: The *Enterprise* makes contact with Moab IV, whose inhabitants are human colonists who left Earth over two hundred years ago to create a "masterpiece society." The colonists have genetically perfected themselves and, as part of their perfection, are genetically predetermined to fulfill specific social roles. All is well until the *Enterprise* crew shows the colonists what life is like outside of their isolated world and, as a result, many choose to leave the colony, which upsets the genetic balance. Captain Picard laments that they may have been more destructive to the colony than the stellar core fragment from which the *Enterprise* had saved it. But why did so many of the colonists want to leave? What did life among the genetically imperfect offer them? Why weren't they content to live their lives in the roles for which they were born and bred? In other words, why did the "masterpiece society" experiment ultimately fail?

In this chapter, we'll explore these and other questions through the lens of *Star Trek*'s myriad episodes and films which deal with genetic manipulation in two different forms: the *enhancement* of an individual's genetic inheritance, and the genetic replication process known as *cloning*. Given that we now have a complete map of the human genome, these previously sci-fi issues will soon become sci-*real*. And while there are a number of nightmare scenarios involving evil geneticists twirling their mustaches on some far-off, isolated island or in an underground laboratory, there's also a great deal of hope that such forms of genetic intervention may be the key to ameliorating or eliminating a number of maladies that afflict millions of human beings. *Star Trek* provides us with glimpses of both the negative and positive features of genetic enhancement and cloning.

"Improve Man, and You Gain a Thousand Fold"

It's natural for us to seek to improve ourselves. Who wouldn't want to be smarter, stronger, disease-free, or to live twice as long, or want these things for their children? Genetic intervention also holds out the promise of bringing below average, or just plain average, human beings up to an above average level. This is what Dr. Julian Bashir's parents did for him—or *to* him:

> I was six. Small for my age, a bit awkward physically, not very bright. In the first grade, when the other children were learning how to read and write and use the computer, I was still trying to tell a dog from a cat and a tree from a house . . . Over the course of the next two months my genetic structure was manipulated to accelerate the growth of neuronal networks in my cerebral cortex and a whole new Julian Bashir was born . . . My IQ jumped five points a day for over two weeks. Followed by improvements in my hand-eye co-ordination, stamina, vision, reflexes, weight, height. In the end, everything but my name was altered in some way. ("Dr. Bashir, I Presume," *DS9*)

This all sounds great and Bashir seems to live a happy life on Deep Space Nine, benefiting from his enhancements—except for having graduated *salutatorian* and not valedictorian from Starfleet Medical. Yet, when forced to face the truth about his genetic enhancements, he labels himself "'unnatural,' meaning 'not from nature.' 'Freak' or 'monster' would also be acceptable." He also considers himself, and all his professional accomplishments, "a fraud."

Not all forms of genetic intervention, however, involve attempts to perfect or enhance human nature. Advanced genetic mapping allows the Doctor on the *U.S.S. Voyager* to extrapolate the future appearance of Tom Paris and B'Elanna Torres's daughter. He's also able to detect an abnormal curvature of the child's spine and repair the defect long before she's born. In fact, the very ability of two persons from different species— humans, Klingons, Vulcans, Trills—to interbreed is a result of complex genetic manipulation ("Tears of the Prophets," *DS9*; "Terra Prime," *ENT*); so we have genetic science to thank for Mr. Spock and B'Elanna Torres, among many others. Let's explore the various promises and perils of this science in more detail.

After encountering the genetically perfected colony on Moab IV, Picard isn't shy about expressing his opinion of it: "They've managed to turn dubious scientific theory into dogma . . . They managed to breed out the unknown, self-discovery, things that make life worth living . . . They've traded their humanity" ("The Masterpiece Society," *TNG*). This is an odd reaction for our typically open-minded captain and it reflects the attitude many have when confronted with a picture of human life that is controlled, designed, determined, or perfected. Does Picard have a well-reasoned attitude to genetic science, especially in terms of the high ideals of the colony's founders?

One benefit of living on Moab IV is that there's no "wasted talent." Each person in the colony is designed to perform certain functions and grows up knowing exactly what their society needs from them. Riker complains that such predetermination "must take some of the fun out of it." But the colony's leader quickly responds, "Not at all. My entire psychological make-up tells me that I was born to lead. I am exactly what I would choose to be." Although the colonists' decisions appear to be predetermined, which is offensive to us who value our autonomy, they do in fact *choose* what they want to do with their lives—it just so happens that what they choose to do is the same as what their "designers" intended for them to do. The colonists' argument isn't necessarily that their way is better; instead they believe that they're no less free than each of us, who are likewise determined to a large extent by our genetic inheritance as well as the environment in which we're raised. The main difference, it seems, between the genetically and environmentally "programmed" choices we make and those that the colonists make is that our programming is the result of a random mixture of chromosomes and external influences largely outside of anyone's control; whereas the colonists' genome and environment are as completely under their control as possible.[1] Is the ran-

---

[1] It's simplistic to assume that we can control our offspring's physical and behavioral traits simply by manipulating their genome, for environmental

domness of nature any more efficient than, or morally preferable to, an unnatural process that's controlled by intelligent
minds?

One argument against the colonists' lifestyle appeals to the
"right to an open future":

> Parents must foster and leave the child with a range of opportuni-
> ties for choice of his or her own plan of life, with the abilities and
> skills necessary to pursue a reasonable range of those opportuni-
> ties and alternatives, and with the capacities for practical reasoning
> and judgment that enable the individual to engage in reasoned and
> critical deliberation about those choices.[2]

Worf, for example, gives lip-service to his son Alexander's
right to an open future when he says that it's up to Alexander
to decide whether he wants to be a Klingon warrior; yet, when
Alexander reaches the age of the First Rite of Ascension, Worf
pressures him to undergo the ritual even though Alexander is
adamant that he doesn't want to be a warrior. Worf makes a
good point, though, in telling Alexander that if he doesn't go
through with the ritual *now*, he'll close himself off to the option
of being a warrior if he ever changes his mind ("Firstborn,"
TNG).

The type of genetic and environmental manipulation that
occurs on Moab IV gives the appearance of preserving the
inhabitants' autonomy. It seems they're doing exactly what they
would want to do with their lives, because their desires have
been manipulated. But respect for one's right to an open future

---

factors, both social and physical, play a large role in determining how one's
genotype is expressed in one's phenotype—a person's observable traits. The
Moab IV colonists, however, have done their best to control relevant environmental factors as well. They reject the *Enterprise* crew's original plan to evac-
uate them claiming that they can't separate themselves from the planet
"without altering who and what we are," and object to a large portion of their
society leaving since they "are integrated and refined to such a degree that
even the slightest change can lead to chaos."

[2] Allen Buchanan, Dan W. Brock, Norman Daniels, and Daniel Wikler, *From
Chance to Choice: Genetics and Justice* (New York: Cambridge University
Press, 2000), p. 175. See Joel Feinberg, "The Child's Right to an Open Future,"
in *Whose Child? Children's Rights, Parental Authority, and State Power*, edited
by William Aiken and Hugh LaFollette (Totowa: Littlefield, Adams, 1980), pp.
124–153.

may prohibit shaping a person's desires in this fashion. An insidious form of such high-tech "brainwashing" is perpetrated by the Founders on the Dominion's Jem'Hadar soldiers. After finding a Jem'Hadar child on Deep Space Nine, Odo attempts to raise him not to be violent and hateful toward other species. Dax offers a word of caution, however: "The Founders may have removed his sense of free will. He may be nothing more than a genetically programmed killing machine." Kira concurs, "That boy was created in a laboratory. His body, his mind, his instincts are all designed to do one thing—to kill" ("The Abandoned," *DS9*). Eventually, Odo's worst fears are confirmed. So while the Jem'Hadar fight as Dominion soldiers in order to fulfill their own desire to kill based on xenophobic tendencies, these psychological features have been bred into them by the Founders as a means of control.[3]

But even if genetic interventions are pursued solely for the purpose of shaping a child's biological, and not psychological, characteristics, the potential for violating the right to an open future remains. When the Doctor shows B'Elanna and Tom a holographic image of their baby, B'Elanna is alarmed to see faint Klingon forehead ridges. She wants to genetically modify her child so she won't appear Klingon and have to suffer the indignities B'Elanna did as a young half-Klingon living among humans. The Doctor balks at her plan, claiming, "There's no reason to arbitrarily remove genetic sequences." And he cautions her about interfering with "genetic sequences that have evolved over centuries." B'Elanna immediately retorts, "Like curvature of the spine?" ("Lineage," *VGR*). Is it hypocritical for the Doctor to genetically modify B'Elanna and Tom's child to ameliorate her spinal defect, but not alter her Klingon appearance?

B'Elanna's concerns for her child echo those of parents who, born deaf, wish to undertake measures so that their children will be born deaf as well.[4] On the one hand, members of the deaf community argue that it'll be easier for parents and children to

---

[3] The Founders also ensure the Jem'Hadar's loyalty by genetically engineering an addiction to a substance—ketracel white—with which only the Founders can provide them ("Hippocratic Oath," *DS9*).

[4] The relevant measures would include the selection of embryos produced by *in vitro* fertilization, to implant in the mother's uterus only those embryos that test positive for the genetic sequence coding for deafness.

relate to one another if the entire family is deaf. Also, many who are deaf—along with others who are categorized as "disabled"—argue that genetically selecting *against* children who are deaf or otherwise disabled perpetuates negative stereotypes concerning the quality of life experienced by members of the disabled community.[5] On the other hand, if deafness is a disability that narrows a child's options for the future in terms of career and lifestyle choices, then deliberately seeking to procreate a deaf child would constitute a "moral harm."[6]

Genetic intervention, though, could be used to *protect* a child's open future by selecting against conditions which would severely limit her future career and lifestyle options. B'Elanna doesn't want her daughter "to start with a disadvantage." So, one could argue in favor of genetic *treatment* for conditions defined as "maladies."[7] Arik Soong—a geneticist who later turns cyberneticist and draws up the initial blueprints for our favorite android—challenges Captain Archer's negative view of genetic "engineering": "How can a supposedly intelligent species reject technology that would enhance ability, relieve suffering?" ("Borderland," *ENT*). He agrees with B'Elanna, who contends that "gene resequencing isn't a weapon, it's a tool," and he compares it to the use of nuclear technology. While such technology "could be perverted into a dreadful weapon"[8] by those with malicious intentions, it can also be a means of bettering human life if used properly. Archer's own father died from a degenerative disease that might have been cured through genetic treatment. Like Soong and B'Elanna, many bioethicists believe, "It is

---

[5] See Adrienne Asch, "Prenatal Diagnosis and Selective Abortion: A Challenge to Practice and Policy" *American Journal of Public Health* 89 (1999), pp. 1649–657.

[6] See Dena Davis, "Genetic Dilemmas and the Child's Right to an Open Future" *Hastings Center Report* 27 (1997), pp. 7–15.

[7] The concept of a "malady" is itself a subject of much debate among philosophers of biology and those in the medical field; see Charles M. Culver, "The Concept of Genetic Malady," in *Morality and the New Genetics*, edited by Bernard Gert (Boston: Jones and Bartlett, 1996), pp. 147–166.

[8] This is David Marcus's concern regarding the Genesis device he and his mother invent to help solve the "cosmic problems of population and food supply" by converting dead moons into living, habitable planets. If used "where life already exists, it would destroy such life in favor of its new matrix" (*Star Trek II: The Wrath of Khan*).

hard to think of any objection to using genetic engineering to eliminate defects, and there is a clear and strong case for its use."[9]

"Superior Ability Breeds Superior Ambition"

Star Trek also presents us with a group of genetically enhanced "supermen" who don't represent simply the perfection of humanity's genetic constitution, as with the Moab IV colonists, but who are designed to be superior to their human progenitors: Khan Noonien Singh and the other Augments. While originally products "of late twentieth century genetic engineering," many Augments were stored as frozen embryos after the Eugenics Wars.[10] Arik Soong had thawed and bred a number of Augments in order to usher in a new era for humanity.[11] He argues to Archer, "They're the future. Smarter, stronger, free from disease, with life-spans twice yours and mine" ("Borderland," *ENT*), and he tells his Augment children, "Someday you will fulfill humanity's promise" ("Cold Station 12," *ENT*).

Star Trek often focuses on the negative effects of genetic enhancement in creating an "us versus them" attitude between "*trans*humans" and the rest of us average human beings. Archer warns Soong that "whenever a group of people believe they're better than everyone else, the result is always the same." And the Augments' evident disregard for human life bears witness as Soong's children turn against even him: "Augments should be led by Augments . . . He'll never be one of us" ("Cold Station 12," "The Augments," *ENT*). Malik, the Augments' leader, tells Archer, "We no longer care what happens to you"—meaning *humanity*—and quotes Friedrich Nietzsche: "mankind is something to be surpassed."

---

[9] Jonathan Glover, "Questions About Some Uses of Genetic Engineering," in *Bioethics: An Anthology*, edited by Helga Kuhse and Peter Singer (Oxford: Blackwell, 2006), p. 190; from his book *What Sort of People Should There Be?* (Harmondsworth: Penguin, 1984).

[10] The term "eugenics" is derived from the Greek word *genos*, "offspring," and the prefix *eu-*, meaning "good."

[11] Arik Soong apparently passed on his deference for Khan Noonien Singh as his great-grandson, Data's creator, is named Noonien Soong. It's ironic, though, that Data is superior to humans in many ways, but "would gladly give it up, to be human" ("Encounter at Farpoint," *TNG*).

But is this a valid interpretation of Nietzsche's famous dictum? A common view is that Nietzsche provides the philosophical foundation for eugenic selection programs, including the Holocaust perpetrated by the Nazis.[12] Paul Cohn, an early promoter of eugenics, asserts,

> A sound system of eugenics will prevail . . . [Science] will be harnessed to the service of the Superman.[13] Thus Nietzsche's true leaders, the men of strong and beautiful bodies, wills and intellects, will be developed.[14]

Nietzsche, through his literary mouthpiece, Zarathustra, appears to agree with this sentiment:

> All beings so far have created something beyond themselves; and do you want to be the ebb of this great flood and even go back to the beasts rather than overcome man? What is the ape to man? A laughing-stock or a painful embarrassment. And man shall be just that for the overman . . . You have made your way from worm to man, and much in you is still worm. Once you were apes, and even now, too, man is more ape than any ape.[15]

Yet, Zarathustra also proclaims, "I love man." The Superman/Overman will *care* for humanity, just as humanity is supposed to care for other animals.

More recent and careful interpretations of Nietzsche note the indissoluble link between the "Superman/Overman" of tomorrow and the human of today:

> The transhuman condition is not about the transcendence of the human being . . . When Nietzsche asks his 'great' question, what may still become of man?, he is speaking of a future that does not

---

[12] See William L. Shirer, *The Rise and Fall of the Third Reich* (New York: Simon and Schuster, 1960), pp. 100, 111.

[13] There are various translations of Nietzsche's term *Übermensch*, including both "superman" and "overman."

[14] Paul V. Cohn, "Belloc and Nietzsche" *New Age* 12 (1913), p. 215; as quoted in Dan Stone, *Breeding Supermen: Nietzsche, Race and Eugenics in Edwardian and Interwar Britain* (Liverpool: Liverpool University Press, 2002), p. 66.

[15] Friedrich Nietzsche, *Thus Spoke Zarathustra*, in *The Portable Nietzsche* (New York: Penguin, 1976), Prologue, §3.

cancel or abort the human, but one which is necessarily bound up with the inhuman and the transhuman.[16]

The key issue for Nietzsche is the unavoidable fact that humanity is continuing to evolve: it's not the *transcendence* of humanity he seeks, but its *transfiguration*. We're not the ultimate species of rational animals to exist on this planet: "Man is a rope, tied between beast and overman—a rope over an abyss [i.e., the real possibility of extinction] . . . What is great in man is that he is a bridge and not an end" (*Zarathustra*, Prologue, §4).

Nietzsche's call for humanity to be "surpassed" isn't necessarily a call for a new, genetically perfected or enhanced, species to replace us. Rather, Nietzsche exhorts humanity to transform itself culturally and philosophically: "I love him who lives to know, and who wants to know so that the overman may live some day" (*Zarathustra*, Prologue, §4). In other words, we're to "engineer," or cultivate, our evolution in *humanistic* and not just scientific ways. The "Superman/Overman" isn't an outsider who will enslave or eradicate humanity: he will *be* the human who transcends his own current nature. As Keith Pearson asserts, "The transhuman only becomes meaningful and intelligible when it involves an affirmation of the totality and fatality of human becoming [i.e., that we're products of natural history]. Considered in these terms genealogy can then be understood as moving beyond the call for any simple-minded, arbitrarily conceived, and uncultivated test of selection" (p. 108). And although Nietzsche calls for us to produce offspring superior to ourselves, doing so requires us to make ourselves superior: "You shall build over and beyond yourself, but first you must be built yourself, perpendicular in body and soul. You shall not only reproduce your self, but produce something higher" (*Zarathustra*, Part I, §20). The key is *mastery* over one's *self*, which is accomplished, not through technical artifice such as genetic engineering, but through *philosophy*:

The philosopher as *we* understand him, we free spirits—as the man of the most comprehensive responsibility who has the conscience for the collective evolution of mankind: this philosopher will make

---

[16] Keith Ansell Pearson, *Viroid Life: Perspectives on Nietzsche and the Transhuman Condition* (New York: Routledge, 1997), p. 163.

use of the religions for his work of education and breeding, just as he will make use of existing political and economic conditions.[17]

Nietzsche considers the human "spirit" to be physiologically based: "But the awakened and knowing say: body am I entirely, and nothing else; and soul is only a word for something about the body" (*Zarathustra*, Part 1, §4). Hence, the spiritual transformation of the species becomes a means to enhancing what we would call the human genotype, since the spiritual progress of each generation passes into the "blood" of their descendants:

> The problem I thus pose is not what shall succeed mankind in the sequence of living beings . . . but what type of man shall be *bred*, shall be *willed*, for being higher in value, worthier of life, more certain of a future.[18]

"It Is the Differences that Have Made Us Strong"

In our own history, we didn't experience the Eugenics Wars,[19] but an international eugenics movement did blossom in the late nineteenth and early twentieth centuries. Long before this, however, the Greek philosopher Plato outlined a program of eugenic breeding for the members of the Guardian class of his hypothetical *Republic*. He contends that "the best men must have sex with the best women as frequently as possible, while the opposite is true of the most inferior men and women" and that "the former's offspring must be reared and not the latter's."[20] Plato stipulates that any misbegotten offspring should be killed: "the children of inferior parents, or any child of the others that is born defective, they'll hide in a secret and unknown place, as is appropriate" (460c1–4). The reference to "a secret and unknown place" is a euphemism for exposing such newborns to the ele-

---

[17] Friedrich Nietzsche, *Beyond Good and Evil* (New York: Penguin, 1990), Part 3, §61.

[18] Friedrich Nietzsche, *The Antichrist*, in *The Portable Nietzsche*, Book I, §3.

[19] According to the *Star Trek* timeline, the Eugenics Wars have already come and gone without our noticing—the media must have been distracted by the latest celebrity debacle.

[20] Plato, *Republic* (Cambridge, Massachusetts: Hackett, 1992), Book V, lines 459d7–e1. Plato's republic, by the way, bears little resemblance to the copycat society on Platonius ("Plato's Stepchildren," *TOS*).

ments and leaving them to die, a practice not uncommon in ancient Greece—particularly in Sparta.

More recent history saw the application of eugenic ideals in laws and social customs devised both to promote those of "good stock" to have many children and to restrict the "genetically inferior" from having any children at all. Examples of the former are the "Better Baby" and "Fitter Family" contests held annually as part of the Indiana State Fair.[21] On the flip-side, those deemed "unfit" by government and health officials were often forced to undergo legally prescribed *sterilization*. This was particularly true of mentally disabled persons in state hospitals. In the notorious U.S. Supreme Court decision *Buck v. Bell* (1927), which judged eugenic sterilization laws to be constitutional, Justice Oliver Wendell Holmes famously stated that "three generations of imbeciles is enough." The eugenics movement ran afoul of world opinion after the horrors of eugenic practices in Nazi Germany came to light during the Nuremberg trials after World War II.[22] It was soon realized the degree to which bad science, racial prejudice, and the overreaching of state authority with respect to reproductive autonomy combined to produce a morally reprehensible practice.[23]

The goals of eugenics need not, however, be tainted by the misguided goals of racial purity and state control over reproductive autonomy. Contemporary genetic selection practices avoid the obviously negative aspects of eugenics while underwriting the exercise of parental autonomy and helping ensure open

---

[21] See Alexandra Stern, "Making Better Babies: Public Health and Race Betterment in Indiana, 1920–1935" *American Journal of Public Health* 92 (2002), pp. 742–752. For further information on eugenic practices in the state of Indiana, where the world's first eugenic sterilization law was passed in 1907, see http://www.bioethics.iupui.edu/Eugenics/index.htm. Indiana, however, was by no means the only U.S. state—nor the U.S. the only nation—to legally and socially sanction eugenic practices in the early twentieth century.

[22] See Benno Müller-Hill, "Lessons from a Dark and Distant Past," in *Genetic Counseling: Practice and Principles*, edited by Angus Clarke (London: Routledge, 1994), pp. 133–141; and Paul Weindling, "The Ethical Legacy of Nazi Medical War Crimes: Origins, Human Experiments, and International Justice," in *A Companion to Genethics*, edited by Justine Burley and John Harris (Oxford: Blackwell, 2004), pp. 53–69.

[23] For an "ethical autopsy" of the eugenics movement, see *From Chance to Choice*, Chapter 2.

futures for born children. Prenatal genetic diagnosis (PnGD) involves testing a sample of fetal DNA obtained through amniocentesis. If the fetus is diagnosed with a serious genetic malady, the parents have the option to treat the fetus prenatally, if a treatment is available, prepare themselves for the birth of a disabled or chronically ill child, or abort the fetus. Preimplantation genetic diagnosis (PiGD) is used in conjunction with *in vitro* fertilization to select embryos for implantation that aren't diagnosed with any serious genetic maladies.[24] The goal of both forms of genetic diagnosis is to provide parents, to the greatest degree possible, offspring who are healthy and won't succumb to early death because of a genetic malady.

A concern shared by many, particularly those in the disabled community, is that genetic diagnosis won't be used only for conditions which result in a disproportionately painful or short life, but for a variety of so-called "maladies," such as Down syndrome, which don't necessarily entail a life that's not worth living. Such reasoning must have stood behind the Augments' treatment of their brother Udar, who was left behind because they considered him "too weak" even though he was perfectly healthy, just not enhanced like his siblings. Bioethicist Adrienne Asch opposes prenatal testing and selective abortion for just the opposite reasons, "that life with disability is worthwhile and . . . that a just society must appreciate and nurture the lives of all people, whatever the endowments they may receive in the natural lottery" (p. 1652).

Geordi LaForge expresses this concern to a member of the Moab IV colony when she reacts to seeing his eyes after he removes his VISOR:

HANNAH: I'm sorry. I didn't mean to embarrass you.
GEORDI: I've never been embarrassed by this, Hannah. Never. I was born blind. I've always been this way . . . guess if I had been conceived on your world I wouldn't even be here now, would I?
HANNAH: No.
GEORDI: No. I'd have been terminated as a fertilized cell.

---

[24] See Bonnie Steinbock, "Preimplantation Genetic Diagnosis and Embryo Selection," in *A Companion to Genethics*, pp. 175–190.

HANNAH: It was the wish of our founders that no one have to suffer a life with disabilities.

GEORDI: Who gave them the right to decide whether or not I should be here? Whether or not I might have something to contribute?

Arguably, there's no *objective* measure of what makes a "life worth living"; it's up to each person to weigh the value of her own life for herself. Only a strict application of the *utilitarian* ethic would render judgments—especially future-oriented judgments—on what types of persons will contribute more to society than take away from it. As it happens, many perfectly "abled" persons might also fall on the negative side of such an equation.

Another potential negative effect of using either selection techniques or direct interventions to enhance offspring is damage to the parent-child relationship. Bashir not only feels like he's "unnatural" and "a fraud," but also like a *product* made-to-order by his parents. His perception is that, before his enhancements, he was a "grave disappointment" to them. After Bashir's "family secret" is discovered and his Starfleet career is threatened, his father is desperate to safeguard him; but Bashir doesn't read parental love in his father's protective scheming: "You're going to lose your only real accomplishment in life: me . . . You used to be my father. Now, you're my architect. The man who designed a better son, to replace the defective one." His mother, though, corrects his misperception:

> You don't know what it's like to watch your son . . . to watch him fall a little further behind every day. You know he's trying but something's holding him back. You don't know what it's like to stay up every night worrying that maybe it's your fault. Maybe you did something wrong during the pregnancy, or maybe you weren't careful enough, or maybe there's something wrong with you. Maybe you passed on a genetic defect without even knowing it . . . You can condemn us for what we did. You can say it's illegal or immoral, or whatever you want to say . . . but you have to understand that we didn't do it because we were ashamed, but because you were our son and we loved you. ("Doctor Bashir, I Presume," *DS9*)

The relevant issue here is *motivation*: Are parents who seek genetic modification for their children, whether treatment or enhancement, motivated out of love, or ego? Arguably, it's on the consciences of parents to decide whether to use genetic technology to treat or enhance their children, and *why* they want to do so; the technology itself is morally neutral.

"Just the One of Us"

In its long history, *Star Trek* has also illustrated the potential uses and abuses of *cloning*. In "Up the Long Ladder" (*TNG*), the *Enterprise* encounters a group of human colonists on the planet Mariposa who needed to clone themselves to survive, but are now experiencing the effects of limited genetic variability in their population and need an infusion of "fresh" DNA donated by the *Enterprise* crew. Later, in *Star Trek: Nemesis*, Picard meets a younger clone of himself who was created by Romulans and raised by Reman slaves.[25] Finally, in "Similitude" (*ENT*), Archer orders Dr. Phlox to create a clone of chief engineer Trip Tucker, which will grow rapidly and experience only a fifteen-day lifespan, so that neural tissue can be excised from the clone and used to treat Trip's fatal head injury. Each story raises a different set of issues related to cloning.

Ever since the famous cloned sheep "Dolly" was born, bioethicists, scientists, and the public have debated the moral permissibility of two types of cloning. *Reproductive* cloning aims at the live birth of a child; whereas *therapeutic* cloning creates embryos from which stem cells may be derived, or on which research can be done to further our understanding of early human development.[26] A number of reasons have been given for allowing cloning to go forward. On the reproductive side, cloning may allow infertile couples to produce biologically related children, prevent inheritable genetic diseases from being passed on from a particular parent, and provide for "rejection-proof" transplants.[27] Therapeutic cloning can be beneficial in

---

[25] For further discussion of cloning in the context of *Star Trek: Nemesis*, see Amy Kind's chapter in *Bioethics through Film*, edited by Sandra Shapshay (Baltimore: Johns Hopkins University Press, forthcoming).

[26] Some of this section is derived from Jason T. Eberl, *Thomistic Principles and Bioethics* (New York: Routledge, 2006), pp. 78–80.

[27] President's Council on Bioethics (PCB), *Human Cloning and Human Dignity: An Ethical Inquiry* (2002), pp. 79–80: http://www.bioethics.gov/reports/cloningreport/pcbe_cloning_report.pdf.

that it results in the production of undifferentiated embryonic stem cells which can be used to grow specialized cells, tissues, and organs to treat or possibly cure diseases such as Parkinson's, Alzheimer's, diabetes, and leukemia, as well as repair spinal cord injury.

There are as many reasons to restrict or ban cloning as to go forward with it. Concerns over reproductive cloning stem from the possibility of psychological harm to the clone resulting from her perception of herself as an individual with no unique identity; the nature of cloning as the "manufacture" of human beings; the possibility that cloning will lead to eugenic selection; the confused family relations a clone may have with her progenitor and other relatives; and the effect cloning may have on society's view of children and on the control one generation may have over the next (PCB, pp. xxviii-ix).[28] Points against therapeutic cloning are that it involves the "destruction" of human embryos to derive stem cells, embryos that have the moral status of persons; that research on embryos—cloned or not—wrongfully exploits developing human life; and that such exploitation is wrong in the further sense that it may harm the moral fabric of society (PCB, pp. xxxiii-iv).[29]

Leon Kass argues against reproductive cloning based on two philosophical concerns: *personal identity* and the right to an *open future*:

Cloning creates serious issues of identity and individuality. The cloned person may experience concerns about his distinctive identity not only because he will be in genotype and appearance identical to another human being, but, in this case, because he may also be twin to the person who is his "father" or "mother"—if one can still call them that. What would be the psychic burdens of being the "child" or "parent" of your twin? The cloned individual, moreover, will be saddled with a genotype that has already lived. He will not be fully a surprise to the world. People are likely always to compare his performances in life with that of his alter ego. True, his nurture and his circumstance in life will be different; genotype

---

[28] See also Dan Brock, "Cloning Human Beings: An Assessment of the Ethical Issues Pro and Con," in *Cloning and the Future of Human Embryo Research*, edited by Paul Lauritzen (New York: Oxford University Press, 2001), pp. 93–113.

[29] From here on, I will focus only on *reproductive* cloning.

is not exactly destiny. Still, one must also expect parental and other efforts to shape this new life after the original—or at least to view the child with the original version always firmly in mind.[30]

Cloning, Kass argues, raises serious questions about personal identity: How distinct is a clone from her progenitor? Would a clone be sufficiently different so that neither she nor her progenitor would consider themselves to be "less" of an individual? This is the thrust of Riker's concern when the inhabitants of Mariposa seek to clone *Enterprise* crewmembers: "One William Riker is unique, perhaps even special, but a hundred of him, a thousand of him, diminishes me in ways I can't even imagine" ("Up the Long Ladder," *TNG*). Riker is imagining multiple Riker-clones walking around—much like the multitude of clone troopers in the *Star Wars* prequel films[31]—and this is accurate given the Mariposans' stated intentions. On Earth, however, no one is seriously considering creating thousands, hundreds, or even tens of copies of a single genotype, and it would be practically impossible to do so without sci-fi technology. But even the real-world example of creating a single clone could validate Kass's concerns. Picard, with knowledge of his single clone, feels "as if a part of [him] has been stolen." Troi counsels him: "What you're feeling is a loss of self . . . We cherish our uniqueness. We believe that there can only be one of us in the universe" (*Star Trek: Nemesis*).

Picard seems to make the same error when reflecting on his clone as B-4 does when he first encounters Data: "You are me." Data gently corrects him: "No . . . I am your brother." Picard's clone is just that: his genetically identical twin brother. The only significant difference between them is that Picard's clone is never the same age as his natural twin sibling would be—a person and his clone don't grow up together. The metaphysical

---

[30] Leon Kass, "The Wisdom of Repugnance," *The New Republic* 216 (1997), p. 22. Given that Kass's overall argument against cloning is based on the general human feeling of *repugnance* toward it, it's interesting to note that the cloned Mariposan colonists have developed a similar reaction to sexual reproduction ("Up the Long Ladder," *TNG*).

[31] For a discussion of cloning in the context of *Star Wars*, see Richard Hanley, "Send in the Clones: The Ethics of Future Wars," in *Star Wars and Philosophy*, edited by Kevin S. Decker and Jason T. Eberl (Chicago: Open Court, 2005), pp. 93–103.

questions regarding a clone and the "original" being different persons invoke both *physical* and *psychological* criteria of personal identity. Clearly, Picard and Shinzon aren't physically identical since they don't have the *numerically same* body—they aren't the same biological organism even though they share the *same type* of body with the same genotype and physical appearance.

In the case of "Sim," Trip's clone, a contrived sci-fi explanation is used to explain Sim's ability to recall Trip's memories as he matures. This leads Sim to consider himself *identical* to Trip: "I have his memories, I have his feelings, I have his body. How am I not Trip?" ("Similitude," *ENT*). In real life, the psychological differences between a clone and his progenitor can be understood by studying cases of identical twins who, even if raised in the same household environment, have personalities which develop distinctly over time. This raises, of course, the old "nature versus nurture" debate concerning how much of one's personality is shaped by genetics and how much by environmental influences. Shinzon, for example, considers Picard and himself to be exactly the same in terms of their psychological *potential*. It's only that they've had different experiences that made their individual psyches different: "You *are* me! The same noble Picard blood runs through our veins. If you had lived my life, you'd be doing exactly what I am. So look in the mirror, see yourself." But Dr. Crusher disagrees: "Right now you're the man you made yourself. Shinzon is someone else . . . Jean-Luc, he is not you" (*Star Trek: Nemesis*).

Carol Rovane clarifies why Crusher is right and why Sim could be identical to Trip only in the sci-fi universe: cloning doesn't create a copy of the same person, since cloning can't reproduce the original's *memories*. "Without such memories, there would be no continuity of consciousness between the original human being and the clone. But cloning certainly does not reproduce such memories. Just as it produces an entirely new and separate animal, so it also produces an entirely new and separate consciousness which possesses no personal memory of the original human life that preceded it," Rovane writes.[32] The concern that cloning violates the clone's right to an open

---

[32] Carol Rovane, "Genetics and Personal Identity," in *A Companion to Genethics*, p. 247.

future rests on a mistaken belief in *genetic determinism*—the thesis that a person's genetic identity fully determines her future traits, both physical and psychological:

> Although genes play an essential role in the formation of physical and behavioral characteristics, each individual is, in fact, the result of a complex interaction between his or her genes and the environment within which they develop, beginning at the time of fertilization and continuing throughout life. As social and biological beings we are creatures of our biological, physical, social, political, historical, and psychological environments . . . In other words, there will never be another you.[33]

Kass acknowledges that "genotype is not exactly destiny," but allows for the misperception on the part of a clone that her future choices are constrained by her progenitor having already, so to speak, "lived her life" to be a compelling reason against cloning. *Star Trek* also calls attention to the idea that the pervasive belief in genetic determinism may cause psychological strife for clones and push them to behaviors designed to set themselves apart from the "original." Although he wasn't cloned, Lieutenant Tom Riker is a duplicate of Commander Will Riker created in one of *Star Trek*'s not-so-uncommon transporter accidents. In "Second Chances" (*TNG*), we see Tom lamenting the career he could've had—the one Will *did* have—if he'd been the one who escaped Nervala IV eight years earlier. When we meet Tom again two years later, we learn that he's joined up with Maquis rebels to fight for a cause he doesn't really believe in so that he can set himself apart from his famous twin. Kira challenges him on his suicidal plan to raid a secret Cardassian base: "This is about you isn't it? You and that other Will Riker out there. The man with your name, your face, your career. You are looking for a way to set yourself apart. Some way to be different . . . you want Tom Riker to go out in a blaze of glory that they talk about for the next ten years" ("Defiant," *DS9*). Shinzon also has issues with his, in his case *elder*, twin: "My life is *meaningless* as long as you're still alive . . . What am I while you exist: a shadow, an echo?" (*Star Trek: Nemesis*).

---

[33] National Bioethics Advisory Commission, *Cloning Human Beings* (1997), p. 32: http://www.bioethics.gov/reports/past_commissions/nbac_cloning.pdf.

"Sometimes You Just Have to Bow to the Absurd"

It's probably inevitable that we'll "tinker" with the human genome in terms of treatment or enhancement, as well as cloning. Various individuals and groups have already announced plans to attempt to reproductively clone a human being.[34] Genetic treatment, enhancement, and therapeutic cloning offer reasonably expectable health benefits that support moving forward with one or more of these endeavors. There are, however, significant moral considerations that must be kept at the forefront of scientific and public consciousness for further discussion, debate, and policy determination. *Star Trek* leaves us with some possible solutions to consider. In the Starfleet policy against genetic enhancement, a clear line is drawn—*how* it's drawn is not so clear—between permissible genetic treatment and impermissible enhancement: "Genetic resequencing for any reason other than serious birth defects is illegal. Anyone who is genetically enhanced is barred from serving in Starfleet or practicing medicine." This policy provides a "firewall" against any future "Khan Singh" being created ("Doctor Bashir, I Presume," *DS9*).[35] And reproductive cloning evidently isn't condoned within the Federation's borders. Hopefully, it won't take us until the twenty-third or twenty-fourth centuries to settle the moral debates of whether to clone or not to clone, and the degree to which we should manipulate the human genome for the purpose of either *mastering* nature or being good *stewards* of it.[36]

---

[34] The Raelians, for example, believe that human beings are clones of a superior alien race and claim to have already cloned a human being. Their claim has never been verified. There's no word yet on whether they're *trekkies.*

[35] For a critique of the moral distinction between genetic treatment and enhancement, see David B. Resnik, "The Moral Significance of the Therapy-Enhancement Distinction in Human Genetics" *Cambridge Quarterly of Healthcare Ethics* 9 (2000), pp. 365–377.

[36] My sincerest thanks to Kevin Decker, Dave Frisbee, and George Dunn for comments on an earlier draft of this chapter.

7

The Enterprise of Military Ethics: Jean-Luc Picard as Starfleet's Conscience

TIM CHALLANS

The mission of Starfleet is peaceful exploration and we come to understand many aspects of our ordinary lives better as we watch these explorers seek out new life. Yet, we also learn about our humanity in extraordinary circumstances, such as war. By the time Captain Picard's crew is following him onboard the *Sovereign*-class *Enterprise-E*, the United Federation of Planets has suffered through engagements with the Borg, the Cardassians, and the Dominion.

Starfleet has always maintained a strong military capability, for even though the four horsemen no longer ride the Earth in the twenty-fourth century, war still gallops across the constellations. In the future, competing empires continue to commit crimes against peace, and the war machines that enact imperial policies continue to commit war crimes against humanity and other citizens of the galaxy. These conditions alone pose fascinating moral quandaries of the gravest consequence for members of Starfleet. But the moral challenges are even greater considering the fact that Starfleet—as benevolent as it appears compared with the rest of its rivals—may not be much more than a military dictatorship, as it is itself an efficient war machine.

One of the reasons that the almost omnipotent Q keeps an eye on Picard is because of his moral character. It's one of the reasons we like to watch him, too. We particularly like to watch him when he does the morally right thing by standing up to senior officers, even at times disobeying their orders. How does an organization such as Starfleet operate with war machine-like efficiency in spite of the independence sported by the captain of the fleet's flagship? Within the *Star Trek* universe, we can learn the most about the enterprise of military ethics from life onboard Picard's starship.

Picard stands as the bearer of Starfleet's conscience and an exemplar of moral autonomy. To live a morally autonomous life is "to live one's life according to reasons and motives that are taken as one's own."[1] Moral autonomy derives a moral understanding for action not from authority or sacred texts, but from justifiable principles arrived at through reason. The eighteenth-century philosopher Immanuel Kant is the luminary who theorized most completely about *moral autonomy*.[2] And Picard makes it look so easy. So that we don't take him for granted, though, let's look at the consequences of a lack of moral autonomy through the lens of Picard's nemesis, the Borg.

"Resistance Is Futile"

The Borg are very scary, primarily because they're unstoppable. The Borg don't just conquer their adversaries; they *assimilate* them into their ranks. Assimilation has a long human history: various ideological military, political, and religious movements have absorbed large numbers of people and assimilated them for purposes that have made our world, through the centuries, a worse place to live. But the Borg don't pose the threat of the ideologies we're now familiar with; they pose a different kind of threat in the way they control their members. The old ideologies kept the members of their ranks filled with passion and irrationalities; the Borg show no feelings and are supremely rational. What should really scare us about the Borg is the fact that even though they have a single consciousness, they're totally without moral conscience. To become a Borg is to lose one's moral agency.

---

[1] John Christman, "Autonomy in Moral and Political Philosophy" *Stanford Encyclopedia of Philosophy*: http://plato.stanford.edu/entries/autonomy-moral.
[2] J.B. Schneewind, *The Invention of Autonomy: A History of Modern Moral Philosophy* (New York: Cambridge University Press, 1997).

Moral authority in centuries past typically came in religious or political flavors, whether sword or scepter, God or Country. Political authority has long been the object of obedience. A political philosopher in the late sixteenth century, Étienne de la Boétie, wrote about the phenomenon of people freely submitting their obedience in a powerful essay titled *The Politics of Obedience*.[3] The subtitle of his work is *The Discourse of Voluntary Servitude*, and it concerns obedience in the political realm—obedience to government and its leaders. Boétie classifies people as either *dupes* or *knaves*. Dupes believe that those in authority are working with the forces of goodness and light, so when dupes follow orders willingly they're not so aware of the harm in which they participate or endorse through their approval, be it explicit or tacit. Knaves are fully aware of their complicity in the evils of their government, but yet submit and go along for a variety of reasons, among them personal glory or gain, or sometimes just simply to implement the lesser of two evils.

In "Tacking into the Wind" (*DS9*), Ezri Dax challenges Worf to confront his own role as a knave in the Klingon Empire when he becomes aware of how corrupt a leader Chancellor Gowron is:

> I think that the situation with Gowron is a symptom of a bigger problem. The Klingon Empire is dying, and I think it deserves to die . . . I see a society that is in deep denial about itself. We're talking about a warrior culture that prides itself on maintaining centuries-old traditions of honor and integrity, but, in reality, it's willing to accept corruption at the highest levels . . . Who was the last leader of the High Council that you respected? Has there even been one? And how many times have you had to cover up the crimes of Klingon leaders because you were told that it was for the good of the Empire? . . . the truth is you have been willing to accept a government that you know is corrupt. Gowron's just the latest example. Worf, you are the most honorable and decent man that I have ever met, and if you are willing to tolerate men like Gowron, then what hope is there for the Empire?

The problem is that both dupes and knaves obey their masters for good or for ill.

---

[3] Étienne de la Boétie, *The Politics of Obedience: The Discourse of Voluntary Servitude* (Whitefish: Kessinger, 2004).

Religious authority has also shared the stage as the object of obedience. Friedrich Nietzsche aptly describes how religious people are herd animals in *Beyond Good and Evil* as well as in his etymological masterpiece on the concept of evil, *The Genealogy of Morals*.[4] Humanity's great impulse to be herded like sheep is the genesis of the slave morality, where values are turned on their head: the mythic and classical virtues of the gods and heroes—pride, strength, and beauty—are replaced by humility and meekness, where the last shall be first and the first shall be last. Unreflective ideology, whether it's of a religious or political variety, can "recruit" large numbers of people to engage in harm of the gravest sort. Perhaps it's our fear of the potential of our own "recruitment" into the ranks of evil that scare us so much. Perhaps we know deep down that the rhetoric of freedom and liberty and independence is only the thin, fragile patina of our real substance, which is malleable and susceptible to the forces of conformity. Just how free and independent are we as individuals and as a species? If we "jump ahead" four hundred years to the political and military scenarios of the *Star Trek* universe, we can begin to answer this question.

As presented to us, the United Federation of Planets is relatively free of religious and political ideologies, at least the type that used to captivate whole cultures several hundred years before the UFP flag flies with its white stars held by two olive branches against a blue field—a future version of the United Nations flag. The rest of the *Star Trek* universe is also largely free of religion, with the few exceptions of the planet Bajor and the Klingon home world Qo'noS. But even the history of the Klingon religious leader—Kahless—was challenged by Worf ("Rightful Heir," *TNG*).[5] There are no chaplains in Starfleet, and it appears that weddings and funerals are free of sacramental religiosity. The universe is by and large a secular place, a representation of Gene Rodenberry's humanistic vision.[6] Peace exists within the Federation because political and religious ide-

---

[4] Friedrich Nietzsche, *Beyond Good and Evil* (New York: Vintage, 1989) and *On the Genealogy of Morals and Ecce Homo* (New York: Vintage, 1989).

[5] For more discussion of Worf's struggle to believe in the face of doubt, see Chapter 13 in this volume.

[6] Ross Shepard Kraemer, William Cassidy, and Susan Schwartz, eds., *The Religions of Star Trek* (Boulder: Westview, 2003).

ologies have given way to more enlightened forms of governance. It took only half a millennium to realize the
Enlightenment's encyclopedist Denis Diderot's recipe for freedom: "Man will never be free until the last king is strangled by
the entrails of the last priest," a demand for the end of rule by
the first and second estates.

Yet sixteenth-century categories still inform the twenty-fourth
century universe. Recall Boétie's distinction between dupes and
knaves. The vast majority of the Borg, those absorbed against
their will, could fall within the category of dupes. In contrast,
most Cardassians appear to be evil and proud of it, making them
good candidates for being knaves, content with their complicity
within an authoritarian hierarchy. Are the Borg Nietzsche's herd
animals? "Hive" may be a more appropriate reference here than
"herd." The hive mind conjures up images of a lower life form
than mammals; the Borg's actions resemble the swarming behavior of insects. They're referred to as residing in a "collective" and
they have a queen, just as bees or ants. We learn from the adventures of the *U.S.S. Voyager* that former Borg drone Seven of Nine
does not easily reclaim her humanity when severed from the
Borg collective, and that she continues to hold a certain degree
of respect and admiration for the efficiency and collective consciousness of her former Borg brethren (or throng). Perhaps the
Borg Queen (*Star Trek: First Contact*; "Dark Frontier," "Unimatrix
Zero," "Endgame," *VGR*), who apparently maintains her own
identity while at the same time being able to connect with the
single Borg consciousness, is capable of moral choice and is cog-
nizant of the moral harm her species exacts throughout the universe. Wouldn't that ability to choose make the Borg Queen
morally autonomous? And if she can wreak great havoc throughout the universe, wouldn't that threaten the whole notion of
moral autonomy as an idea worthy of our consideration?

Yes, the Borg Queen would indeed be morally autonomous,
but no, her moral autonomy doesn't threaten the idea. The twentieth-century philosopher John Rawls—considered important due
to his re-invigoration of Kantian ethics—distinguishes different
types of autonomy.[7] Rational autonomy is only one type of
autonomy and "roughly parallels Kant's notion of hypothetical

---

[7] John Rawls, *Political Liberalism* (New York: Columbia University Press,
1996), pp. 72–81.

imperatives (or the notion of rationality found in neoclassical economics)."[8] Rawls argues that rational autonomy is basically aimed at achieving our interests, economic or otherwise. When we act according to hypothetical imperatives, we act in our own interest. For Kant, such hypothetical imperatives are not morally worthy.[9] The Borg are in pursuit of perfection; that's their interest. When they assimilate whole cultures and planets in order to improve upon their perfection and bring order to what they consider to be chaos, they're acting according to a hypothetical imperative.[10] They also do great moral harm to other species in the process. In pursuing the interest of the collective, the Borg Queen is being autonomous, but only *rationally* autonomous. Individual Borg drones don't share her autonomy; the Borg Queen's authority—as the personification of the Borg collective—is total.

"You Will Be Assimilated"

The Borg aren't the only case of authority having a dampening effect on moral autonomy. In our own twentieth century, Stanley Milgram gave us a damning empirical analysis of the human condition and humanity's predisposition toward obedience. To summarize his work, encapsulated in his *Obedience to Authority*,[11] the human default response to authority is obedience. Milgram conducted a famous experiment that involved an actor playing an authority figure, another actor playing a victim who's electrically shocked at the suggestion of the authority figure, and a series of test subjects who would deliver the shocks without knowing that the others were acting. For all the test subjects knew, the authority figure was a real authority figure, and the victim was receiving real electrical shocks. The test subjects were told by the authority figure that they were participating in

---

[8] John Rawls, "Kantian Constructivism in Moral Theory," in *John Rawls: Collected Papers* (Cambridge, Massachusetts: Harvard University Press, 1999), p. 308.

[9] Immanuel Kant, *Groundwork for the Metaphysics of Morals* (New York: Harper, 1965).

[10] For further analysis of the Borg's quest for perfection, see Chapter 10 in this volume.

[11] Stanley Milgram, *Obedience to Authority* (New York: Harper, 2004).

an experiment to test negative reinforcement with respect to memory recall. They were then instructed to incrementally ratchet up the electricity each time the other person gave the wrong answer to a recall question. Voltage levels were raised by the test subjects, at the behest of the authority figure, up to and beyond the point where the other person would register pain: the "victim" supposedly receiving the shock would yell out in pain, claim that they have a heart condition, and that they were experiencing chest pains. In some cases test subjects administered lethal doses of electricity. The real test was to see how the test subjects responded to authority. The vast majority of test subjects inflicted "pain" and even "death" upon the person being shocked when told to do so by an authority figure. Milgram's experiment showed that a very small percentage of people are self-possessed enough to resist authority when that authority is demanding something bad, illegal, or immoral. The experiment concluded that obedience to authority is natural for most people. One of the few in the experiment to resist authority was Ron Ridenhour, a major source for Seymour Hersh's prize-winning investigative piece about one of America's most notorious massacres.[12] Ridenhour was the soldier who exposed the My Lai massacre during the Vietnam conflict with a letter to Congress when everyone else—soldiers, officers, and even the president—was covering it up, or at least going along with it. The problem with the appeal to authority is that it eliminates the need to examine the reasons for doing something that appears, to all intents and purposes, evil.

What Milgram's work does in disclosing the psychological problem at the level of the individual, Christopher Browning's *Ordinary Men*[13] does for the social-psychological problem at the level of institutional and societal cultures. Browning's book looks at Reserve Police Battalion 101, a mobile extermination unit that operated in Europe during World War II. Outside of academic circles, this book went largely unnoticed because Browning arrived at the uncomfortable conclusion that people from any nation are capable of committing genocide if the conditions are just right. A

---

[12] Seymour Hersh, *My Lai 4: A Report on the Massacre and Its Aftermath* (New York: Random House, 1972).

[13] Christopher Browning, *Ordinary Men: Reserve Police Battalion 101 and the Final Solution in Poland* (New York: Harper, 1993).

rival book, *Hitler's Willing Executioners* by Daniel Goldhagen,[14] looked at the same evidence and came up with the opposite conclusion. Goldhagen asserts that the problem was a German problem, due to their particular history, culture, and nature. The debate continues, but the consensus in the academy has discredited the Goldhagen thesis and supports Browning's. Most people are followers, and many people have a desire to be led. Some contemporary academics theorize that fascism in its most abstract essence is the desire to be led—a disturbingly widespread desire that makes the universal application of the idea of moral autonomy harder to embrace for many people.[15]

Michel Foucault gives us a brilliant analysis of power in his classic work, *Discipline and Punish*.[16] Foucault examines several institutions that have staked out their jurisdictions of power, particularly that of the prison and the military. Alas, for all of the advances we can imagine in the centuries ahead of us, it appears that the problem of violence and armed conflict may persist. Foucault makes a distinction between power and force. Power comes from within an institution or political body, and forces are external to those entities. Institutions of power maintain not only their existence but also their ability to wield power through their very structures, which are based on hierarchies. Institutions of power maintain control over those within via a process through which the members become *docile bodies*. Bodies become docile through physical and mental discipline, through training. The twenty-fourth century has its share of species who do grave moral damage.

The *Star Trek* universe contains examples which illustrate Browning's thesis as well, that conditions go a long way in determining whether people—individually or institutionally— act morally or immorally. Local political and cultural conditions can either spawn species of vast cruelty or nurture others of great kindness. These conditions mean a great deal. We know that the otherwise "warlike, cruel, treacherous" Romulans are

---

[14] Daniel Goldhagen, *Hitler's Willing Executioners: Ordinary Germans and the Holocaust* (New York: Vintage, 1997).
[15] Gilles Deleuze and Felix Guattari, *Anti-Oedipus: Capitalism and Schizophrenia* (Minneapolis: University of Minnesota Press, 1983).
[16] Michel Foucault, *Discipline and Punish: The Birth of the Prison* (New York: Random House, 1978).

biological cousins to the honorable Vulcans ("Balance of Terror," *TOS*; "Unification," *TNG*). In *Star Trek: Nemesis* we see that Shinzon, a clone of Picard with a very different set of experiences, has grown up to have a moral character contrary to the noble Starfleet captain's. Bajorans resisted the Cardassian occupation just as fiercely as the French resistance defied the German occupation on Earth in the twentieth century, and as Iraqi insurgents are resisting the American occupation in the twenty-first century. Given the right conditions, or the wrong conditions, our commonalities as citizens of the universe go a long way in determining the propensity for what we'll do.

"It Was All for the Federation"

In the twentieth century, few soldiers were capable of resisting authority when wholesale, manifest illegal and immoral acts were perpetrated. Ron Ridenhour was one of them, and Hugh Thompson was another. Thompson landed his helicopter between American troops and unarmed civilians to protect the civilians from slaughter in the My Lai massacre. H.R. McMaster's *Dereliction of Duty* examines the utter failure of the highest ranking political and military leaders during the Vietnam conflict as they prosecuted an unjust war in an unjust way without being able to stop it even when they knew it was futile and without any shred of legitimacy.[17]

Are we any better off at the beginning of the twenty-first century, in the face of our senior political and military leaders who haven't been willing or able to stop yet another unjustified war being prosecuted in an unjust way? The current war against terror is similarly morally plagued by lies, torture, and slaughter on the part of the United States. While Heraclitus is famous for saying that one can't step into the same river twice, there are many who reasonably hold that the American war machine hasn't progressed morally since Vietnam. Yet while the war machine—those political and military institutions that engage in organized violence on behalf of the state—is still out of control in the twenty-first century, *Star Trek* shows us a future in which

---

[17] H.R. McMaster, *Dereliction of Duty: Johnson, McNamara, the Joint Chiefs of Staff, and the Lies that Led to Vietnam* (New York: Harper, 1998).

political and military leaders seem to be able to keep it under control. Few people passed Milgram's test in the twentieth century, but we would expect that Jean-Luc Picard would have refused the order to harm the test subject. In fact, Picard passed several twenty-fourth century versions of Milgram's test. He refused illegal orders ("Conundrum," *TNG*) and brought immoral or criminal juniors ("First Duty," *TNG*), peers ("The Wounded," *TNG*), and seniors ("The Pegasus," *TNG*) to justice.

One of his most interesting moral challenges occurs in *Star Trek: Insurrection*, in which Picard and his crew fought against Starfleet itself in order to maintain the azimuth on their moral compass. Picard has to fight not only a clear enemy—the Son'a—but also the military culture in his own Starfleet that forces him to have to disobey in order to do the right thing. Starfleet is self-interestedly conspiring with an immorally self-interested species to remove another species—the Ba'ku—from their homeland (in the end we learn that the Son'a are children of the Ba'ku). The Ba'ku live on a planet with regenerative metaphasic radiation that the Son'a covet. At first, Starfleet conspires to relocate the Ba'ku to another world without the Ba'ku's knowledge or consent. In the end, after the *Enterprise* crew confounds the relocation plan, the Son'a plot to kill the Ba'ku for it.

Data is the first to discover the illegal and immoral plot, and the conspirators attack him to protect their secret. Picard rescues Data and learns of Starfleet's complicity. Lesser Starfleet officers would've gone along with the scheme, as several already had, including Admiral Dougherty and those under his command. Picard objects to the forced relocation, arguing that forced relocations in the past had been among the more heinous crimes in Earth's history. Dougherty responds that the relocation affects only six hundred people. Picard challenges him by asking, "How many people does it take, Admiral, before it becomes wrong?" Picard's is an argument against *consequentialism*, against acting according to hypothetical imperatives, against the infamous slogan that "the end justifies the means." Picard makes a moral argument for acting on *principle*, in this case acting in accordance with the Prime Directive; he contends, "Who the hell are we to determine the next course of evolution for these people?" Picard will go to great lengths to protect the innocent Ba'ku, even if it means fighting his own organization.

It is here that Picard's commitment to full moral autonomy

becomes clear. Consequentialist thinking amounts to only "rational autonomy," but acting on principle amounts to what Rawls would call "full autonomy." Acting according to what Kant calls "categorical imperatives" would qualify a moral agent as being fully autonomous. Categorical imperatives define actions that are good in themselves, and therefore morally worthy. Acting according to the Prime Directive would be good in itself, and its goodness isn't defined by the consequences of the action. While Picard is the greatest exemplar of moral autonomy, other members of his crew possess it, especially Data. Kant didn't know he could've been referring to the starship *Enterprise* when he said he was awed by two things: "the starry heavens above me and the moral law within me."[18]

"Make It So"

One of Data's most impressive features is the advanced nature and reliability of his moral character, thanks to the genius of the moral subroutines programmed into him by Dr. Noonien Soong—one could only speculate that they were *Kantian* subroutines. Consider Data juxtaposed with a Borg. Data is a machine-becoming-human, and a Borg would be a human-becoming-machine. And while Data is moral, a Borg lacks any semblance of morality. Data acts as an autonomous individual, and the Borg act as a group with no individual identities or ability to be morally autonomous, except for the Queen. Most of us have witnessed the dangers of "groupthink," where a group's collective lack of wisdom is capable of great harm—expressed by the ironic maxim, "none of us is as dumb as all of us." Kant's theory of moral autonomy demands that each person use their reasoning through a process of free inquiry while remaining open to revision due to better evidence or better reasoning. As Data has moved from machine-hood toward humanity, he's become more moral; and as the Borg move away from humanity toward machine-hood, they become less moral (for the Queen) or even amoral (for the drones).

So, the Borg's machine-like tendencies rob them of any ves-

---

[18] Immanuel Kant, *Critique of Practical Reason* (New York: Cambridge University Press, 1997), p. 133.

tige of morality. What of the machine-like tendencies of the humans within Starfleet? After all, along with the merging of individual human and machine, at least in certain aspects, comes a merging of society and machine. Organizational efficiency is so good within Starfleet that they appear to have done away with not only paperwork but also bureaucracy altogether.[19] Communication is so precise, language and protocol so regimented that we never see Picard have to say anything more than once. There's no second-guessing after Picard utters his trademark command, "Make it so." Picard fans want to believe that while he's better than other leaders, they can't deny that the rest of Starfleet and the Federation operate at levels of systemic efficiency logarithmically higher than any organization we've experienced in this century; nevertheless, such efficiency can cloud moral judgment, as Picard tells Anij at the end of *Insurrection* that he needs to return to "slow things down at the Federation Council."

Watching the real-world experience of the twentieth century and its wholesale episodes of genocide, we should be somewhat fearful of powerful organizations that are very machine-like, very efficient. Such organizations, particularly powerful ones with military hardware, are capable of great harm if decisions at the top turn out to be bad ones. The psychological casualties of the early twenty-first century's war against terror are much higher than even the cataclysmic wars of the twentieth century because of the moral compromises that warriors make in order to continue to fight in a war that may not be justifiable at any level. Each compromise of moral integrity in war is like the compromise of physical integrity when being absorbed by the Borg collective. Giving up pieces of ourselves, whether those pieces are tangible or not, physical or moral, enables the replacement of the noble with the ignoble. So what changes between the twenty-first and the twenty-fourth centuries that would enable a military organization like Starfleet both to operate with machine-like efficiency, yet at the same time to engage the rest of the universe peacefully without causing great harm, as did the war machines of former centuries? Well, for starters,

---

[19] Starfleet hasn't quite made it to this point by the twenty-third century, as Dr. McCoy gripes that "the bureaucratic mentality is the only constant in the universe" (*Star Trek IV: The Voyage Home*).

Starfleet has the Prime Directive, which prevents it from interfering with the natural development of peoples on other worlds. With the advent of our current national and military strategies, America has never been further from the Prime Directive. The American War Machine today operates more like the Borg than like Starfleet. Never before has thinking been so homogenously regulated and enforced; officers have to retire before being able to disagree with their political or military masters. We have no Picards today.

8

Is Odo a Collaborator?

SANDER LEE

Star Trek: Deep Space Nine broke new ground in the complexity and the moral ambiguity of its characters and situations. With its mature depiction of the after-effects of the brutal occupation of Bajor by the Cardassians, the show was able to deal with issues of transitional justice similar to those raised in the aftermath of the Holocaust, the end of apartheid and white rule in South Africa, and the fall of Communism in Eastern Europe, to name but a few.

While the consequences of the Cardassian Occupation were explored in a number of episodes, perhaps the most profound moral questions were raised by the role played by Odo, the changeling who acted as the head of security on the space station Terok Nor—later renamed "Deep Space Nine"—during the Cardassians' tyrannical rule, which employed slave labor, the use of torture, and religious as well as racial oppression. Long after the collapse of Cardassian rule, Odo comes to flirt with a new form of collaboration as he waffles back and forth between his loyalty to his friends and his attraction to his own people, the Founders. They rule the Dominion with an iron hand and seek to "bring order" to the Alpha Quadrant.

Can Odo's actions be morally justified or was he a changeling regarding his morals as well as his shape? How can his romantic relationship with Kira be understood in the context of Odo's willingness to work with her bitterest enemies at the very times she needs him most? How should we interpret his decision at the conclusion of the series to abandon Kira and rejoin the Great Link?

"I'm Guilty. What More Is There to Say?"

In "Things Past," Odo relives guilty memories from his past service as Head of Station Security during the Cardassian
Occupation. While his colleagues on Deep Space Nine have
always seen Odo as someone who maintained his integrity during the Occupation by acting as an objective defender of justice,
Odo knows that this wasn't always the case. Odo confesses that
he allowed three innocent Bajorans to be convicted and executed unjustly.

Producer Ronald Moore says of this episode:

> One of the things that always drove the writing staff nuts was the
> idea that Odo had been a policeman during the Cardassian
> Occupation, but never had gotten his hands dirty, that he had been
> above it all, and that everyone had trusted him. We never bought
> that. It seemed to me that if I were a Bajoran, I wouldn't trust the
> *cop* who's still on duty from the Occupation. Somewhere along the
> line something bad went down on Odo's watch and "Things Past"
> was the show to say it.[1]

As the story unfolds, we're made increasingly aware of Odo's
anxiety and sense of guilt as he recognizes his own culpability
in what is about to happen. Only Odo appears able to see the
walking ghosts of the three innocent victims and, at one point
while eating, he poignantly sees blood on his hands.

At one point, Odo argues with his past self—in the form of
his predecessor, Thrax. Odo presents Thrax with all the evidence indicating the three Bajorans' innocence. While Thrax
grants the validity of many of Odo's points, he claims that the
overall amount of evidence, although admittedly circumstantial,
is sufficient to prove their guilt. When Odo demands that they
"find the truth, not obtain convictions," Thrax throws Odo's own
words back at him, arguing that the use of terrorist tactics by the
Bajoran Resistance goes "against order, against stability, against
the rule of law."

Odo is desperately trying to lessen his responsibility for the
injustice of having been complicit in the murders of the three

---

[1] Terry J. Erdmann with Paula M. Block, *The Star Trek Deep Space Nine
Companion* (New York: Pocket Books, 2000), pp. 398–99.

innocent Bajorans. As he says, all the evidence of their innocence was "there from the beginning. But I was too busy, too
concerned with maintaining order and the rule of law. I thought
of myself as the outsider, the shape-shifter who cared for nothing but justice. It never occurred to me that I could fail, but I did
and I never wanted anyone to know the truth—that seven years
ago I allowed three innocent men to die." In "Necessary Evil,"
Odo initially accepted the role of constable on Terok Nor solely
for the sake of justice, yet in "Things Past" he admits that, like
his Cardassian masters, he sometimes valued *order* over all else.
Does this make him a collaborator?

"He's Made of Liquid, But He's Very Rigid"

The *American Heritage Dictionary* states that *to collaborate* is
"to co-operate treasonably, as with an enemy occupation force
in one's country."[2] Although he's a changeling and not a
Bajoran, during the Occupation Odo's sympathies certainly
should have been with the Bajoran community. He came to consciousness in a Bajoran laboratory and initially developed his
personality by means of his love-hate relationship with the
Bajoran scientist who raised him, whom Odo comes to accept
as his *de facto* "father" ("The Alternate," "The Begotten"). During
the Occupation, Odo also believed himself to be the only member of his species; he doesn't discover that he's one of the
Founders until long after the Occupation has ended. So while
Odo saw himself as an outsider, neither Bajoran nor Cardassian,
everything in his experience should have led him to see the
Cardassians as the Bajorans did, namely, as brutal enemy occu-
piers of what was in effect "his world": Bajor.

Martin Dean discusses local collaboration with German occu-
piers during World War II—one obvious model for the
Cardassian Occupation:

> As more documentation becomes available, the sharp division
> between studies based mainly on 'perpetrator' or 'victim' sources is
> thankfully being overcome. Instead, there is a growing recognition
> of the need to examine events from the perspective of all partici-
> pants and especially to integrate the viewpoint of the local popu-

---

[2] *The American Heritage Dictionary* (New York: Houghton Mifflin, 2000).

lations of eastern Europe into the narrative. This produces a complex and often painful picture of quite widespread 'local collaboration', as well as sometimes surprising aid for Jews . . . the motives of individuals serving in the collaborationist police . . . add considerably to our understanding of the dynamics of genocide. For it is important to remember that the Holocaust required not only central plans, but also real people at the local level, many of them non-German, for the nightmare to become reality.[3]

If we simply substitute the words "Cardassians" and "Bajorans" for "Germans" and "Jews," we can see the complexity of determining the degree of Odo's collaboration and the moral responsibility he should bear for his actions.

Odo sees himself as someone who values duty over personal preference. In this way, Odo's sense of ethics appears to be "deontological," as opposed to "teleological." Teleologists, like the philosophers known as the "utilitarians," believed that the moral worth of an act is found in its consequences or benefits. On the other hand, deontologists, like Immanuel Kant, believe that the moral worth of an act lies within the act itself.

The difference between these two moral views is brought out in "The Collaborator," in which we learn that Kai Opaka divulged information to the Cardassians that led to the "Kendra Valley massacre" in which her own son was killed. Kai Opaka made this painful decision in order to protect a greater number of innocent Bajorans. From a teleological perspective her decision could be justified as choosing the lesser of two evils. From the deontological perspective, however, her decision to collaborate was inherently wrong. For Kant, the consequences of an act are irrelevant; only the inherent qualities of an act determine its moral worth.

A more light-hearted illustration is presented in "Little Green Men." Quark offers to fly Nog to Starfleet Academy where he's to enroll as a cadet. Suspicious of this act of surprising good will, Odo stows away on Quark's ship to uncover his real scheme. Quark actually intends to smuggle an illegal substance called "kemacite" to sell at a profit. Because of a time travel inci-

---

[3] Martin Dean, "Local Collaboration in the Holocaust in Eastern Europe," in *The Historiography of the Holocaust*, edited by Dan Stone (New York: Palgrave MacMillan, 2004), p. 134.

dent caused by the sabotage of Quark's cousin Gaila—"the one with the moon"—Quark is unable to sell his kemacite, which nonetheless saves them from the initial sabotage and plays a crucial role in returning them to their own time.

From a teleological perspective, it seems a good thing that Quark brought the kemacite along for the ride. Without it, the Ferengi and Odo would've been permanently stranded in the past. As a deontologist, however, Odo morally condemns Quark for his intention to smuggle an illegal substance even though Quark's scheme results in positive consequences. Like Kant, Odo believes that an immoral act is made immoral by one's bad intentions and that the consequences of the act are irrelevant to its moral worth. One should do the right thing for its own sake and not for the sake of any consequences.

Also, like Odo, Kant believed that there rages a war within each of us between our inherent sense of duty and our inclinations or desires. One should always do one's duty in spite of one's desires. Kant calls the intention to act morally a "good will": "Nothing in the world—or out of it—can possibly be conceived that could be called 'good' without qualification except a good will."[4]

In addition to acting with good intentions, in accordance with our common sense of duty, Kant further claimed that for an act to be moral, the command or imperative underlying it should be "categorical" (done for its own sake) and never "hypothetical" (done for the sake of achieving some consequence). For example, "In the Pale Moonlight" depicts Sisko engaging in trickery and deceit—even becoming an accessory to murder—to convince the Romulans to join the war against the Dominion. Kant would unquestionably condemn Sisko's actions and his subsequent decision to delete the log entry containing his "confession." Despite the positive consequences that resulted, the immoral means used to achieve them shouldn't have been tolerated.

Kant's famous "Categorical Imperative" may be stated in two ways. First, moral judgments entail the universal claim that all persons ought to follow the same specific course of action, as

---

[4] Immanuel Kant, *Groundwork for the Metaphysic of Morals*, p. 5. Available at www.earlymoderntexts.com/f_kant.html.

long as they are in circumstances that are identical in all morally relevant aspects. "Act only on that maxim through which you can at the same time will that it should become a universal law of nature," as Kant puts it (p. 23). If I'm trying to decide whether my proposed course of action is moral, I should ask myself whether I think that anyone in a similar situation should do whatever I'm planning to do. Sisko must consider whether he can will to live in a world in which everyone acts as he does; and since he can't will to live in such a world, insofar as no one would trust anyone else, then he can't make himself an exception to the rule.

The second formulation of Kant's Categorical Imperative states that one should "act in such a way as to treat humanity, whether in your own person or in that of anyone else, always as an end and never merely as a means" (p. 28). This requires that each individual person must always be treated with respect. While it's true that Sisko dislikes the Romulan senator, Vreenak, he isn't morally justified in using him for his own ends, no matter how "noble" those ends may appear. Respect for the inherent autonomy of persons requires that we treat each person as an "end" and never merely as "means" to an end.

Returning to "Things Past," we can now decide whether, from a Kantian perspective, Odo should be morally condemned as a collaborator. In retrospect, Odo now concedes that in allowing the Bajorans to be executed he failed in his duty to ferret out the truth, to fight for impartial justice. His explanation for how this could happen—he was too busy, too concerned with order and the rule of law—fits with everything we know about his character; and his remorse and determination to avoid repeating such an error appear genuine and sincere. While Odo is no doubt guilty of a certain level of professional negligence, his moral complicity doesn't seem to rise to the level of collaboration. He didn't ignore the evidence of the Bajorans' guilt to knowingly help the Cardassians frame them. Instead, he experienced a simple failure of professional judgment of the sort that could've happened to any policeman anywhere at any time.

But Odo's actions once he realized his error can't be excused quite so easily. By his own admission, Odo realized three days after the executions that the three Bajorans were innocent; yet he never voluntarily did anything to correct the record. Certainly he owed it to the Bajorans' families to let them know of their relatives' innocence; and his sense of duty should've required him to confess his mistake to the appropriate authorities, if not during the Occupation then afterwards. We know from "Duet" that the Bajoran government did investigate war crimes. Indeed, Odo's contemplation of his hidden guilt comes in direct response to his awareness that he should've confessed his actions at a Bajoran conference on the Occupation, where he was lionized as a hero.

We can argue from a Kantian perspective that Odo's failure to admit his mistake was a violation of both parts of the Categorical Imperative. Odo wouldn't be willing to say that everyone who engages in a miscarriage of justice should hide their guilt. Furthermore, in maintaining the illusion that the Bajorans were guilty, he's using them merely as means to his own end of protecting his reputation. One could even argue that in preserving the cover-up of these unjust executions, Odo is treasonably cooperating with Cardassian efforts to perpetuate the lie that the Occupation wasn't really as bad as the Bajorans claim it to be—a lie we see Garak promoting. If this is true, then Odo is indeed a collaborator; not because of his initial bad judgment, but as a result of his participation in this cover-up.

One could argue that at least he's finally chosen to do the right thing by publicly confessing his sin and setting the record straight. Michael Taylor, however, who wrote the script, makes clear that Odo doesn't voluntarily reveal his guilt: "Odo wouldn't tell anyone about his secret by choice. The only reason he'd tell us is if he was *forced* to tell" (*DS9 Companion*, p. 399). So we can't mitigate Odo's sin by claiming that he freely *chose* to do the right thing. He only told the truth when he had no other choice.

Odo's alter ego, Rene Auberjonois, characterizes the episode this way:

> I loved the script . . . Odo's a character we've come to believe always tells the truth . . . We've tried to be consistent with that. But that doesn't mean that he doesn't lie to himself. He is this wonderfully contradictory character, in that he's made of liquid, but he's very rigid. (*DS9 Companion*, p. 397)

So, from a Kantian perspective, Odo may reasonably be described as somewhat of a collaborator based on his duplicitous actions. But there are degrees of collaboration. While Odo may have helped the Cardassians hide the full extent of their injustice in this one case, he didn't actively participate in the broad array of crimes perpetuated by the Cardassians against the Bajorans on a daily basis.

"Nothing Else Matters"

We should also examine Odo's actions at a different time, after he's publicly concedes his earlier error, to see if Odo has learned from his mistake and is willing to do his moral duty avoiding all hints of collaboration. By the end of the fifth season, Odo has long since discovered his true identity as one of the Founders, the changelings who rule the oppressive Dominion. He's rejected their many attempts to incorporate him into the Great Link and was even temporarily turned into a "solid" as punishment for killing another changeling in defense of his crewmates onboard the *Defiant* ("The Adversary," "Broken Link"). With the beginning of the Dominion War, the Cardassians—now allied with the Founders—have retaken Deep Space Nine. Although officially neutral in the war, the Bajorans, including Kira, are uneasy about tolerating the Cardassians' return. By the end of "Rocks and Shoals," Kira has convinced a reluctant Odo to support the creation of a resistance movement.

Subsequently, however, Odo betrays his promises to his friends in order to link repeatedly with the female changeling, a process that carries undeniable sexual connotations but implies an even deeper level of intimacy. As a result of his infatuation, Odo fails to disable the security alarms and, as a result, Rom is captured and sentenced to death when he attempts to sabotage the station. In "Behind the Lines," Kira angrily confronts Odo:

> **KIRA:** Do you realize what you just did? You just handed the Alpha Quadrant to the Dominion.
> **ODO:** I was in the Link.
> **KIRA:** Are you saying you forgot?
> **ODO:** I didn't forget. It just . . . didn't seem to matter.
> **KIRA:** A lot of people are going to die. Don't you care?
> **ODO:** It has nothing to do with me.
> **KIRA:** How can you say that?

Odo: If you could experience the Link you'd know why nothing else matters.

Kira: The last five years—your life here, our friendship— none of that matters?

Odo: It did . . . once. I wish I could make you understand but you can't. You're not a changeling.

Kira: You're right. I'm a solid.

Eventually, just in the nick of time (this is *Star Trek* after all), Odo comes to his senses, rescues his friends, and helps the Federation successfully retake the station. Odo's actions during this crucial period might seem unredeemable. But Kira obviously had no trouble forgiving him, at least when they became lovers ("His Way").

"I've Never Been Good at Good-byes"

We can now return to our fundamental question, "Is Odo a collaborator?" The answer depends on how we calculate Odo's true relationship to the various parties engaged in the Dominion War. In our earlier discussion of "Things Past," Odo's position was much clearer. During the first Occupation, Odo saw himself as completely neutral in the conflict between Bajoran and Cardassian interests. By the Dominion War, however, Odo's self-image has changed considerably. While he usually espouses loyalty to Bajor and the Federation for moral as well as personal reasons, he now fully recognizes that, even beyond common biology, he's one of the Founders. He frequently refers to them as "his people," and it's quite obvious that he feels a bond of loyalty and obligation towards them even when he feels he must oppose them in their attempt to take over the Alpha Quadrant.

Odo maintains an ongoing debate with the female changeling over whether the so-called "solids" are as deserving of respect as the Founders. She argues that all "solids" are inferior creatures who are guilty of mistreating changelings in the past and are thus unworthy of moral consideration. From her perspective, they're "small," "insignificant" beings who must be "broken" of their desire for freedom and put under the "guidance" of the Dominion ("Favor the Bold"). Her position and arguments are remarkably like those the Nazis presented in defense of their treatment of Jews and other peoples whom they considered to be racially inferior.[5]

To the extent that Odo sees himself as both a biological member of the Founders and a citizen of Bajor, he's like a first-generation German-American living through the Nazi era and forced to decide between his adopted country and his ancestral roots. From a Kantian perspective, it's not difficult to figure out how Odo ought to act. First, it's clear that Kant believed that all rational beings are autonomous and equally worthy of respect. Although Kant wrote a lot about superior and inferior intelligences on other worlds, I don't recall that he ever addressed the question of inter-community relations among different species of extraterrestrials. But he was very aware of the unequal treatment given to those considered inferior in his own time, such as the Jewish people. Kant had a long acquaintanceship with the Jewish philosopher Moses Mendelssohn and supported Mendelssohn's struggle for equal rights.[6] The second formulation of the Categorical Imperative, which demands that all people should be treated with respect as "ends" and never merely as "means," was clearly intended to apply to *all* rational beings.

Furthermore, Kant believed that each person must act autonomously. Blind obedience to the commands of others could never be moral. Odo's duty is clear. Despite his biological and emotional ties to the Founders, he's morally obliged to follow his conscience and actively oppose their attempts to enslave others to bring order to what they perceive as chaos. When he neglects that duty to satisfy his personal desire to link with the female changeling, he's collaborating with evil. Odo's sense of duty eventually wins out and he acts properly before any serious harm is done.

As a deontologist, Kant thought that consequences are irrelevant to the moral evaluation of an act. From this perspective, Odo's actions under the influence of the female changeling are just as evil as they would've been if they'd resulted in catastrophe. To what degree Odo redeems himself by his later actions

---

[5] The Nazis referred to such populations as *Untermenschen* ("sub-human").

[6] For more on this see Francesco Tomasoni, "Mendelssohn and Kant: A Singular Alliance in the Name of Reason," *History of European Ideas* 30 (2004), pp. 267–294.

is a matter of opinion; but there's little doubt that Odo acts, at least twice, as a collaborator with evil.

In "What You Leave Behind," Odo returns to his defeated and sick people to help cure them, both physically and morally. Kant also provides a justification for Odo's decision to return to his people and help them—not only by healing them, but also by educating them about the "solids." Kant's notion of "imperfect" duties includes *beneficence*, a willingness to perform acts of kindness.[7] This duty follows from the second formulation of the Categorical Imperative as Odo's healing and educating the Founders helps them to develop further and flourish as rational, autonomous beings. He accomplishes this by helping them to survive and also to understand the truth about the Alpha Quadrant inhabitants they'd been trying to conquer so they can autonomously reach an informed, rational decision to end the war and live in peace with the "solids."

Even though this means leaving Kira, it's certain that a Kantian would approve of this action. It's now the Founders who are in need of help and only Odo is qualified to give that help. Even if Odo desperately wished to stay with Kira, he'd still be morally required to do all he could to help those in need. So, despite his earlier moral imperfections, we must regard Odo's return to the Great Link, nattily dressed in a tuxedo, as an honest attempt to morally redeem his people, and, in so doing, redeem himself.[8]

---

[7] For Kant, imperfect duties are broad obligations shared by everyone for the improvement of humanity, such as developing our talents or showing kindness to others, while perfect duties are narrow requirements that prohibit certain types of immoral actions such as lying or breaking promises (p. 24).

[8] I wish to thank Jason Eberl and Kevin Decker for their many helpful editorial comments and suggestions.

9

"The Rules of Acquisition Can't Help You Now": What Can the Ferengi Teach Us about Business Ethics?

JACOB M. HELD

Anyone who has ever taught, read, or expressed interest in the field of Business Ethics has heard, at least once, but probably many times, "Business ethics? Isn't that an oxymoron?" This is usually followed by the snickering of someone whose jokes always get a laugh—his own.

Some people seem to think business and ethics are necessarily contradictory. As one scholar notes, "Business pushes one way, ethics the other. If achieving ever-increasing profit is the basic purpose and principle of business, and economic profitability is the primary and overriding factor in strategic business decisions, ethical behavior and business behavior eventually must conflict."[1] This is the conflict any fan of *Deep Space Nine* sees time and time again whenever Quark runs up against an ethical dilemma. Quark usually chooses profit, whereas his more naive brother, Rom, chooses ethical solutions. In "The House of Quark," Quark says that respect is good, but gold-pressed latinum (Ferengi money) is better. In fact, Rule of Acquisition Number 10 states: "Greed is eternal," and Number 109 says: "Dignity and an empty sack is worth the sack" ("Prophet Motive" and "Rivals," *DS9*).[2] When ethics and business interests conflict, the Ferengi favor the side of profit;

---

[1] Ronald Duska, "Business Ethics: Oxymoron or Good Business?" *Business Ethics Quarterly* 10 (2000), p. 112.

[2] There are 285 Rules of Acquisition. These rules are the code of conduct for the Ferengi. For the most part, all of them have to do with success in business and the accumulation of profit.

there's little room for ethical concepts like respect and dignity when latinum is on the line. The problem is that in business, we too often have to make just this type of choice: a choice between success and ethics, and more often than not the answers given sound as though they were written by Grand Nagus Zek himself, for whom efficiency, productivity, and profit take priority over rights, respect, and relationships.

Consider the case for women's rights on Ferengenar as expressed in "Profit and Lace." Grand Nagus Zek promotes women's rights for one reason: It's good business. He isn't concerned with equitable treatment, fairness, or respect. Rather, it makes good economic sense to grant women equal rights: equal rights to work, earn money, consume, and foster economic growth. This seems to be an ideal solution. It's ethical and efficient. Women get what they want and business is helped out in the process. But what if it weren't efficient, what if women's rights would actually hinder the interests of business? Would we still see a Ferengi equal rights movement? Probably not. The same dilemma faces us.

Business appears to be inherently unethical and ethical principles are only operative when they aren't in conflict with the overriding interests of business. And if we leave the matter here, then being ethical in business is agonistic: a constant struggle between morality and business resolved only through compromise where ethics more often than not takes the back seat to functionality and profit.

"Face It Quark, It's Good Business"

The problem is not that we have failed to find the right balance between ethics and business, or that a good compromise solution lies just around the corner and all we need do is keep looking. The problem is that we've separated ethics from business and economics to such an extent that we think business ethics is a new field, a novel creation, as opposed to an ancient practice. Yet economics has been a species of ethics since Aristotle (384–322 B.C.E.). Only today do we think we require an applied ethics in order to integrate the two.[3] Ethics, economics, and pol-

---

[3] See particularly *The Politics* in *The Complete Works of Aristotle* (Princeton: Princeton University Press, 1995).

itics are essentially related. But many people seem to think that these three fields of study are distinct, and this has caused a real problem to arise.[4] If these three areas are distinct, then each demands its own unique approach, which in turn leads to conflict between them. But they don't have to conflict in this way. The debate between which field to privilege, business or ethics, is fundamentally about values: What do we prioritize and why?

The problem with business ethics is its attempt to find the most ethically appealing and efficient answer. Without common ground, or a common bond, resolution of these two often conflicting values is impossible. Recall Commander Sisko's statement to his son Jake, "Human values and Ferengi values are very different. We've never been able to form a common bond" ("The Nagus," *DS9*). It's this lack of a common bond that leads to inevitable, irresolvable conflicts between humans and Ferengi in general, and Sisko and Quark in particular. This is the conflict of contemporary business ethics, and to move forward we must acknowledge the need for a common bond.

"Sometimes the Only Thing More Dangerous than a Question Is an Answer"

Debates in business ethics often follow a certain formula. You identify a problem, like affirmative action, employment at will, or sexual harassment and then choose an ethical theory to apply to the problem. So, for example, you might decide to focus on your particular issue from a *deontological* perspective and emphasize respect and duty. On the other hand, someone else might address the same issue from a *utilitarian* perspective and thus stress results and the greater good. In such a case there will inevitably be an insuperable impasse when the demands of respect don't produce the best results or when the greater good can't be attained because respect is getting in the way. For example, one may argue against employment at will and for due process on the basis that insofar as employees are human beings

---

[4] The belief that ethics, economics, and politics are distinct studies is sometimes called the "Separation Thesis." See Patricia H. Werhane, "Business Ethics and the Origins of Contemporary Capitalism: Economics and Ethics in the Work of Adam Smith and Herbert Spencer" *Journal of Business Ethics* 24 (2000), pp. 185–198.

and demand respect they can't be fired without good reason. Likewise, a utilitarian could argue that employment at will functions best, allowing an employer the flexibility in hiring and firing that will lead to greater efficiency and productivity. At this point, the debate ceases to be about business ethics and becomes more about ethics in general: Should we privilege results or respect? Doing business ethics becomes impossible since both sides are speaking past the other. If both sides agreed on the pre-eminence of respect or the greater good, then headway could be made. But so long as the fundamental value is what is in contention no debate about specific issues can be resolved. One might simply resolve the above debate by asking what would serve the interests of business best, but this would presume that the interests of business take priority over the interests of the employees. There is no common ground between the two sides, and this is the problem.

The inability to resolve this basic disagreement of values is often the root of Quark's problems in *DS9*. In "The Dogs of War," Quark expresses disapproval of some of Grand Nagus Zek's reforms. He claims that taxes go against the very nature of free enterprise, monopolies should be allowed to exist, environmental regulations hamper progress, and labor rights are ridiculous. He sums it all up when he says that business should operate on the principle of unadulterated greed, where the rich get richer and the poor get poorer: survival of the fittest. Rom, Quark's more sentimental brother, often expresses opposing opinions privileging values such as respect, kindness, and love. Why do Rom and Quark disagree? Not because Rom thinks kindness functions better as a business model, or because Quark thinks free markets respect those involved more than regulated markets. They disagree because their presuppositions are different. Quark believes in the free market for its own sake. Rom thinks the economy should foster the well-being of those involved. Until this is resolved they will never reach an agreement. Before any issue can be resolved common ground must be found. So if we are to progress, we have to ask what we fundamentally value. A good example of this is the debate between *stockholder* and *stakeholder* theories, two schools of thought regarding the social responsibilities of a corporation.

The stockholder/stakeholder debate rests on one question: To whom does a corporation have a social responsibility? Milton

Friedman favors the view that the only social responsibility a corporation has is to its stockholders.[5] Basically, since a corporation is created for a single purpose, as an investment, its goal is to benefit the investors, or owners, of that corporation. Managers, therefore, have only fiduciary responsibilities to the stockholders who have given them the right to manage their property according to their express desires, usually the increase of profits. Employees, the local community, environmentalists, or consumers can make no ethical claims against the corporation since the corporation has no duties or responsibilities to them. The only restrictions placed on a corporation are those imposed by law.

As represented by R. Edward Freeman, "stakeholder theory" claims to the contrary that corporations have social responsibilities to either all of those affected by, or those vital to the operations of the corporation.[6] So employees, the community, environmentalists, consumers, and many other groups can make ethical demands against a corporation because corporations have obligations to these groups of individuals. A good example of this perspective occurs in "The Dogs of War." Quark objects to the reforms enacted by the Congress of Economic Advisors. One of these reforms regulates the dumping of industrial waste. Quark finds it ridiculous that they would restrict the actions of business just because dumping waste harms the natural habitat. A stakeholder would respond that we all have an interest in protecting the habitat since it affects us all. These restrictions are, therefore, in all of our best interests, and our best interests should restrict what businesses can and can't do. In fact, the wormhole aliens brainwash Grand Nagus Zek from a stockholder theorist to a stakeholder theorist simply because they see stockholder theory, or the unadulterated pursuit of greed, to be harmful.

Those in favor of stockholder theory have defended it on various grounds. Some argue that privileging stockholder interests is to the greatest benefit of all involved. If the well-being of

---

[5] Milton Friedman, "The Social Responsibility of Business Is to Increase Its Profits," in *Ethical Theory and Business*, edited by Tom L. Beauchamp and Norman E. Bowie (Upper Saddle River: Prentice Hall, 2004), pp. 50–55.

[6] R. Edward Freeman, "A Stakeholder Theory of the Modern Corporation," in *Ethical Theory and Business*, pp. 55–64.

the corporation is of primary concern, business will boom, jobs will be created, and all involved will benefit. Others argue that it is a matter of respect. The corporation is the private property of the owners and this ought to be respected. We can't do what we want with somebody else's property just because we think it would be more beneficial to do so. Others argue that stock-holders are in a unique position of vulnerability when it comes to the health of the corporation. After all, if it fails they lose their money and property. On the other hand, stakeholder theorists argue for their position with similar rationales. Arguing from consequences, stakeholder theorists claim that the general welfare is better served when profit isn't the sole motive. Corporations have a long history of union busting, pollution, labor abuses, and other nefarious activities that result from only looking at the bottom line. Clearly looking only to the interests of the stockholders isn't to the benefit of all those affected. Likewise, with regard to respect stakeholders merely ask, "Who respects the employees or local community who have little say in the operation of the corporation but are directly affected by its decisions?" Surely, there is a tremendous scope of impact that a major corporation like Wal-Mart can have on a community or its million-plus employees. This demands that if these people are to be respected they must be given a say in the operation of the corporation. And finally, with regard to vulnerability, a stockholder with a diversified portfolio comprised of disposable income is likely to be less vulnerable than an employee who depends on her job for her family's health care and rent?

As this debate above rages on, nothing is resolved. Stockholder theorists make their claims and stakeholder theo-rists respond. The problem is that neither side is speaking to the issue at the root of the other's concerns. Business ethicist John Hasnas recognizes this problem and offers the following sug-gestion. "I would ask you to consider that both normative theo-ries share a common feature; they both either explicitly or implicitly recognize the pre-eminent moral value of individual consent."[7] Hasnas means that at the root of the stockholder the-orist's concern for private property rights is a more fundamental

---

[7] John Hasnas, "Two Normative Theories of Business Ethics: A Critique," in *Ethical Theory and Business*, p. 72.

concern with *consent,* or *the voluntary nature of restrictions.* That is, we should have to ask the consent of a property owner before dictating how she may use her property. Stakeholder theorists are also concerned about consent. Stakeholders simply want to make sure that before a corporation is allowed to seriously affect an individual they should have to seek her consent, or at a minimum listen to and consider her concerns. At the root of both, Hasnas recognizes a common value: the pre-eminent moral value of consent. This common value could provide the basis for a common bond. Once such a bond is recognized, fruitful debate can begin. But while Hasnas's idea is insightful, I think the real problem lies even deeper.

Hasnas is arguing about *how* we should do business. But this presumes already that we know *why* we do business. Before we can figure out the best or most ethical way to undertake a practice we must understand why we do it, or should do it, in the first place. This is the question that needs to be asked and understood before business ethics can begin at all.

Do Wise Men Only Hear Profit in the Wind?

Most business ethicists begin from the presupposition that we live in a capitalist society, so any solution to an ethical problem must fit within the constraints of capitalism. They start by looking to the nature of business and capitalism, and go back to the work of Milton Friedman, whose views, as we saw, imply that the property rights of the stockholders are absolute, that there can be no claims made against them in terms of social responsibility. Business is simply about how property functions under capitalism and all ethical problems are thus easily resolved. But this seems feeble. Why do we have this form of property and not another? Society could be organized in some other way. Sure, if you're a capitalist then there are constraints on what can be done with private property. But the problem as phrased above isn't about what we can do within the bounds of the status quo, but how we can question and judge the status quo itself. Quark's mother, Ishka, knows what Ferengi culture and law deems legal and moral, namely, the oppression of women. So she can find answers to problems about women's rights within these bounds. If she asks the question, "Should women be allowed to earn profit?" she can find the answer easily

enough. No they shouldn't because Ferengi culture prohibits it.
But this fails to address the question of whether Ferengi culture
is correct in its judgment that women shouldn't be allowed to
earn profit. Ishka, like us, wants to question the foundations. If
we want to question the roots of business, what better place to
turn than the first Grand Nagus, Adam Smith?

Adam Smith (1723–1790) is mostly remembered for an idea
he never had and wouldn't have endorsed. This is the idea that
an ideal, free market economy is *laissez-faire* (French for "let it
alone"). In such an economy, each person's greed and pursuit
of unmitigated self-interest "miraculously" leads to the public
good due to guidance from an "invisible hand." In this way,
Smith's name is appropriated to the cause of unregulated free
markets, even though he never endorsed unregulated free markets. Although there are numerous quotes people use to justify
this reading of Smith, they're never given in context and are
rarely read with any charity to Smith's clearly stated moral convictions. Take for example the following over-quoted section
from *The Wealth of Nations* about self-interest:

> It is not from the benevolence of the butcher, the brewer, or the
> baker, that we expect our dinner, but from their regard to their own
> interest.[8]

Likewise, another over-referenced notion is the infamous "invisible hand." In this idea, supporters of the free market argue, we
find a clear presentation that unrestrained self-interest will guarantee a mutually beneficial arrangement and, therefore, regula-
tion isn't required. But what is forgotten is that Smith doesn't
think all we need to do is let business look after its own interests and all will turn out for the best. Smith thinks that free markets only work when founded on the *virtue of justice*. Business
ethicist Patricia Werhane puts the point clearly:

> Smith is . . . arguing that people in commerce tend to act in their
> own self-interest . . . But this neither means that people of com-
> merce are, or should be, necessarily selfish of greedy, nor is Smith
> proposing purely laissez-faire markets . . . Smith is arguing that

---

[8] Adam Smith, *The Wealth of Nations* (New York: Bantam Dell, 2003), pp.
23–24.

markets (the famous invisible hand) work best under conditions of economic liberty grounded in commutative justice (the 'rule of law'), when people are parsimonious and prudent, and co-operative as well as competitive. (p. 195)

Free markets only function properly when those operating them are virtuous. Ethics, not greed, regulates the market for the benefit of all.

Smith was first and foremost concerned with ethics and the public good. For him, the market was a mechanism to secure our *welfare*, not profit. The market isn't an absolute good, it serves a greater purpose. Another way of putting this is that free markets are good only insofar as they promote some greater interest, namely, the welfare of all of those affected by them. With respect to Smith's support of markets, Robert Heilbroner notes, "all the grubby scrabbling for wealth and glory has its ultimate justification in the welfare of the common man."[9] As even Quark recognizes, a true Grand Nagus's greed must reflect the best interests of the public ("Ferengi Love Songs," *DS9*).

So Smith really believed that self-interest and avarice function as positive mechanisms for economic progress only when they move the economy in a way beneficial to the public. We can see this idea about the morality behind the market reflected in the first introduction of the Ferengi in "The Last Outpost" (*TNG*). When the *Enterprise* is first made aware of the Ferengi, Picard asks Data for a report on this little-known race. Data offers the following account: "The best description may be, traders . . . likened to the ocean going Yankee traders of eighteenth- and nineteenth-century America." He states that they exemplify the "worst quality of capitalists," specifically the policy of "*caveat emptor*," which Data translates from the Latin as "buyer beware." What this quote clearly expresses is the notion that capitalism can itself be viewed as good or bad, that is, as ethical or unethical. The beginning of our discussion about business ethics shouldn't be about what the system will allow or demand, but whether our economic arrangements themselves are an ethical foundation on which to base our business practices. Nobel Laureate economist and moral philosopher Amartya Sen has

---

[9] Robert L. Heilbroner, *The Worldly Philosophers: The Lives, Times, and Ideas of the Great Economic Thinkers* (New York: Touchstone, 1999), p. 73.

expressed this very sentiment. He reminds us that economics is about values. How we spend our money and distribute wealth is determined by and indicates what we value.[10] It's this bedrock of values that must be resolved before more specific problems can be dealt with.

Consider the Ferengi again. Male Ferengi live by the belief that a Ferengi without profit is no Ferengi at all. They have organized their society based on this. If you were to ask them why profit is so important, they would look at you in confusion. Asking a Ferengi to justify profit is like asking a fish to justify its breathing underwater. Profit is just the mode of existence in which Ferengi live. It's not to be questioned or justified. Profit is a good unto itself. Yet profit *at all costs* is the worst quality of capitalism. In fact, Quark even considers embezzlement to be "pure profit" ("Prophet Motive," *DS9*). When profit is the sole end according to which all else is measured, then ethics takes a back seat. Aristotle may have been the first to understand the nature of this problem.

In his work, *Politics*, Aristotle makes a distinction between economics and chrematistics. Economics, according to Aristotle, is money management for a purpose: the good of the household. In this regard, a good business acumen is to the benefit of all those involved. One needs money to buy things, pay the rent, and generally survive. Money and business serve an end. Chrematistics, on the other hand, is money making for the mere sake of making money. Its end goal is accumulation. However, if this becomes the primary mode of doing business, of prioritizing one's values, then Aristotle sees nothing but trouble on the horizon. Once business becomes primary, humanity is given only a passing glance in the realm of values. At the heart of the problem of business ethics, at the root of any debate needs to be an understanding of the values from which we are beginning.

"There's More to Life than Profit"

What do we value? For Amartya Sen, as for Smith before him, *freedom* is the underlying good that economics and business strive for. According to Sen, "Development can be seen . . . as a process of expanding the real freedoms that people enjoy" (p. 3).

---

[10] See Amartya Sen, *Development as Freedom* (New York: Anchor, 1999).

Sen focuses on the quality of life as opposed to merely the bottom line. This focus has the benefit of not merely judging economic advancement in terms of actual, exercisable freedoms, but also avoiding the pitfall of believing that an increase in gross domestic product or personal income is good in itself. Economics is understood, on this view, as grounded on the well being of those involved, not the promotion of profit or expansion of markets as if they were good above and beyond the welfare of those affected. Quark himself justifies markets in a similar way. In appealing to the wormhole aliens who have brainwashed Grand Nagus Zek, Quark argues how greed serves the greater good by promoting a value beyond itself. He argues that greed fosters growth and development and ultimately a more affluent society ("Prophet Motive," *DS9*). Greed, which underpins free market capitalism, isn't a good in itself, but is good because it serves a larger ideal, namely, human development. In this spirit, Sen understands poverty not simply as an economic condition, one of low income, but as capability deprivation. He states: "What the capability perspective does in poverty analysis is to enhance the understanding of the nature and causes of poverty and deprivation by shifting the primary attention away from *means . . .* income . . . to *ends* that people have reason to pursue, and, correspondingly, to the *freedoms* to be able to satisfy these ends" (p. 90). It's better to be greedy than not because greed is an effective means to promote human welfare. Greed is good when its result is a surplus of goods that afford us a better quality of living. But it is only good as a means to this end. Quark is using this type of argument in an attempt to persuade the aliens who are concerned with welfare above all else. He obviously doesn't believe this entirely, as his practices throughout the series demonstrate. But it emphasizes an important point: Business must be justified with reference to an ultimate value. If freedom is this value, then business practices will be judged in terms of how well they promote this end. Business, once again, becomes a means only and not an end in itself. One can no longer argue for the free market just because we're a capitalist country, whatever this means, or because it's most effective at increasing gross domestic product or productivity. Rather, one has to reference the well being of the people whom the market serves. Quark is right in saying that markets provide not only economic freedom, which is valuable in its own right, but also expanded opportunity, increased wealth, and productivity. But these are good only insofar as they better our collective situation. This is the lesson of the Ferengi: not one they teach, but one we learn from watching.

In any Ferengi-centric episode of *DS9*, invariably Quark, or another Ferengi who serves as a stand-in for Ferengi culture as a whole, is confronted with a conflict between their beloved latinum and some opposing, mutually exclusive value such as respect, love, family, or friends. We then hear the most shocking words come out of the Ferengi's mouth, "It's not about profit anymore." We gasp. How could a Ferengi turn its back on profit? Such a sentiment is anathema for a species that makes no distinction between business and pleasure and who define a "true" Ferengi as one who would sell out his family and friends for a few bars of gold pressed latinum! But we are not really surprised. In fact, when this happens we are pleased that those barbaric and confused Ferengi have learned their lesson: some things are more valuable than profit. Business ethicists need to also learn this lesson. Business ethics shouldn't begin from the presupposition that profit is good in itself and the goal of ethicists is to find the most ethical way to accumulate wealth. Instead, we should ask what we value. Is it love, friendship, family, freedom, or a combination of all or some of these? Then we can ask how profit serves these greater ends, and how we can accumulate profit in a way consistent with these ends. Perhaps I have been unfair to business ethicists and the field of study as a whole, but they have too often unfairly privileged profit over people.

There's no inherent contradiction between business and ethics, just as conflict between Quark and Sisko or humans and Ferengi is not inevitable, a fact of nature. Business is a social practice and just like all other social activities it can and must be evaluated according to an ethical standard. The economy is judged on how well it serves our ends. Business practices are justified with reference to whether or not they're effective means to these ends. The current practice of business ethics needs to be rethought and its foundations need to be assessed before it can provide insight or helpful solutions that are more than mere compromises. The rules of acquisition can't help us now, because the rules themselves are what are in question.

Starfleet Directive
THREE

---

*A United Federation:
Social and Religious
Values of the Future*

10

Inhuman Nature, or What's It Like to Be a Borg?

KEVIN S. DECKER

> **JANEWAY:** I'm having trouble . . . with the nature of individuality.
> **SEVEN OF NINE:** You require a philosophical discussion.
> **JANEWAY:** There's a time and a place for it. This is one of them.
>
> —"Latent Image," *VGR*

The Borg are one of the iconic symbols of latter-day *Star Trek* because they so successfully freak us out. We love to hate this assimilation-crazy collective of drones—the most worthy nemesis of the *Next Generation* and *Voyager* crews—primarily because they assault our vaunted sense of *individuality*: they have a single-minded desire not only to conquer all opposition, but to assimilate the best of all worlds into their collective. Perhaps just as importantly, they are *unnatural*, hybrid cyber-organisms or "cyborgs" (hence, "Borg,") that, by their very nature, transgress boundaries of "human" versus "machine," "nature" as opposed to "artifact," "born" not "made."

We're uncomfortable with processes such as cloning and replacement of original body parts with transplants or prosthetics, even amidst the rapid technological changes of the early twenty-first century. One rationale for this discomfort is the belief that a thing has dignity and deserves respect only if it fits into the categories of "human," "natural," and "born." But the pervasive penetration of technology into our daily lives and even into our bodies, its "matter-of-factness," challenges both these presuppositions by asking us to re-evaluate what "human nature" is. As a result, it's becoming both more difficult to maintain a healthy sense of individuality as well as confidently use distinctions like "natural" *versus* "artificial."

If clones were to walk among us, would they deserve rights to protect their dignity? When can we locate the end of life when most of us may end up on life-sustaining hospital equipment? Because questions like these—and many others—form our most basic speculations about life, death, and human nature, a lack of satisfying answers to them can lead to feelings of alienation from technology as much as from humanity.

Perhaps the Borg shouldn't freak us out as much as they do. The Borg are of a single mind about the need to unify differences and work toward perfection: Does this fact in some way *justify* their assimilations, or at the very least, make them more comprehensible? Is there something inherently wrong with the artificial, cybernetic nature of these enemies of the Federation? The Borg are monsters of the modern age: aside from their pasty, "never-seen-the-beach" complexions, their drone recruitment tactics seemingly gleaned from *Texas Chainsaw Massacre*, and interchangeable parts that would make Henry Ford green with envy, the Borg freak us out because they put us in mind of *our own* transgressions of the distinctions between "natural" and "artificial," "individual" and "collective."

"I Am the Beginning, the End, the One Who Is Many"

As Seven of Nine's adventures aboard *Voyager* show, the essence of the battle between the Borg and humanity is found in the tension between collectivity or unity and individuality or diversity. Does one or the other of these two sides have an advantage in the sense that reality favors their cause? Or in other words, is what is real fundamentally a *unity*, or instead a *diversity* of different things?

In philosophical metaphysics (the study of the "being" of beings), *monism* is the view that there is only one kind of reality, substance, or "stuff" that makes up the world as we know and experience it. Many of the simple theories of the earliest Greek philosophers, the so-called Presocratics, are monistic. In the early sixth century B.C.E., Thales argued that water was the *arche* (or material source) of everything. One of Thales's successors, Anaximander (612–545 B.C.E.) disagreed that the basic stuff of the world could be any specific element, like water or fire. As a result, he conceived of the world as composed of diverse elements, all of which originated from an indescribable *something* that he could only call the "boundless." Just as the Presocratics believed that our basic presuppositions about nature might be challenged by revealing its hidden truths, the "inhuman nature" of the Borg is informed by the collective's own view of perfection.

Of course, most people don't hold a monistic view of reality, simply out of common sense. For example, when Captains Picard or Janeway first beheld the yawning, gloomy interior of a Borg cube, they saw hundreds of different pieces of machinery, pulsing energy, and of course thousands of Borg drones. In their common sense perspective, reality seemed to be full of many different kinds of things, with each kind composed of uncountable individual things. But, seen from the perspective of the Borg Queen, the same cube is a kind of unity: a humming, thriving network of processes and activities. It's a unity which itself comprises a part of a greater whole: the Borg collective itself.

In the history of philosophy, several monists present us with distinct challenges to our sense of our world and ourselves, just as the Borg collective presents a challenge to how we think about our relation to communities and to technology. Parmenides of Elea (515–450 B.C.E.) was the first of these. Parmenides, in thinking about the nature of *change*, did not share with his Presocratic predecessors or with modern scientists the desire to observe the natural world in order to find regularities underlying actual, experienced changes. Instead, he was interested in analyzing the concept of *change* itself: What does it *mean* for some thing X to change into another thing Y? Parmenides's analysis is succinct, if a little cryptic. He tells us:

> Come now, and I will tell you . . . the only ways of enquiry that are to be thought of. The one, that [it] is and that it is impossible for [it] not to be, is the path of Persuasion (for she attends upon Truth); the other, that [it] is not and that it is needful that [it] not be, that I declared to you is an altogether indiscernible track: for you could not know what is not—that cannot be done—nor indicate it.[1]

---

[1] G.S. Kirk, J.E. Raven, and M. Schofield, *The Presocratic Philosophers: A*

When we translate Parmenides's simple argument into the traditional form of a syllogism, it looks something like this:

PREMISE 1: What is, is.

PREMISE 2: What is not, is not.

PREMISE 3: *Change* occurs when something that *is* becomes what it *is not*.

From these three common-sense premises, Parmenides derives a surprising conclusion: Change is impossible! He does this on the back of what Premises 1 and 2 show: that existence is not nonexistence, and vice versa. If something exists, then it cannot pass into the state of nonexistence because, as Premise 2 says, there *is no* "non-existence." A simple illustration shows this. Like any energy source, dilithium loses its capacity to regulate the matter-antimatter reaction and channel energy to power warp engines over time (indeed, knowing facts like this has prevented some of us from getting married and moving out of our parents' basements). Dilithium changes by denaturing, that is, by losing its structure. Apparently, what *is* (its crystal structure) passes into *what is not*, or nonexistence (lack of structure). But where did the structure go? According to Parmenides, there is no "state of nonexistence" for dilithium's crystal structure to pass into. It's logically impossible for anything to change, if change means what common sense says it does. Everything that exists is part of an unchanging, unchangeable whole that we might as well just call "Being."

Parmenides's theory has several implications. First and most obviously, every apparent change—including that of your eyes skipping from one word in this sentence to the next—doesn't really occur. The *appearance* of change is like the illusion of a bent stick in water or the false position of the *Stargazer* during the Picard Maneuver ("The Battle," *TNG*). Second, "Being" is both uncreated and indestructible. This makes sense if you think that "Being" (*what is*) couldn't have come from, and can't turn into nothingness (*what is not*). Finally, "Being" is perfect, or so Parmenides thinks when he says, "Therefore it is right that what

Critical History with a Selection of Texts (New York: Cambridge University Press, 1983), p. 245.

is should not be imperfect; for it is not deficient—if it were it would be deficient in everything" (p. 252). If reality is a single, undivided whole, without change, then there's no basis for making comparisons of better and worse.

Parmenides's monism certainly sounds like a candidate for the official philosophy of the Borg, or at least it is a metaphor for what the Borg yearn for. After all, with a simple argument, Parmenides is able to establish the existence of perfection, which is the Borg's *raison d'être*. The Borg Queen could've quoted Parmenides in *First Contact* when trying to win Data over. "By assimilating other beings into our collective," she says in her alluring voice, "we are bringing them closer to perfection."[2] Yet before we draw such a conclusion, let's sharpen the comparison with a look at another variety of monism.

This is the philosophy of Baruch Spinoza (1632–1677), which the god-like Gary Mitchell (unfairly) dismissed as "simple" ("Where No Man Has Gone Before," *TOS*). Like Parmenides, Spinoza saw himself working at a level more basic than observational science: his metaphysical thinking aimed at finding the logical implications of simple concepts. Spinoza, however, emphasized the concept of *substance* rather than that of change. By "substance," philosophers up to his time didn't mean something weird you might find on the bottom of your boot on an away mission, but rather a *metaphysical principle of individuality and independence*. When Aristotle (384–322 B.C.E.) spoke of "substances" he was referring to individuals ("Neelix," "Troi") as well as natural kinds or groups ("Talaxians," "Betazoids"). For him, substances are the things that *have* qualities or attributes; so "a Bolian" is the substance that "has" the quality "blueness." Substances are also the core of an individual thing, the part that persists despite change: even if our Bolian is assimilated by the Borg and loses his natural blue skin pigmentation, the same Bolian substance remains.[3]

Spinoza, although admitting that there is something called "substance," takes issue in a pretty radical way with Aristotelian

---

[2] The amount of interest the Borg Queen shows in Data is remarkable, given Locutus's verdict in "The Best of Both Worlds, Part II" (*TNG*) that, in the "new order," the android will be "obsolete."

[3] Another way of putting this is that "the Bolian" is still the *numerically identical* individual that he was before the assimilation.

philosophy. Spinoza believes that thinking logically about the nature of substance demands that we admit that there is *only one substance and no more*—a claim similar to, but made for reasons different than Parmenides's belief that reality is unified and unchanging. Here's a simple version of his argument:

PREMISE 1: A "substance" is something that is absolutely independent of everything else.

PREMISE 2: A substance can be different from another substance only if their attributes or qualities can be compared.

PREMISE 3: Attributes or qualities can be compared only if the two substances have something in common.

PREMISE 4: If two substances have something in common, then they are not absolutely independent of each other.

This last premise directly conflicts with the first, which Spinoza saw as the basic definition of substance that all philosophers had accepted. You can't claim that there is substance and in the same breath reason that there is more than *one* such substance, Spinoza declared: you can't have your *raktajino* and drink it too. No, there is only one substance, and given that substance's eternal, uncreated, perfect nature, Spinoza was only too happy to call this "Nature" or "God"—much the same thing, in his view.

Like Parmenides's monism, Spinoza's has challenging implications, perhaps the most mind-blowing of which is that all things—including you, me, and Spock's brain—*are God*, and not just from the perspective of the gullible Eymorg.[4] Spinoza's conception of God resists the tendency of most believers to turn God into a person, a transcendent being who exists separately from the created universe, while retaining this central spiritual truth: the totality of which we are all a part deserves our wonder and awe.

But unlike Parmenides, Spinoza *does* think that change occurs in the world; in fact, every change occurs for a reason.

---

[4] To be precise, we are "modes" or modifications of some of God's attributes like matter and intelligence. Such modes are, according to Spinoza, "in God and . . . can neither exist nor be conceived without God." See Spinoza, *Ethics* (New York: Oxford University Press, 2000), p. 100.

Whose reason? Why, God's of course—since everything *is* God. What God wills, God wills *necessarily*, leading to a world that is as *deterministic* as it is monistic. In such a world, everything happens for God's reasons, so humans—like drones in a collective—don't really have free will. The mind, Spinoza writes, "must be determined to will this or that by a cause, which is also determined by another, and this again by another, etc." (p. 155). And it is in our *understanding* of this fact and its implications that we find out why Spinoza chose the odd-sounding title *Ethics* for a *metaphysical* project establishing the existence of a single substance.

When we *understand* our place within "God" or "Nature," then "it teaches us to expect and to bear with a calm mind both faces of fortune: All things follow from the eternal decree of God with the same necessity as it follows from the essence of a triangle that its three angles are equal to two right angles" (p. 161). Spinoza is saying that such "freedom" as we have is dependent on how well we understand *the whole of which we are merely parts.* This is one statement of Spinoza's *holism*: not only are all the modes or parts of the world related to each other necessarily, but we are doomed to wander in helpless, despondent bewilderment unless we strive to understand the necessary role that we play in something larger than ourselves.

Conversely, Spinoza says, tranquility and enlightenment come with our effort to comprehend the whole. *Star Trek* often presents evidence that Borg drones are anything but "mindless" and that they find something of value in their existence once separated from it. Seven of Nine, for example, often favorably contrasts her former harmonious existence in the collective to life on board *Voyager.* In the collective, it appears, there were "benefits to being a member." Of course, Seven of Nine is not the only *Voyager* crewmember to have had such experiences: Chakotay is temporarily made part of a post-Borg "co-operative" on a planet near the Nekrit Expanse ("Unity," *VGR*) and experiences both the joys of intimate, communal connection as well as the betrayal of having been used as a member of the link. With these thoughts in mind, Parmenides's monism and Spinoza's holism may sound like an excellent one-two combo philosophy for the Borg; but there are good reasons to think differently. What's missing from this collective vision?

"It Is in My Nature to Comply with the Collective"

We have to recognize that, as a race, the Borg are clearly, narrowly, and frighteningly goal-directed or *teleological* in their thinking. Parmenides and Spinoza are not. Consider, for example, the chat-up line that any friendly neighborhood Borg cube would use to establish "diplomatic relations" with a ship it encounters: "We are the Borg. Existence as you know it is over. We will add your biological and technological distinctiveness to our own. Resistance is futile." Clearly, the Borg have a *telos*—the Greek word for goal or purpose—they *aim* at perfection, yet they do not claim to have achieved it (with a few notable exceptions).[5] Nor do they act as if they live in a world that is devoid of change or shot through with necessities. While their familiar mantra that "resistance is futile" *might* be a metaphysical claim that the entire universe is destined to be part of the collective, all we know for sure is that they ruthlessly and mercilessly plow through the galaxy, assimilating others. If we took the Borg's actions as indicators of their beliefs about the world, we would think that, for them, the universe is not "closed," fixed and changeless, but risk-filled and "open" to the possibilities of action, the goal of which for the Borg is to "raise quality of life for all species."[6]

Georg W.F. Hegel (1770–1831) attempted to revise monism in teleological ways. Hegel was strongly influenced by Spinoza's holistic idea of "purpose" as our understanding of being a part within a whole. As a German working during turbulent times (including the French Revolution and the "liberation" of Europe by Napoleon), Hegel focused on the development of what he calls Spirit (in German, *Geist*) throughout history. Rather than seeing "Being," "God," or "Nature" as the lone reality, Hegel reinterprets objective reality in terms of the shifting ways in which *humans perceive the world and act to change it.*

---

[5] In a particularly grotesque scene from "Dark Frontier" (*VGR*), the Borg Queen addresses the severed head of a drone, purring, "It's a shame you're not alive to experience disembodiment. It's the epitome of perfection." Also, Seven's Borg background justifies her elitism toward fellow crewmembers (at least in her own eyes).

[6] Locutus's words, to which Worf indignantly replies, "I like my *species* the way it is" ("The Best of Both Worlds, Part II," *TNG*).

Hegel followed the lead of other German "idealists" in giving up the search for a "God's-eye perspective" from which to define "objectivity." Instead, he insisted upon pursuing philosophy as the study of how specifically human ways of being and perceiving constitute what we take as reality. Hegel's special twist on monism is that Spirit, as reality, is really a *process*, not a thing: it's *mental activity*. Yet this doesn't seem to conform to common sense: What about all those physical objects out there in the world? They, no less than our individual minds, are constructions of the changing consciousness of Spirit, Hegel responds. If, for example, we examine what humans have meant by the word "nature" over the centuries, we'll find a great diversity of opinions that vary from William Blake's sublime universe to Hobbes's view of life as solitary, nasty, brutish, and short. "Spirit" is *everything* in reality, so it is *both* mind and will *and* what our minds perceive and our wills act upon. "It includes all of us and everything in human experience . . . It is simply, the world, aware of itself as a self-conscious and comprehensible unity."[7]

From Hegel's perspective, Parmenides and Spinoza were on the right track—they realized that only *reason* can help us overcome the dualisms that we see, the divisions we experience in life. "Spirit has broken with the world it has hitherto inhabited and imagined," Hegel declared in words that described the instability of Europe in 1807, but which could easily apply to today's world. "The frivolity and boredom which unsettle the established order, the vague foreboding of something unknown, these are the heralds of approaching change."[8] His work reflects a deep concern with how societies and states stick together or fall apart. He sees that it's our ability as reasoners that allows us to glimpse "totality," or in other words, to view the world from a perspective in which we see that there is nothing truly alien to us:

> For it is nothing short of the whole of philosophy that is the knowledge of the universe as in itself *one single* organic totality which develops itself out of its own conception, and which, returning into

---

[7] Robert C. Solomon, *In the Spirit of Hegel* (New York, Oxford, 1983), p. 284.

[8] G.W.F. Hegel, *Phenomenology of Spirit* (New York: Oxford University Press, 1977), §11.

itself so as to form a whole in virtue of the necessity in which it is placed towards itself, binds itself together with itself into *one single* world of truth.[9]

Because Hegelian Spirit develops as history progresses, it also *changes*, overcoming deep divisions and contradictions that always crop up in our limited, context-dependent perspectives on the world. Over time, our understanding of our place in the world changes, Hegel says in an interesting spin on Spinoza, as our own *self-understanding* changes. In turn, when our knowledge of ourselves changes, so does *our world*.

At first glance, Hegel's concept of Spirit, "all of us and everything in human experience" continually developing in reason and unity, doesn't fit well with our everyday experience. Unless what Hegel means by "Spirit" is "God" (and indeed, like Spinoza, this is one of the ways he names the underlying reality), most people don't experience such a force inside each of us, pushing history along. Hegel's ideas seem very strange, yet the *Next Generation* episode "I, Borg" provides a perfect example of how something like Spirit makes progress through individuals. At the beginning of this episode, the *Enterprise* crew has had nothing but terrifying experiences of the Borg that justly lead them to see the race as wholly alien and nothing but a threat. In the wake of Picard's abduction and transformation into Locutus, it seemed that Q had been proven correct in warning, "You can't outrun them. You can't destroy them. If you damage them, the essence of what they are remains. They regenerate and keep coming . . . They are relentless" ("Q Who?" *TNG*). What is wholly alien, wholly other, cannot be reasoned or bargained with. It may not even be capable of being destroyed.

Hegel's monistic doctrine of Spirit, however, tells us that *nothing* is wholly alien to creatures like us. Indeed, the encounters that Geordi, Guinan, and Picard have with Hugh the Borg not only convince them that individual Borg drones may be redeemed, but also create deep-seated changes in their own understanding of what it means to be human.[10] And whereas the

---

[9] G.W.F. Hegel, *Introductory Lectures on Aesthetics* (New York: Penguin, 1993), p. 29.

[10] Although a bit clichéd, Picard's reason for rejecting the paradoxical geometric virus designed by Data and Geordi in the episode is instructive in the

Borg are "merely" treated as highly dangerous (perhaps redeemable) aliens in *Next Generation*, the "progress of Spirit" continues into the *Voyager* series. There we are given new resources to answer the question "What's it like to be a Borg?" from the perspective of Chakotay ("Unity"), Tuvok ("Unimatrix Zero"), the Borg Queen ("Dark Frontier," "Unimatrix Zero" "Endgame") and, of course, Seven of Nine.

Hegel's monism is teleological, and so Spirit has a goal, an ultimate purpose, and it's perhaps this fact that draws Hegel's philosophy closest to the Borg worldview. The Borg's search for perfection occurs on a sweeping, galactic stage: according to Hugh, "The Borg assimilate civilizations, not individuals" ("I, Borg," *TNG*); and from assimilation survivor Guinan we learn that the Borg "don't do anything piecemeal ("Q Who?" *TNG*). Similarly, Hegel examined the history of the great institutions, laws, moral systems, and individuals that define the *Zeitgeist* ("spirit of the times") of particular civilizations, such as ancient Greece and Rome. Spirit moves in great civilizations when "each [culture is] able to appropriate the achievements of its predecessor and accommodate a level of self-consciousness and freedom which its predecessor could not accommodate."[11] Hegel's conception of perfection is thus not found as the conclusion of a logical argument, but at "the end of history," when the internal contradictions, divisions, and dualisms that bring an end to even great civilizations have been reconciled with each other. "The last shape of Spirit," for Hegel, is "Absolute Spirit," or "Spirit that knows itself in the shape of Spirit" (§798). One way of interpreting this would be to say that we achieve perfection when we see other persons and the parts of the world as *necessarily connected*, and not as *opposed to* or *different from* us.

But for those of us who aren't Hegel, perfection is more difficult to envision: it's found in a fleeting moment appreciating art or natural beauty, or discovered in the rarefied atmospheres of philosophical or mathematical worlds. For the Borg, perfection is to be approached by adapting the best elements of assimilated civilizations and casting away the worst elements. What

---

implications it has for self-consciousness: "To use [Hugh] in this manner, we'd be no better than the enemy that we seek to destroy."

[11] Stephen Houlgate, *An Introduction to Hegel: Freedom, Truth and History* (Malden, Massachusetts: Blackwell, 2005), p. 18.

little we know about the ultimate goal of this method is perhaps best stated by Seven of Nine: perfection is, like the Omega molecule, "infinitely complex, yet harmonious," including "infinite parts functioning as one" ("The Omega Directive," *VGR*).[12] The implication here is that the individual contribution of each of Omega's atomic elements creates this harmony, instead of conflict. All internal resistance is overcome. Similarly, Omega's inherent instability comes from its interaction with things non-Omega, elements and energies alien and external to it. A universe in which Hegel's Absolute Spirit finally rested, satisfied with its own self-understanding, expresses the same ideal as a universe in which the Borg had finally conquered all external resistance. Similarly, a universe filled with only Omega molecules would be stable and infinitely complex, with no internal resistance, a picture that resonates with Parmenides's monistic vision of Being.

"The Borg Is the Ultimate User"

If he were alive today, Hegel would likely say that Spirit, understood in terms of radical challenges to our own self-understanding, is on the move in our own time in the rapid advance of technology. And technological development, not just in biomedicine but in security applications (like "chipping" citizens to prevent identity theft) and personal uses (like Palm Pilots and Bluetooth headsets),[13] calls to mind the cybernetic nature of the Borg. Philosophers that take technology seriously find themselves, like Hegel, confronting dualisms—conceptual distinctions that are deeply entrenched in our way of dealing with the world.

---

[12] The Omega molecule hearkens back to the Vulcan IDIC ("Infinite Diversity in Infinite Combinations") philosophy, which presents an alternative picture of harmony in a whole in which individuality isn't suppressed but balanced. Omega also has a correlate in western philosophy: Gottfried Leibniz's *monads* are infinitely complex individual substances which serve as Leibniz's answer to the monistic "heresy" of Spinoza's position. For more on Leibniz, see Robert Merrihew Adams, *Leibniz: Theist, Determinist, Idealist* (New York: Oxford University Press, 1994).

[13] In the BBC series *Doctor Who*, the human-machine hybrids called the Cybermen are analogous to the Borg. In the 2006 episodes of that show entitled "Rise of the Cybermen" and "The Age of Steel," human minds are taken over by the Bluetooth headset-like "earplugs" manufactured by Cybus Industries, headed by Cybermen-creator John Lumic.

Donna Haraway is a contemporary feminist philosopher of science who, like Hegel, is concerned about the role that dualisms play in producing social fragmentation. Our either/or ways of thinking, she writes, have been the cornerstones of the "domination of women, people of color, nature, workers, animals." According to Haraway, these dualisms include: "self/other, mind/body, culture/nature, male/female, civilized/primitive, reality/appearance, whole/part, agent/resource, maker/made, active/passive, right/wrong, truth/illusion, total/partial, God/man."[14] Thinking in terms of these dualisms seem natural to us, because we believe that each of these either/or terms accurately describes a certain category of things that is exclusive of its "opposite." While the dualisms are very abstract, Haraway, as well as many other critics of traditional ways of philosophizing and of the cultural *status quo*, think that they have concrete, *practical* consequences.

Some people, though, feel apprehension at attempts to "fuzz up" the differences between sides of dualisms of the natural and artificial. This feeling may rest on what Leon Kass, chairman of President Bush's Council on Bioethics, has called "the wisdom of repugnance."[15] This seems like an odd reaction when we consider it, as Spinoza and Hegel would demand, in wider context: the context of the medical technology that grants life daily to prematurely born children in neonatal care units of hospitals (who could forget the "Borg baby" in "Q Who?" (*TNG*)?); or the context of prosthetics, pacemakers, and the culture of psychoactive medication that use physical or chemical technology to re-establish "normalcy" for an ever-increasing number of people.[16]

---

[14] Donna Haraway, "A Cyborg Manifesto: Science, Technology, and Socialist-Feminism in the Late Twentieth Century," in *Simians, Cyborgs, and Women: The Reinvention of Nature* (New York: Routledge, 1991), p. 177.

[15] The phrase forms the title for Chapter 5 of his *Life, Liberty, and the Defense of Dignity* (Lanham: AEI, 2004). Kass applies this notion to the possibility of human cloning.

[16] Broadening the context even further, we could ask why we would care about the security of our pets enough to "chip" *them*, but not our children; why processed foods largely made of artificial ingredients now intuitively taste better on the palate than natural ones; and why we spend increasing amounts of time and money immersing ourselves in the virtual environments of television, the internet, and video games (the human equivalents of Unimatrix Zero, surely!).

Kass justifies the "wisdom of repugnance" by relying on a familiar distinction in biomedical ethics between the use of technology to *treat* humans who have naturally occurring diseases or biological defects, on the one hand, and using it to *enhance* human capacities beyond what is considered normal.[17] But this distinction is highly debatable for at least two reasons. First, there doesn't seem to be anything inherently repugnant about enhancing human capacities through technology, so the burden of proof is on those who think we should usually steer clear of enhancements. Beyond this, however, if we don't unnecessarily limit our understanding of technology (think: fire, the plow, the printing press), a case can be made that the use of enhancing technology is actually part of the human condition. Although much of our technology does its work outside the bounds of the human skin (unlike most biomedical technology) why is the former more ethically acceptable than the latter?

Haraway takes this one step further. She believes that, with biomedicine and genetics, virtual reality and prosthetics, the cyborgs are already among us, and *we are them*. "Late twentieth-century machines have made thoroughly ambiguous the difference between natural and artificial, mind and body, self-developing and externally designed, and many other distinctions that used to apply to organisms and machines," she writes. "Our machines are disturbingly lively, and we ourselves frighteningly inert" (p. 152).[18]

Haraway's words bring into sharp relief the cultural distance between today and how audiences viewed computers and artificial intelligence in the original *Star Trek* series forty years ago, and why there were no Borg, and nothing like the Borg, in that show. For example, in the original *Star Trek* series, the treatment of the M-5 ("The Ultimate Computer") or Landru ("The Return of the Archons"), the androids of "What Are Little Girls Made Of?" or "I, Mudd," as little more than overblown calculators depicts the difference between "natural" and artificial intelligence as so

---

[17] For more on this distinction as it applies in genetics, see Chapter 6 in this volume.

[18] Consider, for example, the "liveliness" of performances in the two categories of actors—computer generated ones and real, live humans—in the second *Star Wars* trilogy, Episodes I through III.

great that it's an absolute gulf. In *The Next Generation,* that distinction is fuzzed by Picard's assimilation, by artificially intelligent life forms that qualify as persons ("The Measure of a Man," "Quality of Life," "Emergence"), and most pre-eminently by Data's quest to be human. By the time of *Voyager,* the distinction has all but been erased as we are asked to struggle alongside a holographic Doctor and a former Borg drone with the issues of constructing individuality and a new life. We can clearly envision a future in which Kass's repugnance has little or no wisdom left to it.

"Obviously, the Borg Can't Hold Their Liquor"

In the cyborgs portrayed in science fiction, Haraway finds that "nature and culture are reworked; the one can no longer be the resource for appropriation or incorporation of the other" (p. 151). This implies that it's wrong to see the Borg assimilation of other civilizations as a fight between machines and "natural" life forms, since the civilizations targeted by the Borg are, as we have seen, also products of the assimilation of technology into culture and the body.

If the theories of Parmenides, Spinoza, and Hegel mean anything in this context, they must give us a basis for questioning our thinking in terms of such fundamental oppositions as those we've discussed. All three philosophers would agree that what's most fundamentally real—the basis for our living and thinking—doesn't support dualisms like "natural" *versus* "artificial." Spinoza and Hegel would likely question whether or not "freedom" (a central value prized in all the *Star Trek* series) and "collectivity" are irreconcilable. Spinoza might find truth in Seven of Nine's criticisms of the anarchic and fragmentary individuality of her fellow crewmembers—for her, individuality is the Alpha but not the Omega of self-perfection. And Hegel in particular would find poignancy in Q's statement that the Borg are "the ultimate user," since, as we've seen, Spirit has the ability to come to terms with what was apparently alien to it that leads it ever onwards toward self-knowledge and greater freedom.

At first glance, the Borg freak us out because the "wisdom of repugnance" tells us that we would never want to encounter, never want to become what they portray in our conveniently fictional, and therefore "safe" *Star Trek* universe. Yet today, 150 years out from when Starfleet begins to explore the galaxy, the dense intermeshing of the technological and the natural in our lives should make us stop and think: if we *are* the Borg, then resistance truly is futile.[19]

---

[19] This chapter has been improved thanks to the attention of Karl Erbacher and Jason Eberl; my thanks go to them.

11

Recognizing the Big Picture: Why We Want to Live in the Federation

JASON MURPHY and TODD PORTER

Why is *Star Trek* such a cultural phenomenon? Why does it instill such deep devotion? This dedication can be seen in examples such as the Klingon Language Institute's translation—or reclamation of the Klingon original—of *Hamlet*, recreations of *Trek* sets in homes around the globe, and the shocking dollar figures that a recent auction of memorabilia at Christie's generated—the six-foot studio model of the *Enterprise-D* sold for half-a-million dollars. One explanation may be *Star Trek*'s capacity to isolate themes that the creators of the various incarnations of the show find most important.[1] Viewers can be hooked by either the particular, "small" story, or the background, "big" story.[2] At both levels, *recognition*—an idea in political philosophy by which someone is seen as a citizen, peer, or simply a rational person—is a prominent theme throughout *Star Trek*. We'll show how this notion of recognition makes the society depicted in *Star Trek* so appealing to fans, because we'd all like to live in such a society that allows the rich development of its citizens' talents.

"You Have Helped Me to Recognize the Better Parts of Myself"

The idea of recognition has played an important role in social and political philosophy since the nineteenth century. At that

---

[1] By "creators," we refer to the contributions of directors, editors, producers, script writers, and actors working to achieve a single voice.

[2] We're not referring here to the frequent use of "A" and "B" plots in *Trek*

time, Georg W.F. Hegel (1770–1831) emerged as the primary theorist of recognition, but the term is also used in the present day by critical theorists such as Jürgen Habermas and Axel Honneth. Recognition can be understood by first looking at it in a relatively simple light. In daily life, to get something done we often need to be *recognized as entitled* to do that work. Badges, degrees, knighthoods, job titles, and uniforms are examples of formal recognition, which entitle those recognized to enter specific places or do certain tasks. Starfleet Medical personnel wear blue uniforms, while Cardassian Guls are known for their form-fitting leather. There are also a host of *informal* sorts of recognition, examples of which include greetings, rhetorical forms, and etiquette, like the Vulcan salutation "Live long and prosper." These also reflect entitlements that are expressed by those who give them. Imagine saying "hello" and getting only a stare. In this case, the blank look may be a sign that its wearer doesn't recognize the greeter as entitled to be there or to talk to him— of course, ignoring "*Qapla'*" may only indicate that you don't speak Klingon. Referring to Captain Picard as "Jean-Luc" in any but the most intimate situations indicates that the speaker doesn't recognize the authority or station of the *Enterprise's* commanding officer.

When philosophers speak about recognition, they're also referring to the most fundamental sorts—recognition as a fellow citizen or, more fundamental yet, as someone who's entitled to ask for an explanation behind an assertion. Denying someone such recognition is effectively denying them the capacity to participate in reasoning, to be a factor in the assessment of claims. Whether Data is *recognized* as a tool or a person determines his role within the Federation. If a tool, he has no "self" and is simply a very useful encyclopedia. If a person, he has rights and responsibilities within society. In "The Measure of a Man" (*TNG*), Data is declared a person and thus recognized by Starfleet as possessing all rights and responsibilities inherent in that status.

---

episodes. Instead, we refer to the interactive relation between particular episodes and events with overall narrative themes. On one side there is the Mirror-universe, the Borg, Q's interventions. On the other side there is the triumph of the "human spirit," meritocracy, respecting difference (IDIC), and ethical obligation. The big story is often assessed in relation to how we think reality "really works."

In Hegel's work, the "struggle for recognition" is a basic part of his explanation of awareness itself.[3] A simple way of putting his view is that a person can't be aware of anything unless she's aware *that* she is aware. Before Hegel, most philosophers described our awareness as given, part of some capacity that each individual possessed. The most famous example is found in Descartes's assertion, "*Cogito, ergo sum*" or, "I think, therefore I am." While Descartes attempts to prove his own existence in this way, his view can't directly explain how he can move from knowing himself to knowing that other selves also exist, which is called the "problem of other minds." But Hegel points out that self-awareness always depends upon the awareness of *another.* The "phenomenology" in Hegel's title refers to a "journey" in which a knowledge-seeker tries different "routes" to knowledge, keeping what's good and rejecting what fails in each step. In what scholars of Hegel call the "master-slave dialectic," the pursuit of knowledge leads the seeker to wholly dominate others as a means of controlling and understanding his world. Hegel shows that this approach fails, ironically, because the master ends up needing the slave while the slave has no use for the master. Because of this, the master becomes incapable of surviving independently of the slave.

The problem of domination indicates that we're ultimately dependent upon a community of free people if we're to effectively and rationally pursue science and ethics. *Trek* enthusiasts will recognize the relationship of Romulans and Remans depicted in *Star Trek: Nemesis* and the Stratos-Troglyte relationship featured in "The Cloudminders" (*TOS*). These examples can be seen as thought experiments that confirm Hegel's assertions that ethics, politics, and science are not matters of "enlightened self-interest" or even the sum of separate individuals' sets of interests. Real recognition isn't going to come from someone who lacks the freedom to say "no." If the slaves are able to free themselves of masters, they can possibly develop venues in which no one dominates efforts to develop a true account of the world.

Of course, all of this is riddled with political consequences. At the beginning of his *Philosophy of Right*, Hegel lays out

---

[3] Georg W.F. Hegel, *Phenomenology of Spirit* (New York: Oxford University Press, 1977), §178–184.

what's missing from the ideas of liberal and libertarian political philosophies, like those of John Locke and many modern political thinkers.[4] They have a tendency to see society as made up of wholly independent political agents, co-operating only for the sake of common interests. This view is typically referred to as political or social "atomism" because individuals are conceived of as independent "atoms" with no deep connections to each other. Often liberals and libertarians treat political life as if its goals were no more than to secure the freedom of citizens from force and fraud. Such freedom is often summed up by the phrase "negative liberties," examples of which include Americans' freedom of speech or religious expression. Yet recognition requires more than just the negative liberties of a society in which everyone is simply forbidden to interfere with each other.

For recognition, others must be capable of challenging your claims, or you'll have no reason to trust your reasons regarding what's fair, good, or true. This means that skills must be developed, venues for communication must be organized, and resources have to be guaranteed so no one can buy their way into office or out of a debate. A society without interference could still be one in which there was less freedom if some people have little or no access to important debates; alternately, there could be important debates in which all options were already narrowed down to suit those in power. Therefore, recognition requires some "positive liberties"—like education, the guarantee of open debates, and the development of capacities to participate in such debates—in order to function properly. We're less free while anyone is in bondage, desperate, ignored, or mute.

Hegel is often pegged as a precursor to totalitarianism, when, in fact, he campaigned for progressive reforms throughout his life.[5] The most plausible reasons for this totalitarian interpretation come from Isaiah Berlin, whose essay on "negative" and

---

[4] See Hegel, *Philosophy of Right* (Oxford: Clarendon, 1952); John Locke, *Second Treatise of Government* (Oxford: Blackwell, 1956). See also Charles Taylor, *Hegel and the Modern Society* (New York: Cambridge University Press, 1979).

[5] See Terry Pinkard, *Hegel: A Biography* (New York: Cambridge University Press, 2000).

"positive" liberties remains a classic. His concern, stoked by communist and fascist threats to liberty and humanity, was that positive liberties must entail some sort of ideal of individual perfection imposed by the state. Berlin located the meaning of "perfectionism" in the words of the prominent British Hegelian, T.H. Green, who claimed, "The ideal of true freedom is the maximum of power for all the members of human society alike to make the best of themselves." Berlin, however, doesn't agree:

> Apart from the confusion of freedom with equality, this entails that if a man chose some immediate pleasure—which (in whose view?) would not enable him to make the best of himself (what self?)—what he was exercising was not "true" freedom: and if deprived of it, would not lose anything that mattered. Green was a genuine liberal: but many a tyrant could use this formula to justify his worst acts of oppression.[6]

But not all thinkers who seek to promote mutual recognition agree with Berlin's characterization of "positive freedom." Charles Taylor would endorse Green's principle, adding a phrase like "make the best of themselves *by their own lights.*"[7] Self-mastery by all citizens is a principle that would hardly be of use for any tyrant. Recognition isn't attained by means of a common understanding of what's good, nor is it necessarily involved with any common good feeling. Recognition is more fundamental than that: without it, one's reasons won't count as reasons in the eyes of others. The unrecognized aren't entitled to challenge anyone's opinions, including any views about *them.* As an example, prior to the present day, gays and lesbians were often considered mentally ill despite their own claims to the contrary. Their claims didn't "count" because they weren't recognized as capable judges. Until people recognized as clearly sane "came out of the closet" and sought an

---

[6] Isaiah Berlin, "Two Concepts of Liberty," in *Contemporary Political Philosophy*, edited by Robert E. Goodin and Philip Pettit (Oxford: Blackwell, 2005), p. 385, n10. The T.H. Green quotation is from his *Lectures on the Principles of Political Obligation* (New York: Cambridge University Press, 1986).

[7] See Charles Taylor, "What's Wrong with Negative Liberty?" in *Contemporary Political Philosophy*, pp. 387–397; and *Hegel* (New York: Cambridge University Press, 1975), pp. 15–29.

extension of that recognition to their choice of partner, the cycle wasn't broken.[8]

Star Trek rhetorically shifts the positions in "The Outcast" (*TNG*), when Commander Riker seeks to rescue Soren, a sexless J'naii scientist, from culturally ordered brainwashing after s(he) falls into heterosexual love with him. The impassioned Riker argues in front of a J'naii court that Soren isn't ill, but should be recognized in hir unique orientation. Certainly, the value of recognition in culturally uncomfortable situations is easier to accept in sci-fi.

Some charge that such a principle mixes up equality and freedom—but one just isn't free if others aren't recognizing you. Abolishing slavery was considered "impossible" just as long and in as much as slaves were denied recognition. To the Romulans, the Remans' complaints aren't worth considering. In our society, feminist political demands are sometimes met by jokes and parodies that enact a denial of recognition. For there to be recognition, a state must have policies that secure for citizens the capacities to challenge each other out of mutual respect and acknowledge each others' beliefs and talents. While liberal negative liberties—such as an absence of state interference in matters of speech and opinion—can play a crucial role, they aren't sufficient for recognition. In the utopian future of *Star Trek*, perhaps the Federation functions as a paradigm of recognition, or so we shall see.

"You Have Kept My Course True and Steady"

Saying anything about the political atmosphere of *Star Trek* is difficult, as the show is one that largely avoids Federation politics. In fact, what little we see can be disturbing from a democratic point of view. For example, in the original series, there's no election coverage, nor other suggestions that the main characters are part of a participatory political structure. With the advent of the films, a political body comes into view, though it seems

---

[8] Gays and lesbians still aren't recognized as capable of marrying one another in most U.S. states. Also, *Star Trek* needs to answer for the fact that somehow gays and lesbians seem to have been wiped out of Federation society. This is exemplified in Beverly Crusher's reaction to her Trill lover being placed in a new female body ("The Host," *TNG*).

to have many military figures within it. In *Star Trek VI: The Undiscovered Country*, the Federation president is nearly assassinated by a cabal of Federation, Klingon, and Romulan military officers interested in maintaining the antagonistic *status quo*. Because the only active Federation players in plotting and in preventing the murder are military officers, we get the message that the political branch is, to some degree, naive if not helpless.[9]

On *The Next Generation*, a coup orchestrated by worm-like entities takes over Starfleet Command, but is thwarted by the officers of the *Enterprise* strictly out of the public eye ("Conspiracy"). On *Deep Space Nine*, elections on Bajor are always presented as an annoying impediment to Sisko's work. While it's true that the recovering culture of Bajor is important to Sisko—despite his discomfort with his role of Emissary—it's also clear that the politico-religious struggles of an entire planet are of secondary importance to the military administration of the space station. The military hierarchy is sometimes questioned, but ultimately affirmed, in *Voyager*. There are no elections to determine who should govern their new arrangement, as we see in the re-imagined *Battlestar Galactica*. When Janeway decides to blow up the Caretaker's array rather than allow it to fall into Kazon hands—and thereby strand both the *Voyager* and Maquis crew in the Delta Quadrant—B'Elanna Torres protests, "Who is she to be making these decisions for all of us?" Chakotay, still a Maquis renegade and not yet Janeway's First Officer, responds, "She's the *captain*" ("Caretaker"). There are none of the political wranglings and constitutional debates found throughout series like *Babylon 5* or *Firefly*. So, why would we want to argue that there's a political dimension to a show that lacks democratic detail? The answer lies in the pervasive notion of recognition.

Leonard Nimoy, in an interview with Charlie Rose, says the key to the success of the series was the presentation of a crew of competent professionals who worked together to solve serious problems.

---

[9] This notion is played out more overtly in the original *Battlestar Galactica* series, with Apollo and Adama always correct, while the Quorum of Twelve are always wrong. The Moore-Eick re-imaging of this series pits the military and civilian governments against each other in a more nuanced way.

Everybody gets the same breaks. Everybody gets the same education. Everybody gets the same kind of household and family life
and so forth. Everybody gets the job that they are qualified to do
and holds the job if they do it well. Simple. Plain and simple.
There's no rhetoric. There's no backstabbing. There is no political
infighting, no political agenda on anybody's part. And this is the
Star Trek world if you stop and think about it. It's a morally struc-
tured society, and I think it is a very, very, desirable society. I
wouldn't mind living that.[10]

The moral implications of Nimoy's idea allude to equality and
recognition. The *Star Trek* universe is one "where things worked
out properly, where people who are professional would work
together to solve the problem . . . Start at square one, and what's
the next problem?" Such professional problem-solving provides
a prime example of recognition. Yet Nimoy's vision is another
example of *Star Trek*'s strangely anti-political tone concerning
life in the Federation. Despite its advantages, do we really want
to live in a world in which no one has a "political agenda"?

This is an important question, because dedicated viewers
would want, like Nimoy, to live in the Federation and work on
the *Enterprise*, but not because life there would be easy. This
desire isn't based in a yearning for utopian ease. Borg attacks
and Ricardo Montalban can disturb the good life, even with
those natty Corinthian leather-upholstered cybernetic augmenta-
tions. The *Enterprise* crew is in constant danger, but their lives
are taken seriously. As Picard does when he calls Riker "my right
arm," they're recognized.

In sci-fi, recognition is more important than in other genres
such as, for example, the western. Even in a "Wagon Train to
the Stars,"[11] a "lone gunslinger" soon ends up dependent on others in outer space. Thus, a show greatly influenced by westerns
ends up very different in its ethical feel. The virtues that mark
the great hero of the wild west just aren't as helpful when you're
stranded in deep space with a limited air supply and depleted
warp nacelles.[12] Technology and scale impose co-operation and,

---

[10] *Charlie Rose* (Broadcast on PBS, 23rd November, 1995).

[11] This is how Gene Roddenberry originally pitched *Star Trek* to network producers.

[12] The ethical warp and woof of the western and the sci-fi drama is thematized
brilliantly in Joss Whedon's *Firefly* and *Serenity*.

if that co-operation is to be successful over time and under pressure, recognition must occur.

All of the heroic captains throughout the series have what political theorists might call a "consultation regime," in which the expertise of individuals is explicitly recognized as the team gathers around a physical or metaphorical table to make a decision. Being at that table matters. Captain Kirk may be a transitional figure (informed by westerns and an idea of Shakespearean drama) that doesn't fit this description as well as the others, but even he enables his crew to develop their talents and be recognized as valuable. Kirk may lead very different sorts of meetings around the conference table—consultations being a core element of *The Next Generation, Voyager,* and corporate offices around the world—but his reliance on his crew is no less based in recognition. During any given episode, Kirk explicitly calls on his crew to do the impossible. Be it Scotty's warp drive or McCoy's skills as a doctor (or bricklayer), Kirk regularly reminds viewers and crewmembers alike that the lives of more than four hundred men and women depend on their actions. While the captain is duty-bound to be responsible for the lives of his crew, Kirk recognizes his command staff in their skills, knowledge, and abilities which, taken alone, can save lives. His insistence on their performing to the best of their abilities, though, is in no way a shirking of his own responsibility. He's certainly willing to destroy his ship while on board or jump in front of a phaser beam; but when the only person who can save the ship is Scotty, Kirk is quick to recognize that value. He doesn't fly to Engineering to realign something or other at the drop of a hat. The captain's faith in his individual crewmembers demonstrates an implicit "promotion"—suddenly the crewmember is as capable as the captain—and recognizes the individual as worthy of their Starfleet uniform.[13]

In Federation society, a person can find recognition for his or her interests and talents both within and outside of the workplace. Thus, the viewer could desire life in this society without a clear picture of its actual political governance. As they observe

---

[13] This recognition is also exemplified by Captain Janeway when she allows, after initially refusing, the Doctor to develop his "Emergency Command Hologram" subroutine so that he could effectively command the ship in an emergency situation ("Tinker, Tenor, Doctor, Spy," *VGR*).

specific events marked by recognition, viewers can fill in their idea of the good society—militarist, capitalist, socialist, or what have you—referring to the one that they believe promotes recognition well. Yet some facts about how the Federation has promoted the value of recognition for its citizens seem clear. It seems, for one, to have somehow secured economic and political freedom. Economic want is off the table. Characters casually make it clear that no one has to worry about such basics as food and shelter. As Picard points out in *First Contact*, "The acquisition of wealth is no longer the driving force in our lives. We wish to better ourselves and the rest of humanity." The only "currency" in this universe is the recognition of others from within the Federation.

But how did humanity advance to such a point? In "Past Tense" (*DS9*), the story of human political progress is marked by a drastic act that leads to a quantum leap in recognition. Problems with chroniton particles and the *Defiant*'s transporter send Sisko, Dax, and Bashir back in time to 2024, when Earth society is shown to be deeply divided between rich and poor. The unemployed are shunted into "sanctuary districts," which are spoken of by the wealthy as if they were voluntary. The "Bell Riots" (lead by a reluctant Commander Sisko standing in for the real, murdered Bell) erupt, hostages are taken, and demands issued to release sanctuary residents and reinstate the "Federal Employment Act." Sanctuary residents put their life-stories out on "Channel 90," owned by a media mogul who has the hots for Dax. While not in time to save those killed by government troops, the sanctuary dwellers' testimony renders the public sympathetic to their cause and even to those who kept hostages in order to strike back. In this way, the sanctuary residents achieved recognition as human beings, instead of being seen as "dims" (the mentally ill) or "gimmies" (the unemployed). We see that recognition is the beginning of good politics, and that some political measures are needed to recognize humans as such—like health care, housing, and employment.

Between times on duty, Federation citizens have a rich cultural life. We see characters acting, playing instruments, engaging in careers outside their main area (such as archaeology or botany), playing sports, and writing—Lieutenant Sulu was notorious on the original *Enterprise* for having a different hobby each week and trying to get others interested in them. In fact, characters even use their free time to struggle with deeper philosophical issues through simulation. Data spends time on the holodeck as Sherlock Holmes or a Shakespearean hero in what is, essentially, a practice of simulating humanity with the hopes of achieving it. He's rehearsing recognition with his cohorts' help.

In day-to-day Federation life, this freedom is secured, as we've seen, in part because all the basic needs of individuals are met. Certainly there are a number of social and military hurdles along the way: the *Enterprise* series gave us several of them, and Khan Noonien Singh was a notable example of another. But ultimately, in the world of *Trek*, we're reminded that the world's problems were solved long ago, and that Federation citizens pursue only that to which they're drawn. Jonathan Frakes is fond of quoting Gene Roddenberry's saying that, "In the twenty-fourth century, there will be no hunger and there will be no greed"—Ferengi aside.

This lack of economic need does not, as we see, result in a world of poor musicians who would make better engineers. Each profession seems to be filled. This implies that there's some value derived by citizens from their primary job; rather than simply pursuing hobbies that are a respite from the weary drudgery of a dull, meaningless job. In addition, recognition isn't limited to Federation citizens alone: Garak, Quark, and Odo are all fully realized inhabitants of Deep Space Nine, yet none of them seek Federation citizenship. Odo is drawn to his own people through a return to the Great Link, while Quark hopes to rise in prestige among the Ferengi while constantly remaining on the economic outside. In "Body Parts" (*DS9*), Quark is banned from trading with the Ferengi Commerce Authority. Despite rather good prospects for doing business with non-Ferengi, Quark seeks to restore recognition from those who know him best.

Ironically, given Nimoy's comments about recognition and expertise, the only sympathetic characters that *don't* seem to understand recognition are Vulcans. For instance, in "Journey to Babel" (*TOS*), Sarek makes clear that "one does not thank logic." In human societies, the expression "thank you" recognizes another as having achieved the task at hand or as having done something worthwhile. Vulcans, of course, probably have a salute and proverb they say upon such occasions. Greetings and farewells are also a matter of recognition. There's nothing illogical about everyday speech-acts of recognition. Insisting on only one style of recognition (certain salutes and proverbs) constitutes a failure to recognize in its own right. No wonder Bones gets so hot under the collar when he can't perform the Vulcan salute! Sci-fi is great precisely because it investigates prospects: we quickly see that the exclusiveness of the Vulcan way *couldn't* be maintained because no organization could be conducted without recognition. During "Who Mourns for Adonais?" (*TOS*), with the entire communications system out to lunch, a god running about in a sheet, and Uhura underneath her console with a soldering iron, Spock, true to the Federation model of recognition, makes it clear that though the stakes are high and the work is delicate he "can think of no one better equipped to handle it." Uhura is a little surprised. After all, the explicit Vulcan position on recognition makes such statements unlikely. However, the need for social cooperation aboard a Federation starship implicitly makes such statements just as necessary.

"Its Continuing Mission"

Captain Kirk straddles the divide between the individualist virtues of the western story and the cooperative virtues needed in a large-scale technologically complex enterprise, while Picard more clearly exemplifies the latter. The move from Kirk to Picard as a leader-figure parallels changes in the world that have altered the primary project for all of us as citizens of a democratic state. Once, securing negative liberty in terms of equality under the law and non-interference was at the center of democratic politics. The movie western often depicted the transition from anarchy to law in the guise of a solitary, resolute sheriff or a no-name, cheroot-smoking drifter in a poncho. Of course, even basic liberty requires a tremendous amount of social organization, which could distract from the drama of the western genre. In *Star Trek*, the social organization we've examined provides the basis for positive liberties—the freedom to exert and develop one's capabilities—and recognition, the new focus of democratic political life.

In much of the *Star Trek* series, but most often in *TOS*, the central plot is an encounter with a new form of social organization. This week, they travel to Ardana, a planet that's heavily stratified class-wide, with a civilization in the clouds and one in the mines ("The Cloud Minders"). The miners have the sort of ironic power that Hegel attributes to the slave. Next week, they confront Bele and Lokai, obsessed over arbitrary racial differences ("Let That Be Your Last Battlefield"). In each case, Kirk acts in order to implement a new regime of recognition on the planet-of-the-week. We want to live in the Federation because such a society transcends the struggle to meet our physical needs with a new struggle to see what we can really do, find out what we really want, and ultimately who we really are . . . truly a Final Frontier.[14]

---

[14] Special thanks to Jason Eberl and Kevin Decker for episode references and other recommendations.

12

Why Not Live in the Holodeck?

PHILIP TALLON and JERRY L. WALLS

In *Star Trek: The Next Generation* the holodeck presents challenges to the crew in various stories. In more than one episode, things turn deadly as a computer glitch or human error releases the "mortality failsafe," making the realistic simulations dangerous to the holodeck's hapless inhabitants. Besides being a good setup for a "technology-run-amok" story, the holodeck gives us the opportunity to explore scenarios that compare the value of the world that exists with fantasy worlds of our own choosing.

In one of the best "holodeck-out-of-control" episodes ("Ship in a Bottle"), Picard, Data, and Barclay are trapped unknowingly by a rogue holodeck character, Dr. Moriarty, the evil genius of the Sherlock Holmes stories. Given sentience in another episode ("Elementary, Dear Data," *TNG*), Moriarty's program is accidentally reactivated by Lieutenant Barclay. Once back in action, Moriarty ingeniously traps Picard, Data, and Barclay in the holodeck by making them think they are *not* in the holodeck. Holding them hostage, Moriarty uses his leverage to try and get out of the holodeck and into the real world. Even remaining free to roam about the holodeck is an unattractive option for him. When Picard tries to sympathize, saying, "I understand your frustration," Moriarty snaps back, "Do you really? When this is over, you will walk out of this room to the real world and your own concerns and leave me here trapped in a world I know to be nothing but illusion. I cannot bear that. I must leave."

In contrast to Moriarty, Lieutenant Barclay seems to have the opposite desire. In "Hollow Pursuits" (*TNG*) we see Barclay develop an unhealthy holodeck addiction. Disappointed with life on the ship, because of his painful shyness, Barclay shirks his engineering responsibilities and retreats into swashbuckling simulations in which he surrounds himself with virtual representations of the *Enterprise* crew, alternately besting simulacrums of the ship's male officers at swordplay and smoothly impressing the female ones. Barclay's real-life job performance suffers as he become more engrossed in the pleasurable Musketeer-world of his own creation. Finally, Barclay's problems come to a head when Geordi, Riker, and Troi discover his fantasy life. Vowing to turn over a new leaf, Barclay is helped along by Geordi, who once struggled with similar problems. "You're going to be able to write the book on holodiction," Geordi says, while adding sympathetically, "Look, I know how easy it is to get caught up in it. I fell in love in there once" (referring to "Booby Trap," *TNG*). Barclay responds, "You know, the people that I create in there are more real to me than anyone I meet out here."

Nearly anyone—especially *Star Trek* fans—can sympathize with Barclay's obsession with a fictional world. What's striking about the juxtaposition between these two examples are the opposite impulses displayed by Moriarty and Barclay. One desires to be outside the "illusion" of the holodeck, and the other desires to be caught up in it. Which is the more reasonable desire? If we were in Barclay's shoes, should we try to live life in the constructed illusion of the holodeck, or are there benefits to the real world that outweigh the pains of daily life? Presumably, it's at least possible that in the future we could live entirely within a simulated environment of our own choosing. Now, it seems unlikely that this would be an *actual* dilemma for anyone reading this essay, but the question is still a fascinating one with relevance for philosophy: Could a simulated world be more satisfying than the real one? These may become quite pressing questions in the twenty-fourth century, while still quite theoretical in our own. Nevertheless, a large body of literature, stretching back for centuries, has grappled with this issue by asking a different question: Given the pain and suffering of this world, is there a better world that could have been created?[1]

---

[1] Much of the discussion of this question in the modern period centers around

Gottfried Wilhelm Leibniz (1646–1716) asked this question when he famously defended the idea that this world was the "best of all possible worlds," meaning that our universe couldn't get any better. Others have been less optimistic than Leibniz, questioning whether our world is optimally, or even minimally good. For many philosophers, the "problem of evil" has marked the dividing line between belief and unbelief in a perfectly good and all-powerful God who created this universe. Among the evils which raise this problem is the amount of pain we experience: Why would a benevolent God bring about such pain if he had the power to create a less pain-filled world? Since we can easily imagine a much safer and happier world than this one, if a perfectly good and powerful God existed, this God surely would have created a better world rather than this one with all its pain and misery.[2] Taking Barclay's dilemma as a guide, would it be better, on the whole, to live in the holodeck—in many cases, a less-painful world—or not? If we answer that a virtual life would be better, then this would be a rather unique way of questioning belief in a good God as creator.

Hume in the Holodeck

If one were given the chance to live in an environment of their own choosing, the first thing they should ask is, how successfully might it provide for their well-being? Exactly what constitutes well-being is up for debate, of course. Some philosophers have weighed the quality of life on a pleasure/pain scale, seeing a good life as one where the former outweighed the latter. In his *Dialogues Concerning Natural Religion*, David Hume (1711–1776) asserts that this world is less than the best because of the amount of *pain* that it contains. Hume acknowledges that pain serves a function—to motivate feeling creatures to action—but proposes that pleasure might do this just as well:

---

a comment by King Alfonso X in 1252: "If I had been God's counsel at the Creation, many things would have been ordered better." See Susan Neiman, *Evil in Modern Thought* (Princeton: Princeton University Press, 2002), pp. 14ff.

[2] See Michael Peterson, *The Problem of Evil: Selected Readings* (Notre Dame: Notre Dame University Press, 1992); and William Rowe, *God and the Problem of Evil* (Oxford: Blackwell, 2001).

> Now pleasure alone, in its various degrees, seems to human understanding sufficient for [exciting all creatures to action] . . . Men pursue pleasure as eagerly as they avoid pain; at least, they might have been so constituted. It seems, therefore, plainly possible to carry on the business of life without any pain.[3]

Why, in the best world, would there have to be so much pain? Couldn't the basic shape of common life remain the same while simply increasing pleasure and decreasing or eliminating pain? Hume's suggestion sounds a lot like what the holodeck could do. By creating a pleasurable and safe environment, people can pursue their interests without worry of harm. Given the choice between the real world and the holodeck, Hume would probably side with Barclay.

But questions arise about the likelihood of Hume's "painless world." For one, humans are quick to become spoiled, so wouldn't the absence of pleasure simply replace pain as the most unpleasant feeling? Drug addicts between fixes can experience a kind of suffering even in the absence of pain. Wouldn't we come to expect pleasure, and suffer in its absence? Problems with Hume's hypothetical world, however, need not concern us as the holodeck presents an environment which supplies many sorts of pleasurable experiences with very low levels of pain. With the holodeck's safety settings in place, we could enjoy the thrill of sword fighting (as Barclay *obviously* does) while avoiding the agony of stab wounds, as well as enjoy romantic liaisons (as Barclay *presumably* does) while never worrying about having one's heart broken or getting any sort of disease. But even if one *could* experience life without the suffering of swinging between existential highs and lows, doesn't a part of us desire this polarity? A number of examples from *TNG* and a few from *TOS*—such as "This Side of Paradise"—make the point that perpetual pleasure isn't necessarily the highest good.

Whitehead and the Mortality Failsafe

In "Elementary, Dear Data" (*TNG*), Data and Geordi dress up as Sherlock Holmes and Watson to solve crimes by gaslight in the

---

[3] David Hume, *Dialogues Concerning Natural Religion* (Indianapolis: Hackett, 1980), pp. 69–70.

holodeck. Once there, however, Data is able to solve the crimes easily, since the mysteries are all derived from the Arthur Conan Doyle stories which he's memorized. Geordi quickly grows frustrated and explains that there's little point in solving a mystery if one already knows the answer to it: "If there's no mystery, there's no game. No game, no fun." Dr. Pulaski backs up Geordi's point: "To feel the thrill of victory there has to be the possibility of failure." Getting the idea, Data doffs his Deerstalker cap and heads back for the holodeck, where he will "dare" the computer to defeat him.

What follows *is* more exciting, as through a mix-up of language, Geordi asks the computer to "create an adversary capable of defeating *Data*," rather than capable of defeating *Holmes*. The virtual character of Moriarty is thereby given sentience and the "mortality failsafe" is turned off, making the holodeck a truly dangerous place.[4] Imaginative interest in this kind of scenario presents one possible response to Hume: it suggests that there are other goods—such as the *intensity* derived from the possibility of pain—which would be missing in a pain-free world.

Among advocates of the value of intensity stands Alfred North Whitehead (1861–1947), a mathematician, philosopher, and theologian who draws on aesthetic categories to show the value of a dangerous world. For Whitehead, the highest form of beauty consists in *harmony*, together with *intensity*. He differentiates between "minor" beauty, which is *merely* harmonious— "the absence of painful clash"—and "major" beauty, which is bigger and better because it contains *contrasts*. Whitehead writes (with a style that's reminiscent of *Star Trek* techno-babble), "These contrasts introduce new conformal intensities natural to each of them, and by so doing raise the intensities of conformal feeling."[5] Contrasts raise the level of intensity and make beauty *bigger*. For Whitehead, all of life is like a big work of art, so it's no surprise that he sees the purpose of the universe in the same way that he views beauty: "God's purpose in the creative advance is the evocation of intensities."[6]

---

[4] Similar peril confronts the *Enterprise* crew in "The Big Goodbye" and "A Fistful of Datas."

[5] Alfred North Whitehead, *Adventures of Ideas* (New York: Free Press, 1967), p. 252.

[6] Alfred North Whitehead, *Process and Reality* (New York: Macmillan, 1929), p. 161.

Aristotle (384–322 B.C.E.) agrees that a beautiful object needs more than an "orderly arrangement of parts"; it also needs "magnitude."[7] In Aristotle's prescriptions for tragedy, for instance, there needs to be a major "reversal of fortune." If Aristotle were commenting on an episode of *TNG*, he would no doubt agree that any holodeck episode needs a similar reversal of fortune— where the playful becomes perilous—in order to have a proper degree of *magnitude*. Imagine how dull an episode would be where the crew simply has an enjoyable time playing in the holodeck with no real conflict or difficulty. Might a completely safe world be similarly dull? If nothing serious was ever ultimately at stake, if we could *never* suffer, wouldn't our actions all seem a bit trivial? Given our interest in "holodeck gone bad" stories where human lives are endangered, it seem likely that in the long run we might find a truly safe world aesthetically unsatisfying. In Barclay's case, we can easily imagine that his enjoyment of the holodeck would decrease as time goes on, ending in severe boredom. But from Barclay's story we don't get the idea that it's only pleasure that he's after and pain that he's avoiding. Barclay also seems to prefer the absence of *responsibility* the holodeck provides, and this might also be a valuable factor to consider.

Swinburne in the Nexus

Star Trek: Generations begins with the commissioning of the new *Enterprise-B*. Within minutes of its "quick run around the block," however, the *Enterprise* is called to rescue two transport ships from a dangerous energy ribbon. The ship's new captain, John Harriman, is timid about taking risks and James T. Kirk, onboard for publicity purposes, quickly grows anxious to be in control. Finally, Harriman asks for advice and Kirk tells him to bring the *Enterprise* closer to the energy ribbon to transport the other ships' inhabitants over. Harriman worries about the risk, but Kirk replies, "Risk is part of the game. You wanna sit in that chair."[8]

---

[7] Aristotle, *Poetics* (Mineola: Dover, 1997), p. 14.

[8] This echoes Kirk's famous declaration to his crew in "Return to Tomorrow" (*TOS*): "Risk is our business. That's what this starship is all about. That's why we're aboard her."

Kirk clearly has no problems taking risks. Siding with Geordi and Dr. Pulaski, he savors the peril of adventure. In a deleted scene from *Generations*, the sexagenerian Kirk is seen skydiving from space at amazing speeds. Scotty and Chekov watch as he zooms toward the ground from orbit. Scotty comments, "Rappelling crystalline trench, rafting down lava flows, orbital skydiving. It's like the man's trying to run a decathlon across the galaxy." Later in the film, Kirk and Picard find themselves in the blissful Nexus where individuals are given whatever they want. Kirk seizes the opportunity to go back to his ranch home. Once there, however, he's clearly unsatisfied. Taking a jump over a Nexus-gorge on his Nexus-horse, Kirk muses to Picard about how, in the real world, that jump used to scare him: "I must have jumped that fifty times. Scared the hell out of me each time. Except this time. Because it isn't real." But a lack of intensity in the Nexus isn't the root of Kirk's dissatisfaction; rather, it's that "nothing here matters." The Nexus is a metaphor for Kirk's retirement, "Ever since I left Starfleet, I haven't made a difference."

Picard senses a weak spot and exploits the opportunity to get Kirk to come back with him and stop Soran, an obsessed El-Aurian, from destroying an inhabited planet in order to get himself back into the Nexus. Though the situation looks grim, Kirk replies, "You know, if Spock were here, he'd say that I was an irrational, illogical human being for taking on a mission like that. Sounds like fun." Though Kirk is obviously a risk-junkie, his desire to help Picard can't be chalked up to an *illogical* desire for adventure: he derives personal meaning from making the world better. Kirk exhorts Picard, "Don't let them do anything that takes you off the bridge of that ship, because while you're there, you can make a difference." Here we find a good that can't be replicated in the holodeck. While the holodeck could be programmed to allow for danger, it can't provide a genuine sense of responsibility. Since holodeck simulations feel no agony, suffer no distress, and can't experience even the faintest inklings of real joy, we have no obligations to them. Of course, not all of us *enjoy* having big responsibilities. But even when responsibilities are a burden, we often derive a great deal of meaning from fulfilling them.

British philosopher Richard Swinburne places a high value on responsibility in a way that's reminiscent of Kirk's reflections. In true science fiction tradition, Swinburne imagines possible worlds—various states of affairs that could constitute the universe—where humans enjoy varying levels of responsibility, ranging from tending to plants, to taking care of one's own body, on up to the wider scope of responsibility most humans actually experience. Like Kirk, Swinburne is a big champion of "making a difference":

> It is of course good for us to be able to mould the inanimate world, but clearly a much greater good is to have responsibility for other animate beings—and that serious responsibility involves again the ability to benefit or harm them.[9]

The context here is theological—defending God's purposes in creating this world—but Swinburne's words sound so similar to Kirk's philosophy that one can almost hear William Shatner reading them in his staccato delivery: "But . . . *what* an awful world it would . . . *be* if the only . . . good or *harm* we could do was to our . . . *selves.*" Swinburne's point is that a world where we could only harm or benefit ourselves would be one without much meaningful responsibility, and therefore automatically inferior to worlds that allow a wider range of significant choices.

Responsibility, like intensity, is a value that the real world possesses which is likely to be missing from life in the holodeck. But just as with intensity of experience, responsibility carries with it the possibility of pain and suffering. Genuine responsibility entails that we might, intentionally or unintentionally, cause *others* to suffer. So even if meaningful responsibility is, as Kirk and Swinburne seem to suggest, a very valuable element of this dangerous world, it can also be a very serious burden. Like the timid captain of the *Enterprise-B*, we too might worry about the danger of giving anyone—ourselves included—responsibility for others' well-being. But what's the alternative? Perhaps there are more *pleasurable* things to do than fulfilling our responsibilities; but if Kirk is even mildly representative of human desires, it seems likely that a merely pleasurable life will be *unsatisfying.*

---

[9] Richard Swinburne, *Providence and the Problem of Evil* (Oxford: Clarendon, 1998), p. 147.

Hick in the Q Continuum

Besides Barclay, one of the most popular characters on *TNG* is Q, a roguish being with god-like powers who torments the *Enterprise* crew from time to time. Because of his powers, Q is free to do as he pleases safe from danger. He's thus a good example of what to expect from a person whose character is formed in a holodeck-like environment. The result isn't good: besides being insensitive and troublesome, Q's emotional life seems unpleasant, and oscillates from bored to angry to fleetingly amused.[10]

In "Déjà Q" (*TNG*), Q is expelled from the Q Continuum—a pantheon of god-like beings—for bad behavior. As punishment, Q is placed in impotent human form on the *Enterprise*. But even as a wimpy human, Q is still quarrelsome and cantankerous. He explains his bad attitude when Data tells him that part of being human is learning to work in groups, "I'm not good in groups. It's difficult to work in a group when you're omnipotent." Q hits the nail on the head. The root of his immaturity lies in the fact that he's never been *obliged* to behave well. Q has never had to *work* at anything.[11] Now powerless, Q, for the first time, must adjust to human limitations and learn to cooperate with people in order to survive. To satisfy his hunger pains, he must rely on Guinan for food. When he wrenches his back, he must go to Dr. Crusher for medical treatment. When Q's enemies (the grudge-holding Calamarain) come seeking revenge on the once-godlike prankster who "tormented" them, Q absconds in a shuttlecraft to *protect* the *Enterprise* crew. Seeing his newfound maturity, the Q Continuum sends one of its own to restore Q's powers: "Sacrificing yourself for these humans? Do I detect a little selfless act?" Q dismisses the suggestion as preposterous, "You flatter me. I was only trying to put a quick end to a miserable existence." Despite his denial, it's obvious he really is being selfless for once, the result of his difficult experience aboard the *Enterprise*.

---

[10] For a perspective on Q that reinforces this interpretation, see Chapter 5 in this volume.

[11] A similar situation occurs in "Q2" (*VGR*) where Q again learns how poor the Q Continuum is as a developmental environment when he sees how troublesome his adolescent son is turning out.

We earlier heard from David Hume, who finds the world a very ill-designed place, and wittily compares it to a house where the "windows, doors, fires, passages, stairs, and the whole economy of the house were the source of noise, confusion, fatigue, darkness, and the extremes of heat and cold" (p. 68). Hume accuses this world of being poorly designed for human habitation. As agile as Hume's intellect is, however, he seems to miss the potential value that adversity might have as a means to human growth, and ultimately, fulfillment and happiness. Instead of a world filled with difficulties, Hume imagines a world where ships with beneficial purposes always met with fair winds, and persons born to power were always just-minded: "A being therefore, who knows the secret springs of the universe, might easily, by particular volitions, turn all these accidents to the good of mankind and render the whole world happy." But what of such characters as Q, for whom a life without pain and difficulty has brought about an immature, selfish, and ultimately miserable existence?

John Hick responds to Hume by rejecting the idea that pain and difficulty are *always* detrimental. Hick defends the world—and, by extension, God—by arguing that pain and hardship may be quite helpful in developing *moral character.*

> Such critics as Hume are confusing what heaven ought to be, as an environment for perfected finite beings, with what this world ought to be, as an environment for beings who are in the process of becoming perfected.[12]

The world's value "is to be judged, not primarily by the quantity of pleasure and pain occurring in it at any particular moment, but by its fitness for its primary purpose, the purpose of soul-making" (p. 295). Hick's Christian theology informs his terminology. He's thinking, not just of one's moral character in this world, but of the soul and its ultimate home in heaven. But Hick's ideas are nonetheless poignant as a reminder that suffering often helps us grow into mature, happy people. In the case of Q, we see directly how his godlike powers have prevented him from developing positive traits such as patience and kind-

---

[12] John Hick, *Evil and the God of Love* (London: Collins, 1979), pp. 293–94.

ness. We also see clearly how being forced to deal with tangible difficulty helps him to grow personally.

When we recall how Barclay's personal problems prevented him from coping well with the real world, both in dealing with his responsibilities and with human interaction, we can see how the holodeck wouldn't foster his ability to overcome these problems. If Barclay is in need of personal development, then being forced to deal with real life pains and disappointments may help him to develop his character. In fact, Barclay later does have to deal with turbulent situations, such as overcoming his own paralyzing transporter phobia ("Realm of Fear," *TNG*). Despite thinking that he's being attacked by worm-like creatures when he's dematerialized, Barclay persistently carries on his work and is able to discover that these creatures are actually humans trapped in "transporter limbo." Barclay's bravery ultimately leads to their rescue. On *Voyager*, Barclay has become even more confident and mature, and his tireless work studying the lost ship is instrumental to its ultimate return ("Pathfinder"). This isn't the same Barclay as before. He's grown in many significant ways, and is no doubt a happier, better person in the end. That Barclay even *uses* the holodeck as a tool in bringing *Voyager* home is significant, as it shows how he's no longer using the *virtual* world to escape from the *real* one—although he still admits to Troi that he finds the holodeck recreations of the *Voyager* crew easier to relate to than his real-life co-workers.

Death on Veridian III

Besides intensity, responsibility, and character development, there are other related and overlapping benefits, such as genuinely loving relationships, which also seem to exist only in the real world.[13] But for all the benefits of the real world, the drawbacks are undeniable and challenging. If we heard Kirk earlier affirming the problems of the virtual world, the rest of his story elucidates the problems of the real one. Emerging from the

---

[13] True love can't be simulated, as a teenage girl named Amanda discovers when she uses her newly discovered Q-powers to make Riker "love" her in "True Q" (*TNG*). The disenchantment Amanda suffers would undoubtedly be shared by any of us who tried to have a genuine, long-term relationship in the holodeck.

Nexus, Kirk and Picard stop Soran from destroying the Veridian system, thereby also saving the stranded *Enterprise-D*. In the process, Kirk sacrifices his own life. Crushed by a collapsed bridge, Kirk asks Picard, "Did we make a difference?" Picard answers, "Oh yes. We made a difference. Thank you." Kirk's last words are, "It was . . . fun," followed by the mysterious, "Oh, my," and then his eyes glaze over in death. Even with his optimistic last words, Kirk's passing adds a small, cautionary warning to any overly-confident dismissal of virtual life, or any overly-confident affirmation of the value of the real world. Humans endure all kinds of agonies every day, much worse than Kirk's, and there's no guarantee, no matter how safely we live, that we won't experience a great amount of pain in life.

Yet it's suggestive that when *Star Trek*'s creative force turns its collective imagination to the question, the real is consistently championed over the virtual. In "This Side of Paradise" (*TOS*), Kirk reflects, "Maybe we weren't meant for paradise. Maybe we were meant to fight our way through. Struggle, claw our way up, scratch for every inch of the way. Maybe we can't stroll to the music of the lute. We must march to the sound of drums." Despite a thousand flights of fancy, the show, like Kirk, never questions the value of reality.

In Barclay's case we see several valuable factors that would be missing from a life of simulated experience. These three key elements—*satisfying intensity, meaningful responsibility,* and *development of character*—all present compelling reasons for choosing not to live in the holodeck. They present the basis for a defense of this world's value, and help us grapple with the problem of evil. If we could hold a "Best Universe" competition, it seems unlikely that any of us would be fit to act as perfect judges. But if we must choose between this world and immersion in a virtual reality environment like the holodeck, these benefits present a strong case for giving the virtual world "runner-up," and thereby confirm the intuitive judgments of *Star Trek*'s writers. At the very least, Barclay's dilemma helps us see more clearly a part of a philosophical discussion that should be, for all of us, a continuing mission.

13

The Second-Coming of Kahless: Worf's "Will to Believe"

HEATHER KEITH

Do you ever wonder what it's all about? Do you ever worry about what happens after death? Do you ask the big questions, like "Does God exist?" Do you wonder what to believe when it seems as though there can never be an answer? If you do, then you have something very important in common with Klingons, or at least with Starfleet's favorite Klingon: Lieutenant Worf of the starship *Enterprise*.

In "Rightful Heir" (*TNG*), Worf does what many of us do when we go to college, enter into rich religious debate with others, or simply sit down and start thinking about the big issues: He questions his faith and whether he can have certainty about spiritual things. In the episode's opening scenes, we find Worf shirking his duties because he's seemingly lost his faith entirely. Worf explains to Captain Picard that this is the result of his attempt to educate isolated Klingon youths about their religious and cultural traditions and beliefs ("Birthright, Part II," *TNG*). And the zeal he witnessed in these young Klingons made him realize how apathetic his own spiritual life had become.

"I have felt empty," Worf tells Picard, because he suspects that he doesn't have answers to central questions concerning Klingon religious traditions. He fears that he may doubt the existence of Kahless, the spiritual leader overdue to make a comeback. Like Jesus, Siddhartha Gautama, Muhammad, and other great religious figures from Earth, Kahless provided Klingon civilization with leadership, hope, and, most importantly, a code of behavior. He defined the honorable Klingon life. Without believing in the existence of Kahless, and the possibility of his return,

Worf might find it difficult to imagine a meaningful Klingon way of life. When Picard asks him whether he's lost his faith, Worf worries, "To lose something, one must first posses it. I am not sure I ever had a true belief." Being the sensitive captain we all know and love, Picard invites Worf to take a sabbatical to a Klingon religious retreat center to see if he can't get his mind right—and get back on the job. Little does Worf know that truth won't be the only thing revealed, but that Kahless himself in all his physical glory will appear!

Questions, Questions: "Worf, You're Not Alone"

At Boreth, a Klingon monastery on the world where Kahless promised to return, Worf tries unsuccessfully for several days to summon a vision of Kahless. As he watches a younger, less experienced Klingon find his spiritual path, he becomes even more dejected and starts packing to go home. Koroth, the high cleric, gently admonishes Worf for giving up so soon and tells him, like a good philosopher, "You came to us seeking answers, but this is a place of questions." Koroth persuades Worf to keep trying for a vision with an open mind and a ready heart.

As so often happens on television, when our hero Worf tries hard enough, he eventually succeeds. A vision appears to him with arms spread wide and announces, "I am Kahless, and I have returned." Surprisingly, this isn't just Worf's private spiritual vision. Kahless appears to everyone. He's *real*, and apparently really has returned on a spiritual and moral mission of his own: "I have returned because there is a great need in my people. They fight amongst themselves in petty wars that corrupt the glory of the Klingon spirit. They have lost their way, but it is not too late. I have returned, and I will lead my people again."[1] Worf, the skeptic, does what any smart Starfleet officer would do: He gets out his tricorder and checks this guy out. After all, in the twenty-fourth century, Kahless could be a hologram, a shape-shifter, an android, a bioreplicant, another

---

[1] Have the Klingons lost their way? Note the participation of the Duras family and their supporters in the Romulan-backed attempt to instigate a Klingon civil war ("Redemption," *TNG*) for an important example of Kahless's professed concern.

Klingon surgically altered to look like Kahless, or any other breed of phony. But no, Kahless seems, physically at least, to be The Real Thing.

If you're as clever as Worf, however, and live in such a technologically advanced culture, you'd be skeptical that this *is* The Real Thing. Even when faced with a person who seems real, knows things from fifteen centuries past, and even understands his own private religious experiences, Worf still questions the truth of the second-coming of Kahless because there are so many possibilities for deceit. Worf can't help his skeptical outlook any more than he can help his bumpy forehead, even though he may wish for things to be otherwise—though who wouldn't love that forehead! Like the great "warrior for wisdom" Socrates (469–399 B.C.E.), who in ancient Athens stood his ground in defense of intellectual freedom even when the death penalty was hanging over his head, Worf keeps asking difficult questions. This leads him to an argument with Kahless in front of other, more blindly believing, Klingons:

> **KAHLESS:** Something still weighs heavy on the brow of the son of Mogh. Are you contemplating yet another question for me? . . .
>
> **WORF:** Questions are the beginning of wisdom, the mark of a true warrior.
>
> **KAHLESS:** Do not forget that a leader need not answer questions of those he leads. It is enough that he says to do a thing and they will do it. If he says to run, they run. If he says to fight, they fight. If he says to die, they die.
>
> **WORF:** If the commander is worthy of that trust.

They battle it out with *bat'leths*—Klingons' weapon of choice— and eventually, when it's beginning to seem that the man might not match up to the myth, Kahless stops the battle and peps up the audience with a rousing cheer of "We are Klingons!"

Worf still isn't sure about all this. This vision looks like Kahless, speaks like a Klingon leader, fights like a warrior, and has spiritual power over his followers; but Worf remains skeptical while still allowing for the idea that this really could be Kahless. When both are picked up by the *Enterprise* for further study and speculation, Worf gets a little time to do some deep thinking. Enter philosophy.

William James and "The Important Things"

As Wesley Crusher points out, the ideas of the American philosopher and psychologist William James (1842–1910) probably won't be found on the Starfleet entrance exam. "The important things never are," Picard laments, insisting that Wesley read an early edition of one of James's books which Picard himself returns to often ("Samaritan Snare," *TNG*). A return to James's ideas might serve Worf well also as he sorts out his response to this current religious conundrum. Worf might have found some comfort, or at least some advice, in James's "The Will to Believe,"[2] in which he explores the question of what we do when faced with a choice of believing or not believing in a situation where we have no real intellectual grounds pointing us one way or the other.

Worf might ask himself whether his belief in the second-coming of Kahless is even a "genuine" option for an educated Klingon. Genuine options are "living," "forced," and "momentous." For example, a *living*, rather than *dead*, option makes sense within the wider web of one's beliefs. For myself as a member of American society, among my living options might be that I believe (or not) in the possibility of a Christian Heaven. This option is live because it's genuinely a question for me, and one that my culture makes available through traditions, popular beliefs, and religious teaching. If you were to suggest to me that I ought to believe in the possibility of *Sto-vo-kor* (the afterlife for honorable Klingons), or perhaps *Sha Ka Ree* (the Vulcan version), I would probably view these as dead options because I know—or at least I say this in public—that the *Star Trek* universe is imaginary. Believing in *Sto-vo-kor*, however, *is* a live option for Worf, since his culture accepts its existence as a genuine possibility.

According to James, Worf's options must also be either *forced* or *avoidable*. If Riker tells Worf that they can meet either in Ten Forward or on the bridge, this is clearly avoidable since Worf can suggest that they meet on the holodeck or elsewhere on the *Enterprise*, or even that they don't meet at all. But Worf's options regarding Kahless seem more forced

---

[2] William James, *The Will to Believe and Other Essays in Popular Philosophy* (New York: Dover, 1956).

than that—either Kahless has returned or he hasn't. There's no avoiding this particular dilemma; for Worf not to decide is, in fact, a decision—effectively a decision to act as though Kahless isn't a deity.

Finally, James suggests that options are either *momentous* or *trivial.* Whether to eat *Rokeg* blood pie or heart of *targ* for his afternoon snack may be, in the grand scheme of things, a pretty trivial question for Worf. However, if Kahless has indeed returned to the Klingon people, it would be a pretty big deal, as would the homecoming of any supernatural being who would restore honor, meaning, and order to his people. So the question of Kahless is live, forced, and momentous to Worf—all ingredients for "genuine" options for belief. Now comes the hard part: deciding what, from these options, to actually believe.

"A Matter of Faith"

James may have something to say about this issue, but so does our android philosopher friend Data. Excited by anything resembling a human emotional struggle, Data asks Worf, "In the absence of empirical data, how will you determine whether or not this is the real Kahless?" Worf replies, "It is not an empirical matter. It is a matter of faith." Data continues, "Faith. Then you do believe Kahless may have supernatural attributes. As an android, I am unable to accept that which cannot be proven through rational means. I would appreciate hearing your insights on this matter." Yet the big Klingon blows him off, clearly uncomfortable with his own faith.

James differs from Data and Worf in that he doesn't feel the same discomfort about faith when empirical evidence is wanting. There are cases, especially those involving morality, love, metaphysical issues, and one's own psychology, where James argues, "Faith creates its own verification" (p. 97). It's like a self-fulfilling prophecy: If, say, Will Riker fancies a love relationship and assumes that the object of his affection, Deanna Troi, reciprocates his love, then he may ask her out, making it much more likely that a reality will unfold in which the relationship will work. If, on the other hand, Will assumes that a smart woman like Deanna would never, ever, love a sop like him, then he'll avoid the risk of declaring his love and the relationship may never get started.[3] Likewise, James suggests that if you're out hiking in the mountains and find yourself in the unfortunate position of standing on the edge of a scary abyss from which your only means of escape is a "terrible leap," you're much more likely to make it if you assume that you can: "Refuse to believe and you shall indeed be right, for you shall irretrievably perish" (p. 59). If you doubt your abilities and hesitate at the last minute, you may tumble to your death. You may tumble to your death anyway, but by believing in the possibility of success, you at least give yourself a chance.

For Worf, this isn't a life or death question for him personally, but it could mean renewal or tragedy for Klingon society. Since, according to James, the question of faith is left open when there isn't evidence one way or the other, Worf can continue to entertain the possibility of Kahless's return. As one of the founders of a tradition in American philosophy called "pragmatism," James believes that truth is simultaneously found and made, discovered and constructed—a mixture of hard evidence and contextual perspective, such as the perspective, individual or cultural, that determines whether or not options are live. Truth is what "works" for us as we constantly struggle to make sense of our varied physical and cultural environments. It's what we put our trust in and the world answers back favorably. This is a little different than many earlier philosophies of knowledge that assume there's one objective truth that transcends human experience. In that case, truth is what can be seen from the perspective of some kind of "God's eye view." Rather, truth for pragmatists is a vast and varied relationship between the perceiver and the social-cultural-physical environment in which she finds herself. Absent any empirical evidence from such an objective, God's eye view, we're left with our own perspectives. This allows James to assert the controversial claim that it's reasonable to believe in cases of spiritual truth, even in the absence of any kind of recognizable evidence that's sufficient to objectively verify what one believes.

This may be all fine and well about truly metaphysical issues, where we'll never have much evidence offered up by the nat-

---

[3] In "Parallels" (*TNG*), Worf similarly explores a relationship with Deanna, but only after he views their marriage in an alternate reality. Poor Deanna—she sure gets a lot of male attention on this show!

ural world, but what about issues when science may have something to say? I might believe that my existence has meaning and purpose. My experience of the natural world doesn't offer much evidence regarding this claim; so I'm left to contemplate the practical benefits of having this belief *sans* a scientific analysis. However, if I believe that I can survive without oxygen for more than a minute or two, a little experimentation would easily provide evidence to the contrary. James is very clear that good philosophers must take the experiences the world offers us into account, even when the evidence is contrary to what we'd like to believe. I may wish to believe that it's a bright sunshiny day, but when I don't take an umbrella and the raindrops start falling on my head, my wishful thinking isn't going to do much work for me.

Worf may wish to believe in the return of Kahless, but his ponderings take a less metaphysical direction when Gowron, the political leader of the Klingon Empire, arrives on the *Enterprise* with a sure-fire way of proving, one way or the other, the truth about Kahless. With what's believed to be a sample of the original Kahless's blood—itself a matter of faith—Gowron suggests, you guessed it, a DNA check. Ah, would that all tricky dilemmas could be so easily solved! Worf, Gowron, Koroth, and Kahless himself (or whoever he is) can finally get some truth about whether this particular spiritual leader really did transcend death.

After some testing, more fighting (these are Klingons, remember), a good bit of soul-searching, and a whole lot of arguing, it comes out that "Kahless" is actually a clone of the original. For Worf, this changes everything and causes an even greater personal crisis. He now has scientific evidence that demands his attention, but he retains a passionate desire to hang on to his belief in Kahless—a belief which, if shared by other Klingons, could lead to the reunification of his people. What's a Klingon to do?

Real Things and Rightful Heirs

First, Worf has it out with Koroth, the "creator" of Kahless-the-clone. Perhaps with the best of intentions, Koroth cloned Kahless, somehow imprinted this version with knowledge of the sacred texts and even some of the original's memories, and staged his "comeback." But as an educated person, Worf has to consider the physical evidence even when Koroth poses the interesting question, "How do you know that this was not the way the prophecy was to be fulfilled?"

How indeed? What if Worf were to do what Koroth suggests: lie to the Klingon people about the cloning of Kahless? On the one hand, the Klingon people would experience immediate joy, hope, and a return to honorable ways at the appearance of their beloved *messiah*. On the other hand, even with good intentions Worf risks at the least a serious lack of personal integrity. Furthermore, as is sometimes the case when politicians lie to the public, the falsehood will probably be found out, causing disharmony and distrust. Clearly, this belief may not work as well as Koroth plans. If truth, as the pragmatists teach, is what works in light of our best understanding of the world, including the future consequences of our present ideas and actions, then it seems that Worf must decide between what's immediately exciting and expedient versus what will contribute to a more honorable society in the long run.

Under these circumstances, James might suggest that we consult his friend, Charles S. Peirce, also a pragmatist, who argues that some methods of believing are better than others. Peirce describes several ways of "fixing" beliefs—our beliefs become "fixed" like plaster, or we get "set" in our beliefs.[4] One of the troublesome ways people form beliefs, Peirce suggests, is *via* the method of "tenacity," in which people act like ostriches with their heads in the sand, believing whatever they like while ignoring all evidence to the contrary. Another problematic method is that of "authority," in which people blindly follow the ideals and actions of others. It doesn't take long to think of historical examples of the dangers of these methods: the execution of Socrates, Nazi Germany, the terrorist attacks of September 11th, and the ease with which the American government convinced its citizens about weapons of mass destruction in Iraq quickly come to mind.

If he were a lesser Klingon, Worf could run away and hide his head in the sand, believing that Kahless had returned even

---

[4] Charles Sanders Peirce, "The Fixation of Belief," in *Philosophical Writings of Charles Sanders Peirce* (New York: Dover, 1955).

when the evidence says otherwise, or he could follow the advice of Koroth—an authority—and help convince the masses to believe in a lie; but Worf is incapable of avoiding reality. Fortunately, Peirce has a method that might work a little better: the method of science, or the "experimental" method, in which we use *doubt* as the starting place for developing beliefs about the world that are strong, trustworthy, and useful.[5] In this way of fixing our beliefs, we explore evidence, ask hard questions, become members of a "community of inquirers," and fight for the right to seek truth without hiding our heads in the sand or blindly following orders:

> There are Real things, whose characters are entirely independent of our opinions about them. Those Reals affect our senses according to regular laws, and, though our sensations are as different as are our relations to the objects, yet, by taking advantage of the laws of perception, we can ascertain by reasoning how things really and truly are. (p. 18)

For us, as for Worf, reality can't be avoided.

James and Peirce both offer realistic and creative ways of forming beliefs that balance human experience with the empirical evidence the world offers us. While the very questions we ask often reflect our own little windows on the world, we must take care that our truths, in order to work for us, reflect the widest possible perspectives. Although it's true, for James, that the "trail of the human serpent is thus over everything"[6]—that we come to form beliefs from our own unique encounter with the world—he and Peirce both argue that the truth that works best will be the one that embraces the real, hard facts of existence. As a Klingon warrior of honor and integrity, Worf is used to hard facts, and, even if he thought it would be a spiritual

---

[5] For an extensive, much earlier, version of the method of doubt, see René Descartes, *Discourse on Method and Meditations on First Philosophy* (Indianapolis: Hackett, 1998). Descartes's approach to doubt is quite intentional and universal—he doubts everything in order to closely examine his beliefs. For Peirce, doubt emerges from perplexing circumstances. Doubt about everything all at once is impossible. About Cartesian doubt, Peirce says, "Let us not doubt in philosophy what we do not doubt in our hearts." ("Some Consequences of Four Incapacities," in *Philosophical Writings*, p. 40).

[6] William James, *Pragmatism* (New York: Penguin, 2000), p. 33.

boon to his people in the short-run, he just can't hide the truth about Kahless.

Worf now wonders whether his only option is to expose Kahless as a fraud, or whether he can retain the hopefulness of his initial belief in the leader's return. In a heart-to-heart chat, our favorite android again waxes philosophical on the topic of faith and belief, this time much in the style of James:

> **DATA:** I once had what could be considered a crisis of the spirit . . . The Starfleet officers who first activated me on Omicron Theta told me I was an android, nothing more than a sophisticated machine with human form. However, I realized that if I were simply a machine, I could never be anything else. I could never grow beyond my programming. I found that difficult to accept, so I chose to believe that I was a person, that I had the potential to be more than a collection of circuits and subprocessors. It is a belief which I still hold.
>
> **WORF:** How did you come to your decision?
>
> **DATA:** I made a leap of faith.

Likewise, James offers a personal example of when he laments that he can't answer with any certainty the question of whether he has free will, since this is a metaphysical, and not a scientific, issue. Taking his own advice about faith creating its own verification, and in the absence of any evidence, James decides that the better and more optimistic course of action is to believe in the truth of free will, since that might actually make it a reality. If he doesn't believe, and he does have free will, then this freedom won't make any difference, because it won't be actualized—in Data's terms, he'll never grow beyond his programming. If, however, he acts in a hopeful spirit with the assumption of free will, then his freedom might actually become a reality.

So, even with scientific evidence, perhaps there's still a little room for humanity—"humanoidity"—or even faith, and Worf finds that there are more than two horns to his dilemma. In the end, he offers what James might think of as a pragmatic solution that balances the realities of empirical data—that Kahless is a clone—with the need for meaningful experience.

"Something to Believe In"

While Gowron, sensing a threat to the political status quo, demands that Kahless be exposed, and Koroth wishes to allow the vast majority of Klingons to blindly believe in the second-coming of Kahless, Worf works out a creative alternative that accounts for both scientific truth and the quest for meaning. He proposes that the Klingon people be told the truth, but that Kahless be accepted as an *emperor*—a spiritual and moral leader charged with bringing honor and integrity back to Klingon culture, a political solution to what was initially a religious puzzle. Kahless-the-clone has the imprinted memory of the teachings of the great leader, as well as his DNA; so he's in the unique and powerful position of being able to spread and exemplify those beliefs. It's like passing down the *dharma* in Buddhist traditions—it's the teachings that are meaningful, not necessarily the messenger. As Worf suggests, perhaps the people don't need the real Kahless, "They need something to believe in . . . something larger than themselves, something that will give their lives meaning." Our Kahless may not be the real Kahless, but "he is the rightful heir to Kahless." The people, Worf claims, "will make a leap of faith."

Though we don't worry, at least not yet, about the cloning of religious heroes, perhaps Worf's dilemma isn't too different from what many of us face everyday. We wish to make sound decisions about how to get along in the world based on good reasoning and a desire to live meaningfully. We thus have to learn to balance what we'd like to be true with what we know to be true in cases where empirical evidence is present. Finding hope, meaning, and even faith in our everyday existence while embracing reality as it constantly presents itself to us through our senses and scientific ponderings could truly lead to a creative response to the world. In this, truth—a trustworthy method of believing—really is what works.

Striking the right balance, however, between evidence and hope is often very difficult and perhaps is itself a matter of experimentation. Though Worf has faith in his plan to offer Kahless as an emperor to the Klingon people, he still entertains doubts regarding its integrity and workability. Kahless-the-clone responds to Worf's skepticism:

Kahless left us, all of us, a powerful legacy, a way of thinking and acting that makes us Klingon. If his words hold wisdom and his philosophy is honorable, what does it matter if he returns? What is important is that we follow his teachings. Perhaps the words are more important than the man.

For James, as a pragmatist, this makes sense; as long as we're true to what we know about the world, what becomes important is what we *do*—since our actions are the consequences of what we believe. Perhaps Worf's faith in the possibilities of Kahless's moral leadership and the future of the Klingon Empire is more important than the genuineness of Kahless's origins.

Despite all this, in the end Worf is still skeptical, questioning whether this "leap of faith" will work, and wondering whether he's been truthful to himself, the Klingon people, and the "real" Kahless—should he exist somewhere in *Sto-vo-kor*. Ah, such is the life of a philosopher. And the world of the honorable philosopher is, like the Klingon monastery at Boreth, a place of questions instead of answers. *Qapla'*, philosophers![7]

---

[7] I'd like to thank the many, many Introduction to Philosophy students I've thus far had the privilege to know. Each time I enter into conversation with students about issues such as faith, belief, hope, and reality, I learn something new, and my "will to believe" optimistically in the future of humanity grows stronger. This also happens when I watch *TNG*.

14

Cardassian "Monsters" and Bajoran "Freedom Fighters"

MARNIE NOLTON

Star Trek episodes are often morality plays providing allegories for social issues like race, gender, the nature of war, and religion. The result is a United Federation of Planets with a message of progress, integrity, and optimism that has sustained audiences throughout the years. *Deep Space Nine* takes these Federation ideals a step further by deliberately placing its characters in situations that question some of these grand ideals, often in terms of dilemmas that aren't easily reconciled. *DS9*'s questioning and further exploration of boundaries occurs specifically through its use of conventional ideas regarding religion, mental illness, and most dramatically, the concept of *difference*.

"Difference" here means more than just "surface dissimilarity." It points to deep level problems in how we understand such things as community, our relationships with others, and ourselves. It reminds us that what we might perceive as different is often lost, distorted, repressed, or reduced in importance, a process that's often defended in the name of some identity we consider worth preserving. For instance, the distinctions we create and maintain around our ideas about what it means to *be* Ferengi or Vulcan or Human extends beyond the physical dissimilarities of our lobes. Consider the ways Ferengi society tries to uphold "Ferengi-ness" with its insistence on the pursuit of profit or the subjugation of women.[1] In *DS9*, this problem of dif-

---

[1] Recall Quark's vexation that Rom's son, Nog, is busy studying for his entrance exams into Starfleet Academy instead of working at the bar and

ference is exposed by looking at the diplomatic, socio-economic, and military relations between Cardassia and Bajor, as mediated through the Starfleet personnel serving on Deep Space Nine.

The space station's situation itself—formerly the Cardassian mining facility Terok Nor—is particularly well suited to an exploration of identity and difference, given that it's a (largely) stationary site through which many different species interact. We should also remember Bajor's strategic position near the wormhole, which Bajorans refer to as the "Celestial Temple," the home of the Prophets. Of equal importance is the Federation's insistence that Bajor become a member of this grand alliance "by any means necessary." In this situation, not only are Starfleet's General Orders regularly abandoned, but the Articles of the Federation are themselves temporarily set aside or suspended, which Sisko alludes to in "The Maquis, Part II"[2]:

> The trouble is Earth . . . On Earth, there is no poverty, no crime, no war. You look out the window of Starfleet headquarters and you see paradise. Well, it's easy to be a saint in paradise, but the Maquis do not live in paradise. Out there, in the Demilitarized Zone[3] all the problems haven't been solved yet. Out there, there are no saints, just people—angry, scared, determined people who are going to do whatever it takes to survive whether it meets with the Federation's approval or not.

Sisko recognizes that there are no easy solutions to the complexities of life on and around DS9. We see this most clearly as

---

helping them make a profit. "That's how it begins," Quark laments. "All it takes is for one impressionable youngster to join Starfleet, and the next thing you know a whole generation of Ferengi will be quoting the Prime Directive and abandoning the pursuit of latinum. It's the end of Ferengi civilization as we know it" ("Family Business"). Quark is claiming that a particular kind of Ferengi identity is worth maintaining—the one that pursues gold-pressed latinum. "Rules of Acquisition" is another episode in which this notion of Ferengi identity is jeopardized.

[2] All episode references are from *DS9*, unless otherwise noted.

[3] The Demilitarized Zone is the result of the armistice between Cardassia and the Federation. A number of planets were traded between the two governments as part of the treaty, resulting in a number of colonies finding themselves in each other's redefined territory. Some were offered relocations, but this was met with resistance by a small group of Federation colonists who later became known as The Maquis ("Journey's End," *TNG*; "The Maquis").

the Federation's democratic ideals fracture and shift uneasily between its two roles: one as beneficent host and defender of peoples, planets, and principles; the other as strategic opportunist, concerned with maintaining stability and security near the awesome potential of the Bajoran wormhole.

In "Duet," Major Kira interrogates Aamin Marritza, a Cardassian accused of war crimes against the Bajoran people during Cardassia's occupation of Bajor. It's revealed that hundreds of thousands of Bajorans died at the Gallitep labor camp, and that Marritza is somehow associated with this camp; although it isn't clear immediately to what extent. Kira helped to liberate Gallitep twelve years prior and feels compelled to punish anyone who served there. She believes that a trial would give Bajor satisfaction. Marritza, in turn, accuses Kira of not wanting to seek the truth: "It's not the truth you're interested in. All you want is vengeance." To compound the situation, Starfleet's Commander Sisko and Cardassia's Gul Dukat discuss the potential implication that relations between their two governments may suffer if Marritza is handed over to the Bajorans. All parties are at an impasse, and no amount of discussion will be able to satisfy everyone. Hence, the possibility of justice—and questions surrounding notions of justice, retribution, and recompensation—become highly problematic. The questions arise: Are all Cardassians "monsters"? Are all Bajorans "righteous freedom fighters"?

"A Masterpiece of Meticulous Exactitude"

The Cardassian occupation of Bajor is similar to the Nazi and Soviet models of occupation, experimentation, and extermination carried out in concentration camps and gulags ("Necessary Evil," "Wrongs Darker Than Death or Night," "Things Past"). During the occupation, and despite ongoing resistance, the Cardassians plundered Bajor's natural resources, murdered Bajorans in labor camps, suppressed their religion, kept them as personal slaves and mistresses, and used them in medical experiments ("Nothing Human," *VGR*). After fifty years, the Cardassians, perhaps having grown weary of Bajoran "freedom fighters" and mindful of their relatively new treaty with the Federation, made the political decision to withdraw from Bajor. Some Cardassians were furious at leaving the mining station

Terok Nor and the remaining resources. The fragile Bajoran Provisional Government asked the Federation to establish a Starfleet presence in order for Bajor to begin rebuilding ("Emissary"). Thus, *DS9* begins with a tenuous Bajoran Provisional Government, a hostile Cardassian Empire, and all the diplomatic problems the Federation might expect from such a situation, in which its own peaceful coexistence with Cardassia is new and fragile.

The tension is thick, with Cardassians who loathe the Bajorans whose resistance hindered Cardassia's progress. In turn, the Bajorans revile all things Cardassian and reject any opportunity for cooperation with Cardassia, despite Federation meditation. Kira sums up her people's feelings in "The Darkness and the Light": "None of you belonged on Bajor. It wasn't your world. For fifty years, you raped our planet and you killed our people, you lived on our land and you took the food out of our mouths and I don't care whether you held a phaser in your hand or you ironed shirts for a living. You were all guilty."

Faced with Bajoran and Cardassian hostility, the Federation is at an impasse because it's essentially unable to enforce its Directives and Articles.[4] There are numerous instances in *DS9* when Starfleet officers deliberately break with Federation protocol—just a few examples would be the crew's easy compromise of temporal integrity in "Trials and Tribble-ations"; O'Brien's actions in "Time's Orphan"; and Sisko's manipulation of the Romulan government into joining the Federation's side of the war in "In The Pale Moonlight," where he readily admits, "I'd pay any price, go to any lengths because my cause was righteous. My . . . intentions were good." The Federation is severely compromised by both its increasingly torturous moral justifications[5] and its irrelevance to the reality of life on DS9. Michael

---

[4] The Articles of the Federation are from the non-canonical *Star Trek Starfleet Technical Manual* by Franz Joseph and are only hinted at, but never explicitly stated, in *Star Trek*. "Non-canonical" refers to the manual as a fictional reference with a colorful history of consensus, use, and later rejection by Gene Roddenberry.

[5] Section 31 is an example of the darker side of morality with which *DS9* engages. Section 31 is a covert Federation security operation that appears to work outside of the ethical protocols we're used to in *Star Trek*. It's revealed that Section 31 is responsible for the disease that's killing the Dominion's Founders ("Tacking into the Wind," "Extreme Measures"). High-ranking Starfleet officers even collude with Section 31 to manipulate Romulan politics

Eddington—a former Starfleet officer turned Maquis—gives a scathing critique of Federation policies:

> Why is the Federation so obsessed about the Maquis? We've never harmed you, and yet we're constantly arrested and charged with terrorism. Starships chase us through the Badlands and our supporters are harassed and ridiculed. Why? Because we've left the Federation and that's the one thing you can't accept. Nobody leaves paradise. Everyone should want to be in the Federation. Hell, you even want the Cardassians to join. You're only sending them replicators because one day they can take their rightful place on the Federation Council. You know, in some ways, you're even worse than the Borg. At least they tell you about their plans for assimilation. You're more insidious. You assimilate people, and they don't even know it. ("For the Cause")

Starfleet, indeed the Federation itself—situated far away from DS9 on Earth—can't possibly appreciate the complexity of the local situation on Bajor. Sisko recognizes this all too clearly when he's compelled to ignore Federation orders in the best interests, religious and otherwise, of Bajor ("Rapture," "Tears of the Prophets"). Starfleet shares DS9 with the Bajorans. It's a space station and not a Federation starship, and the sheer volume of visitors and trade demands that rules of negotiation and hospitality necessarily differ from previous examples of *Star Trek*. Michael Piller—co-creator, with Rick Berman, of *DS9*—indicates that this was both a strength of and a challenge in creating and maintaining the series:

> One of the things about [*DS9*] . . . is that it has a true social conscience. And the nature of the challenges that face the crew of [*DS9*] is in some ways more difficult than the challenges that face the crew of [*TNG*]. Because at the end of every hour of [*TNG*], they get on their horse and ride out of town. But the people who are on [*DS9*] are stuck there to face the problems that are there week after week.

---

in order to protect Federation interests ("Inter Arma Enim Silent Leges"). Another example of the Federation's questionable moral actions is when Sisko reflects on his own behavior: "I lied. I cheated. I bribed men to cover the crimes of other men. I am an accessory to murder. But the most damning thing of all . . . I think I can live with it. And if I had to do it all over again . . . I would" ("In The Pale Moonlight").

If you want parallels to contemporary society and the problems that we live with, you will find that they are much easier to adapt to [*DS9*] than they are to [*TNG*]. These are the stories we wanted to do for years on [*TNG*] that we could never quite figure out how to do: the pollution show, or the AIDS show, or topics like that. The difficulty in doing those shows is because it's hard to come into somebody else's town or somebody else's planet and start fixing them and curing them and telling them what to do. It's not what *Star Trek* is about.

But when you deal with, say, the influx of refugees through the wormhole at [*DS9*], it's an immediate problem. It has to do with where we live, and where we're stationed, and the people who have different agendas coming together to argue about what's right and wrong.[6]

"Duet" highlights these tensions between Bajor, Cardassia, and the Federation. We see them played out in debates over Maritzza's identity, over who should have jurisdiction in this matter, and whether there might be a way to satisfy everyone. Consider these exchanges:

KIRA: . . . the Federation has no right telling us how to deal with our criminals.
SISKO: If it turns out that he is a criminal then he'll be yours, and you're welcome to him. Until then, he's just a traveller under suspicion.

DUKAT: This Bajoran obsession with alleged Cardassian improprieties during the occupation is really quite distasteful.
SISKO: I suppose, if you're a Bajoran, so was the occupation.
DUKAT: I might remind you that neither one of us is Bajoran and I would hate their bitterness to cause conflict between Cardassia and the Federation.

French philosopher Jean-François Lyotard's work, *The Differend*,[7] can help us better understand the antagonism between Cardassia and Bajor, and the impasse faced by all three

---

[6] Judith and Garfield Reeves-Stevens, *The Making of Deep Space Nine* (New York: Pocket Books, 1994), p. 279.
[7] Jean-François Lyotard, *The Differend: Phrases in Dispute* (Minneapolis: University of Minnesota Press, 1988).

parties. Lyotard's concept of the *differend* can be understood by what he calls *agonism*—the conflicts and problems which arise out of competing views of reality. The idea of agonism suggests that we look past simplified pictures of two diametrically opposed and equally weighted enemies, such as found with the Federation-Cardassian conflicts or Captain Kirk's longstanding tiff with the Klingon Empire. Instead, the kind of conflict that Lyotard speaks of is more like the interaction between the Borg Collective and other species they assimilate. Just as individuals are involuntarily assimilated into the Collective by having cybernetic implants inserted into their bodies, Lyotard describes the differend in terms of a playing field so incredibly unfair, that one player's advantage overwhelms the other's. One side completely strips away the other's capacity to engage competently or even to speak in its own defence. Lyotard speaks of practices that attempt to silence other voices by advocating general rules or criteria which exclude the opposition, leading to their marginalization from the game itself. One party is left silent, with no comeback or recourse to justice possible, a situation that Lyotard argues is untenable and unjust:

> The differend is the unstable side and instance of language wherein something which must be able to be put into phrases cannot yet be . . . What is at stake in a literature, in a philosophy, in a politics perhaps, is to bear witness to differends by finding idioms for them. (p. 13)

From this starting point Lyotard uses the differend to argue that these silences must be "attended to"—that they must be put into language and affirmed.

The differend identifies conflicts that result in massive injustices. One of the first steps in identifying and then dealing with them is to recognize that it's the current "framing"—the express character and boundaries—of the situation which makes it impossible for one party to take a stand or defend itself. And simply providing this party with the opportunity to speak isn't enough. After all, in terms of the dominant framing of the situation some issues may be "unpresentable"—invisible, effectively "off the table." In the example of the camp at Gallitep, many horrific experiences can't be spoken of, can't be accurately captured in words within Cardassian reports or databanks—no matter how good their filing system may be. Hence, as Lyotard tells us, a whole new idiom is needed, which requires recognizing that there are always alternative ways of framing any situation. Indeed, there are alternative possibilities for any given reality (a Federation, say, in *Star Trek: Insurrection* that protects rather than exploits the Ba'ku); yet these possibilities are typically masked by such systemically-maintained silence.[8] It's tragically true that not every possibility can be fulfilled in any given situation—and this is the very point with which Lyotard is concerned. Either the Ba'ku are removed and their planet is rendered inhabitable or not; either Federation or Ba'ku interests are satisfied, not both; and whichever are satisfied means that the others are denied, perhaps unjustly.

"I'm Asking for All the Bajorans Who Can't Ask"

The conflict between Cardassia and Bajor is a deeply difficult example of Lyotard's *differend*. The success or validation of Bajor necessarily excludes that of Cardassia, and vice versa. For example, Lyotard's theory supposes that when we speak of Bajorans as "victims" or "righteous freedom fighters," or Cardassians as "monsters" or "butchers," the language we use presents people, their actions, and their interests in ways that suit us. But these ways are not always truly representative of whom we speak, and point to the power of language when used to impose the significance that *we* see in a situation.

Lyotard's work on how language and meaning are constructed, and may be established to exert pressure, can help us better understand the impasse between Bajor, Cardassia, and the Federation. After all, it's through our use and privileging of language—in particular, descriptions—that important things such as relationships and reality are presented. Think of the way Klingon phrases or sentences privilege certain notions of reality. When Kang exclaims to Kor, Koloth, and Dax, "May Kahless guide us on this day of vengeance," the way he expresses him-

---

[8] Picard's mutiny against the Federation to protect the Ba'ku, ironically, works to affirm the Federation Prime Directive—a doctrine of non-interference. Picard's willingness to face a court martial, where he believes the truth will be heard, works in favor of the marginalized Ba'ku and against the personal interests of some who live in the Federation.

self prioritizes certain ideas about the world over others ("Blood Oath"). He expresses the idea that vengeance is good and desirable. The aim of vengeance is further legitimated by reference to the legendary warrior, Kahless. This phrase also implies the notion of a tiered reality, the domain of everyday life and, above or behind it, the mythic domain of legendary warriors such as Kahless who may be drawn upon to validate certain actions and behaviors as the norm in Klingon life.

Since we commonly ask why particular statements or views are true, important, or ultimately worthwhile, Lyotard's interest in the language we use to justify the validity of statements and ideas about the world is significant. To ask our starting questions again: Are all Bajorans freedom fighters? Are all Cardassians monsters? What if only one of these is true? If both are true, then productive dialogue between Cardassia and Bajor would seem impossible. Productive dialogue requires that both parties be able to understand the other's position or "reality." Here, though, the realities of Bajorans and Cardassians would seem to be irreconcilable and unpresentable in each other's idiom.

Arising from the unpresentable in both positions, the lack of dialogue between Bajorans and Cardassians shows that there are *several* differends in the battle over whose view and interest should count. This battle gives way to a war between the Bajoran Provisional Government and Cardassia's Central Command for prominence, authority, and recognition from third parties, like the Federation. Thus, a Lyotardian "agonisitic construal" exists in the irreconcilable relationship between Bajor and Cardassia. The agonistic construal is expressed primarily in the use of language, especially in the ways each side chooses to express or hide certain things. Think of the way in which Gul Dukat—the Cardassian Prefect in charge of Bajor during the occupation—refers to Bajorans as "ungrateful children," even going so far as to lament the fact that there's no statue of him on Bajor to recognize all that he did for them during the occupation ("Sacrifice of Angels"); language is also used to construe Bajorans as "simple folk" compared to Cardassians despite the fact that Bajor has an advanced culture that's much older than Cardassian civilization ("Explorers").

Let's zero in on exactly how this agonistic construal is played out in "Duet." When an unknown Cardassian arrives at DS9, he's held by the Bajorans as a war criminal, simply because of his affiliation with Gallitep. Kira attempts to explain her intense feelings about him to Sisko:

> Commander, if you'd been there twelve years ago when we liber-
> ated that camp—if you'd seen the things I saw—all those Bajoran
> bodies, starved, brutalized . . . Do you know what Cardassian pol-
> icy was? Oh, I'm not even talking about the murder. Murder was
> just the end of the fun for them. First came the humiliation. Mothers
> raped in front of their children, husbands beaten until their wives
> couldn't recognize them, old people buried alive because they
> couldn't work anymore.

Yet there are "neglected, forgotten, or repressed possibilities"[9] on both sides—in this case, the Cardassian's own story of being only a file clerk. The Cardassian prisoner hits a nerve with Kira when he accuses her, "It's not the truth you're interested in. All you want is vengeance." Kira admits to Dax that she doesn't want to believe that the Cardassian—self-identified as Marritza— is merely a file clerk. If Marritza is more than a clerk, if he's a war criminal, this will somehow give Bajor satisfaction. Kira's hope for satisfaction, or vengeance, is problematic for a number of reasons. In Lyotard's view, there can be no satisfaction, or vengeance, for Bajor; the crimes and injustices Bajor suffered under the Cardassian occupation were so great and terrible as to be unpresentable. Not only are they unpresentable, nothing could possibly make amends for such deliberate, purposeful decimation and genocide—it wouldn't matter how many war criminals the Bajorans prosecute. As the Cardassian prisoner states, "You can never undo what I accomplished. The dead will still be dead."

As "Duet" unravels, much confusion abounds as to the iden-tity of this Cardassian prisoner. Initially claiming to be a filing clerk, he's later revealed as the "Butcher of Gallitep" himself: Gul Darhe'el. As Darhe'el, the Cardassian provokes Kira with some of the Cardassian attitudes behind the occupation: "What you call genocide, I call a day's work," he boasts. When Kira delves deeper, however, she finds evidence of cosmetic alter-ations, coupled with reliable reports that Darhe'el is dead. When

---

9   Jean-François Lyotard, *The Postmodern Explained to Children: Correspondence 1982–1985* (Sydney: Power, 1992), p. 136.

she confronts the Cardassian prisoner with this new information, he becomes hysterical, tries to ignore her, and then calls for security to rescue him from Kira's questioning. It turns out that this Cardassian *is* the filing clerk Marritza after all. When Kira confirms that Darhe'el is dead, Marritza becomes increasingly agitated and eventually his story and his assumed personality break down:

> That's not true. I am alive. I will always be alive! It's Marritza who is dead. Marritza, who was good for nothing but cowering under his bunk and weeping like a woman. Who, every night, covered his ears, because he couldn't bear to hear the screaming for mercy of the Bajorans. Covered my ears every night, but . . . I couldn't bear to hear those horrible screams. You have no idea what it's like to be a coward . . . to see these horrors . . . and do nothing. Marritza's dead. He deserves to be dead.

Kira's shaken by his story and can't understand Marritza's deception. She even begins to forgive him for his minor role in the occupation: "You didn't commit those crimes and you couldn't stop them. You were only one man." Marritza pleads with her to maintain the charade, "No, no, don't you see? I have to be punished. We all have to be punished . . . Cardassia will only survive if it stands in front of Bajor and admits the truth. My trial will force Cardassia to acknowledge its guilt and we're guilty, all of us. My death is necessary."

DS9 shows us the overpowering guilt of a Cardassian who was by all accounts completely powerless to prevent the injustices for which he blames himself. Kira's recognition that Marritza isn't a Cardassian "monster" is dramatically highlighted against the events after the public revelation of his true identity. On his way to departing the space station, Marritza is killed by a Bajoran who wasn't even at the Gallitep labor camp. "He's a Cardassian!" the Bajoran explains, by way of exculpating himself, "That's reason enough."

"You Can Never Undo What I Accomplished"

Lyotard's theory of the differend reminds us that there's always more than one set of interests at stake, and that these stakes are often irreconcilable with each other. In the case of *DS9*'s moral and political situation, we could argue that, for the Federation, what's at stake is the stability and security in the Alpha Quadrant that they've worked hard to establish through their treaty with Cardassia. Their offer to protect Bajor through its transition to Federation membership has benefits for them, particularly in terms of Bajor's proximity to the wormhole. What are the possible stakes for Cardassia? First, *survival* prompted Cardassia's expansionist policies as Cardassia Prime ran out of natural resources and her people were dying of starvation and disease. The military saw that the only way to stop death and disease was for Cardassia to expand its borders and become a powerful force. It thus sent warships to invade other worlds and steal their natural resources, territory, and technology ("Chain of Command, Part II," *TNG*).

Second, since Cardassia pulled out from Bajor, its reputation has taken a beating. Despite their well-deserved reputation for brutality and a strong social and military order—for example, the work of the Obsidian Order, Cardassia's secret intelligence organization, and the intensive indoctrination that Cardassian children undergo—it's perceived that Bajor "beat" the Cardassians. The success of the Bajoran resistance in contributing to Cardassia's decision to withdraw from Bajor effectively undermined them as a power base in the Alpha Quadrant.[10] Lastly, the greatest resource at stake for Cardassia is the Bajoran wormhole. Had they been able to maintain their position on Bajor, or even mount a successful campaign against both the Federation and Bajor, they could reclaim Terok Nor (DS9's Cardassian name) and control access to the wormhole, opening up a whole new quadrant from which to acquire natural resources, territory, and technology, and thereby re-establish their position as a powerful empire. That Cardassia accomplishes such feat only after joining forces with the Dominion must have taken some of the sweetness out of their victory ("Call to Arms").

The stakes for the Bajorans are different, though no less important. They're rebuilding their world and reasserting their cultural practices. The Provisional Government struggles to

---

[10] Something similar might be said with regard to the Maquis's undermining of Federation authority ("The Maquis," "For the Cause").

assert its right of sovereignty, of self-regulating governance. Also at stake is Bajoran culture, coming to grips with the havoc wrought by fifty years of occupation that sought to suppress religious devotion and cultural heritage. This interest is often in tension with another stake for Bajor: its potential membership in the Federation. Bajor is precariously balanced between the full rights and privileges afforded Federation members and those who are non-Federation compliant. Federation, Cardassians, Bajorans—each group's claims will be of paramount importance to that group and given priority over and above the interests of others.

For Lyotard, these different interests, as they inevitably compete for prominence, authority, and recognition, express themselves in different "realities" relative to those interests. One way of ending the competition is by "totalization": any one group's set of norms—say, the standard Federation set of practices and values—could be offered as a universal standard for the intergalactic rights of all. But this may lead to great injustice when applied to species or communities that don't share or wish to share the Federation's ideals or ways of doing things. Quark, for example, balks at first when newly-appointed DS9 commander Sisko asks him to keep his bar open on the Promenade: "How could I possibly operate my establishment under Starfleet rules of conduct?" ("Emissary"). Also, when the Federation first broaches peace with the Klingon Empire, Chekov commits a *faux pas* by referring to the Federation's concept of "inalienable human rights." Azetbur, daughter of Klingon Chancellor Gorkon, retorts, "'Inalien,' if you could only hear yourselves. 'Human rights.' Why, the very name is racist. The Federation is no more than a *Homo sapiens* only club" (*Star Trek VI: The Undiscovered Country*).

Lyotard's philosophy thus reminds us of the fundamental importance of difference in the face of the pressure for totalizing or universalizing standards—standards that typically claim to have incontestable authority over diverse beliefs and practices. It's totalizing to say that all Cardassians are monsters, or claim that all Bajorans are victims in the context of the occupation. Totalizing standards—even Federation law—are also often used to make claim to 'the truth' or the 'right' way of doing things. *DS9*, however, presents us with what might be called a loss of confidence in the truth, in the form of the Federation's inability to regulate other parts of the galaxy. This is particularly striking in contrast to the other *Star Trek* series, and suggests that there's more than one way, more than one law, and more than one species to take into account as we look to the future. It's worth noting here the Dominion's goal in "totalizing" its power over both the Gamma and Alpha Quadrants. They, like the Borg, wish to introduce their own brand of "order" to the perceived chaos of the rest of the galaxy.

DS9's political and cultural dynamics are a powerful example of Lyotard's theory of agonistics, showing us ongoing contests between incommensurable interests. Federation Directives go head-to-head with a range of other legal, ethical, and political systems in a galactic context. Ferengi political economy, for example, competes for control of commodities and services against other economic systems on a local level (DS9), a planetary level (Ferengenar), an interplanetary level (the Federation), and even a galactic level (Quark's dealing with the Dosi who reside in the Gamma Quadrant in "Rules of Acquisition").

"He's a Cardassian! That's Reason Enough"

"Duet" is a serious and significant piece of the agonistic construal that is the Bajoran and Cardassian relationship. This agonistic relationship is particularly entrenched by the construction of identities by both sides—the Cardassian overlord or the Bajoran victim—which operate to displace the other as either Cardassian monster or Bajoran freedom fighter. And at even broader levels, we've seen how agonistic conflicts have been used both to legitimate certain stakes and identities, while marginalizing and displacing others.

The parties in "Duet" have reached an impasse—unable to move beyond certain assumptions about themselves and others as a result of the occupation. This impasse can be better understood through Lyotard's theory of agonistics and the differend. His theory is suspicious of, and argues for the destabilizing of, closed traditions and totalizing claims and beliefs, whether they be Federation Directives, Cardassian military stratagems, or Bajoran faith claims. Lyotardian "difference" becomes a useful tool for understanding the contextual nature of claims to truth offered by the various parties involved in and around the struggle for the rebuilding of Bajor and its claim to the wormhole.

It's important to recognize that agonistics frames issues which are ongoing concerns. "Duet" isn't concerned just with things that occurred during the occupation of Bajor. It isn't solely about past wrongs or injustices that might "lessen" with the passage of time. Some differends, such as the occupation, are so entrenched that they continue to exert pressure well after the events occur. The episode "Cardassians" is further case in point, where a war orphan is caught up in the impasse between Bajor, Cardassia, and the Federation. The situation is made more difficult by the fact that the Cardassian orphan—Rugal—is ashamed of who he is. O'Brien points this out to the boy's newly-discovered Cardassian father, Pa'Dar: "The boy hates everything he is. He hates Cardassians, he hates being a Cardassian." The Cardassian tailor/spy, "plain, simple" Garak, also a pariah from his own people, could be a sympathetic ear to Pa'Dar; but he's little interested in the truth of Rugal's heritage, or indeed anything else. Garak might have been quoting Lyotard when he tells Bashir: "Truth, Doctor, is in the eye of the beholder. I never tell the truth because I don't believe there is such a thing. That's why I prefer the straight-line simplicity of cutting cloth . . . But you don't need me to tell you, my friend. Just notice the details. They're scattered like crumbs all over this table we regularly share."

Garak's little speech is an example of what *DS9* does so well in the face of agonistic construals: it offers responses that are best described as "transgressive"—it subverts accepted and acceptable norms. The characters of *DS9* try out possibilities that transcend the limits set by any one idiom, whether it be the Articles of the Federation, the Ferengi Rules of Acquisition, the Obsidian Order's machinations, or the Bajoran Provisional Government's struggle to be less "provisional." *DS9*'s commitment to transgressive subversion of the familiar reminds us that agonistic relations, closed boundaries, and limited identities are always open to subversions that point to a consequent shift beyond impasse. The differend is not only an urgent call to recognize silenced voices, it's also a call to create new idioms, new ways of presenting reality that might be able to overcome the differend. In Marritza's motivations for impersonating Darhe'el, in Kira's shift to understanding and forgiveness, "Duet" is an excellent example of transgression and subversion. One Cardassian and one Bajoran move beyond the longstanding conflict between them, and their bravery is found in their will-ingness to transgress and subvert.[11] *DS9*, although in many ways a dark, questioning series, is also an exercise in intergalactic hope.

---

[11] Kira's journey along this line continues with her relationship with the Cardassian Ghemor ("Second Skin," "Ties of Blood and Water").

Starfleet Directive
FOUR

Multiple Enterprises: *Metaphysical Conundrums from A to E*

15

Time—The Final Frontier

AMY KIND

Writing in the early years of the fifth century, St. Augustine grappled with the nature of time in his autobiographical work, *Confessions*: "What, then, is time? I know well enough what it is, provided that nobody asks me; but if I am asked what it is and try to explain, I am baffled."[1]

We can only imagine how baffled Augustine would have been had he encountered the Bajoran Prophets of *Deep Space Nine*. However difficult time is to explain, there's one feature of our experience of time that seems non-negotiable, namely, that it flows, with each present moment receding into the past. Moreover, the flow of time seems to us to move in only one direction; future moments become present, but present moments never become future. Yet here, *Star Trek* renegotiates the non-negotiable, forcing us to call some of our most deeply held beliefs into question. For the Prophets, a non-corporeal species revered by the Bajorans as their spiritual protectors and guides, time doesn't flow. This alien species has no understanding of *linear* time. They don't experience any distinction between past, present, and future—every event that occurs is as much in the *now* as any other event.

We're introduced to the Prophets in "Emissary" (*DS9*), the pilot episode of the series. While *en route* to the Denorios Belt in a runabout, Commander Benjamin Sisko and Lieutenant Jadzia Dax are sucked into a previously uncharted wormhole.

---

[1] Augustine, *Confessions* (London: Penguin, 1961), p. 264.

The Prophets, who live in the wormhole, soon make contact with Sisko. They communicate with him by taking on the appearance of people from his life, like his late wife Jennifer, his son Jake, or his colleagues from Starfleet. But the Prophets have trouble making sense of Sisko and the temporal nature of his existence:

> **PROPHET:** (*appearing as Jennifer*) It is corporeal! A physical entity . . .
> **SISKO:** You and I are very different species. It will take . . . time for us to understand one another.
> **PROPHET:** (*appearing as Jake*) What is this . . . time?

As Sisko's encounter with the Prophets continues, he tries to explain:

> **SISKO:** It can be argued that a human is ultimately the sum of his experiences.
> **PROPHET:** (*appearing as Jake*) Experiences ... what is this?
> **SISKO:** Memories. Events from my past, like this one.
> **PROPHET:** (*appearing as Jake*) Past?
> **SISKO:** Things that happened before now. You have absolutely no idea what I'm talking about.
> **PROPHET:** (*appearing as Jake*) What comes before now is no different than what is now, or what is to come. It is one's existence.

Sisko sizes up the situation very quickly, realizing that the Prophets must not experience time as we do. Rather, for them, time is not linear. Even before the discovery of the Prophets living in the wormhole, *Star Trek* had flirted with the possibility of non-linear time. In "We'll Always Have Paris" (*TNG*), the *Enterprise* crew experiences a temporal distortion caused by Dr. Paul Manheim's experiments with non-linear time. Manheim, who believed that the universe consists of infinite dimensions, was working to change the linear nature of time in an effort to open up a window into a dimension other than our own. And in *Star Trek: Generations*, both Captain Kirk and Captain Picard end up in the Nexus, a distortion in the space-time continuum in which there's no linear time. As the two captains discover, time has no meaning in the Nexus, and as a result, they can experience both the past and the future whenever they like.

The idea sounds enticing. But can we really make sense of the notion of non-linear time? What would it mean to experience time as the Prophets do? Or would it be better to say that these beings don't experience time at all?[2] This chapter attempts to shed some light on these questions by examining the nature of time. To understand what time is like for the Prophets, we first need to understand what time is like for us. In this enterprise, *Star Trek* proves to be a remarkable resource.

Time's Arrow

Philosophers have often viewed time as being mysterious, especially in comparison with space. Unlike space, time seems to have a "flow" or "passage." Anticipated events in the future get closer and closer, until they become present, while events in the present seem to flow right by us, receding farther and farther into the past. Time can be aptly described using a metaphor from Spock: "time is fluid . . . like a river with currents, eddies, backwash" ("The City on the Edge of Forever," *TOS*). We couldn't describe space the same way. There's no spatial analogue to the flow of time—*here* doesn't automatically become *there* the way that *now* becomes *then*. Though we move past points in space, moments in time move past *us*.

The mystery surrounding time is deepened by the fact that it flows in only a single direction. Unlike space, time has a built-in order. One object in space isn't inherently to the right or left of another; we need a third object to serve as a reference point. From the perspective of Picard in the captain's chair, Wesley Crusher sits to the right of Data. But from the perspective of the television viewer looking in from the front the bridge, Crusher sits to the left of Data. In contrast, two objects in time have an order independent of any reference point. We all share

---

[2] Similar questions also arise about God's atemporal mode of existence. For example, the medieval philosopher Boethius (around 475–526), in claiming that God exists eternally, thought of God as existing outside of time, simultaneously and completely possessing limitless life. For further discussion of the notion that eternity plays in philosophical theism, see Eleonore Stump and Norman Kretzmann, "Eternity" *Journal of Philosophy* 78 (1981), pp. 429–458.

the same perspective when we note that the *Enterprise*'s first encounter with Data's brother Lore ("Datalore," *TNG*) occurred *after* their first encounter with Q ("Encounter at Farpoint," *TNG*) but *before* their first encounter with the Borg ("Q Who?" *TNG*). This inexorable directionality of time is often referred to as time's "arrow."

These mysterious features of time have led to quite a divergence of philosophical opinion about its nature. Generally speaking, philosophers writing on time divide into three different camps. There are some who claim that time exists objectively, some who claim that time exists subjectively, and some who deny that time exists at all.

To say that something exists objectively means that it exists independently of any mind. Consider a tree on Earth. Even if humans never existed, the tree could still exist. (Whether it would still make a sound when it falls in the forest is another matter entirely.) So the claim that time is objective means that it is not mind-dependent. In contrast, something that has only subjective existence is mind-dependent. Consider Captain Pike's suffering after being captured by the Talosians, a telepathic race capable of producing powerful illusions directly in the minds of their "specimens" ("The Cage," *TOS*). At one point, Pike experiences a fire raging all around him. However, the fire doesn't have objective existence; no one other than Pike senses the fire. As an illusion projected into Pike's mind by the Talosians, it has only subjective existence.

Sir Isaac Newton (1642–1727) and Gottfried Leibniz (1646–1716) viewed time as existing objectively, though they took very different positions on what time is. Newton advocated a position known as *absolutism.* According to absolutism, time exists independently of the events that occur in time. Newton saw time as a kind of infinite container for events. As Newton claimed, "Absolute, true and mathematical time, of itself and from its own nature, flows equably without relation to anything external."[3] Leibniz, in contrast, offered a *relationist* picture of time, in which time is conceived as merely a set of relations between events. For Leibniz, time is sort of like marriage. Just as

---

[3] Isaac Newton, *Philosophiae Naturalis Principia Mathematica* (Berkeley: University of California Press, 1934), pp. 6–12.

a marriage is a relation between individuals, and couldn't exist without the individuals who are married, time is a relation between events, and couldn't exist without the events that are related.

Since an absolutist like Newton thinks that time is a kind of container, he might have to deal with the possibility of the container's being empty—that is, he's committed to the possibility of a temporal *vacuum*, a time in which no events whatsoever take place. There's something very intuitive about the idea of a temporal vacuum. "When time seemed to stop"—that's how Anij in *Star Trek: Insurrection* describes the notion of a perfect moment to Picard, and perhaps this is what a temporal vacuum would be like. But how could it seem to us that time has stopped? How could we even notice this? Once we think a bit about these questions, we can see why relationists such as Leibniz find the idea of a temporal vacuum incoherent.

Leibniz might ask us to suppose there were a temporal vacuum, a period of time in which nothing happens. Since a temporal vacuum is a period of time, it's natural to ask: How long did it last? How long was the period of time during which nothing took place? The problem, however, is that it appears that these questions can have no answers. The only way to measure a period of time is in terms of the changes that take place during it.[4] If nothing changes during a temporal vacuum, then in principle there's no way we can notice it. Just think: For all you know, a temporal vacuum might have occurred between the time you started reading this sentence and the time you finished reading it. There's no way for you to tell. If by chance one occurred, there would be no way to measure its duration. As the Vulcan Science Directorate would likely say, given their negative ruling on the possibility of time travel in the twenty-second century, the very idea of a temporal vacuum seems illogical.

In contrast to both Newton and Leibniz, some philosophers deny the objective existence of time. This was the position that Augustine ended up adopting. In thinking about the nature of events, Augustine noted that anything we experience is present only for a moment—as soon as it occurs, it becomes part of the

---

[4] Aristotle, in fact, defined time as the measure of change in his *Physics* (Oxford: Oxford University Press, 1999), Book 12.

past. This means that our sense of time, and our measurement of it, can't be based on the events themselves—they don't exist to be measured. Whenever we experience an event, however, it leaves an impression in our minds. The impression lasts even once the event has passed. Our measurement of time, then, must be a measurement of impressions in our mind. Using this reasoning, Augustine drew the conclusion that time is mind-dependent: it exists only subjectively.

Time and Again

It's not easy to settle the matter decisively between the objective and subjective conceptions of time. Some of our experiences appear to favor Augustine's side in the debate. For example, time always seems to pass more quickly when you're doing something fun, like vacationing on Risa or chancing your luck at the Dabo wheel, than when you're doing something boring or unpleasant, like going over duty rosters or having dinner with Lwaxana Troi.

We also might think that we can make better sense of the Bajoran Prophets if we accept that time exists only subjectively. Time for them can exist differently from the way it exists for us. And *Star Trek* provides many other examples in which time is depicted subjectively. In "Wink of an Eye" (*TOS*), we're introduced to the Scalosians, aliens for whom time passes much faster than it does for us, as Kirk discovers when he's "accelerated" to their temporal experience. In "The Inner Light" (*TNG*), an alien probe causes Picard to experience more than three decades of life on the planet Kataan—he gets married, has children and grandchildren, and grows old—during a period that feels like less than half an hour to the rest of the *Enterprise* crew. Finally, in "Hard Time" (*DS9*), the Argrathi tinker with Miles O'Brien's mind, implanting over twenty years of memories. For everyone else, just a few hours have gone by. But for O'Brien, it feels like he's just spent two decades locked away in an Argrathi prison. All of these occurrences suggest that the passage of time is somehow mind-dependent.

On the other hand, we can also draw lots of evidence from across the *Star Trek* series in favor of the objective conception of time. People in the twenty-third and twenty-fourth centuries have no more control over time than we do. They can't slow down the clock, even when they really need just a few more seconds—and this suggests that time exists objectively. Think of Data urgently trying to replace the isolinear chips in the *Enterprise*'s computer banks before the ship is hit by debris from a stellar explosion ("The Naked Now," *TNG*), or Scotty desperately trying to beam Kirk off the *Constellation* before it self-destructs ("The Doomsday Machine," *TOS*). What gives situations like these their dramatic tension is the force of time passing objectively, utterly outside of our control. Even the *Enterprise*'s "miracle-working" chief engineer can't change the laws of physics when he needs thirty minutes to restart the warp engines ("The Naked Time," *TOS*).

So it looks as if *Star Trek* doesn't definitively classify time as either subjective or objective. Some philosophers, however, would say it's a mistake to classify time in either of these two ways. Rather, we should simply accept that time—or at least, time as we know it—doesn't exist at all.

Timeless

The philosopher most commonly associated with the position that time doesn't exist is J.M.E. McTaggart, who argues that we can't account for the flow of time without contradiction.[5] Thus, time must not exist. There are typically two ways that we order temporal events—first, in terms of the notions of *past, present,* and *future;* and second, in terms of the relations *earlier than* and *later than.* If time were to exist, then we must be able to explain it in one of these two ways; McTaggart calls them the *A-series* and *B-series,* respectively. But McTaggart denies that we can do this—time can't be explained in terms of either of these series. If he's right, then time must not exist.

How can McTaggart hold such a radically counterintuitive picture about time? To see this, we have to look at each series individually. First, note that an event's position in the A-series is constantly changing. Consider Tasha Yar's death ("Skin of Evil," *TNG*). This event still lies in the future when Yar and some of her crewmates beam down to Vagra II to rescue Deanna Troi,

---

[5] J.M.E. McTaggart, "The Unreality of Time," in *The Philosophy of Time*, edited by Robin Le Poidevin and Murray MacBeath (Oxford: Oxford University Press, 1993), pp. 23–34.

whose shuttlecraft has crashed on the planet's surface. Upon their arrival, the away team has to tangle with the malicious slimelike entity Armus. When Armus directs his evil energy towards Yar, she's instantly killed—her death becomes present. By the time the crew manages to escape from Armus's forcefield and depart from the planet's orbit, the event of her death has receded into the past.

In contrast, when we consider these same three events— Yar's death, the away team's arrival on Vagra II, and the *Enterprise*'s departure—with respect to the B-series, their ordering doesn't change. The first of these events occurs later than the second but before the third. Even as time passes, this ordering never alters. Unlike the A-series, the B-series is *fixed*.

This fact about the B-series, however, means that it can't account for the passage of time. In the B-series, nothing flows; there's no change. But as McTaggart notes, it's "universally admitted that time involves change" (p. 25). How, then, could we explain time in terms of the B-series? The B-series is also unable to account for the *specialness* of the present moment, the "nowness" of it. You could know everything there was to know about the B-series, you could know the complete ordering of events, and you would still not know which event was occurring *now*. Thus, if we're going to be able to give an explanation of time, we'll have to use the A-series.

But McTaggart suggests that the A-series is also incapable of accounting for time. The problem is that the A-series requires objects to have incompatible properties, which violates the laws of logic. (And if Scotty thinks changing the laws of physics is hard, he should just try to change the laws of logic!) A basic presupposition of our thinking is that nothing can have incompatible properties. It's impossible, for example, for a Klingon to have both a smooth forehead and a ridged forehead at the same time; or for a Vulcan to simultaneously have both pointy ears and rounded ears. Of course, someone could have one pointy ear and one rounded ear—perhaps if he were a Ferengi-Vulcan hybrid?—but a single ear cannot be both pointy and rounded, at least not in the same way at the same time. Just as being rounded and being pointy are incompatible properties, so too are being past and being present, or being past and being future. Nothing can be both past and future. This, however, is required by the A-series as any given event moves from future, to present, to past. Thus, since the A-series embodies a contradiction, it can't provide us with an adequate explanation of time.

The basic form of argument that McTaggart uses against the A-series should actually be immediately familiar to any fan of *Trek*. Think of Kirk's many efforts to talk a computer to its own destruction, which he does successfully to the machine Landru in "The Return of the Archons," (*TOS*), the space probe Nomad in "The Changeling" (*TOS*), and the M-5 computer in "The Ultimate Computer" (*TOS*). Perhaps the best example of this form of argument comes in the climactic confrontation of "I, Mudd," when Kirk relies on an instance of what philosophers call the *Liar's Paradox*:

> **KIRK:** (*to the android Norman*) Everything Harry tells you is a lie. Remember that. Everything Harry tells you is a lie.
> **HARRY MUDD:** Now listen to this carefully, Norman. I am lying.
> **NORMAN:** You say you are lying, but if everything you say is a lie, then you are telling the truth. But you cannot tell the truth, because everything you say is a lie. But . . . you lie . . . you tell the truth, but you cannot, for you lie. Illogical. Illogical.

No statement can at one and the same time be both true and false. When trying to consider this contradictory state of affairs that Kirk and Mudd have suggested, Norman becomes completely incapacitated.[6] Confronted by McTaggart's argument against time, we too may feel completely incapacitated—even if our ears are not literally smoking. How on earth could time be unreal?

Past Tense

It should come as no surprise that most philosophers have been extremely reluctant to accept McTaggart's conclusion that time doesn't exist. Some philosophers attempt to shore up the idea of the A-series by showing that it doesn't contain the contradiction McTaggart supposes. Roughly speaking, they argue that we

---

[6] For further discussion of Kirk's mastery of the destructive paradox, see Chapter 18 in this volume.

must take grammatical tense seriously. Events aren't past, present, and future at the same time; rather, an event currently occurring *was* once future, now *is* present, and soon *will be* past. Sisko appears to defend the A-series, and the importance of grammatical tense, when conversing with the Prophets:

> **PROPHET:** (*appearing as Jennifer*) She [Sisko's late wife Jennifer] is part of your existence.
> **SISKO:** She is part of my past. She's no longer alive.
> **PROPHET:** (*appearing as Jennifer*) But she is part of your existence.
> **SISKO:** She *was* a most important part of my existence, but I lost her some time ago.

It's only by understanding the importance of tense that the Prophets will be able to understand what Sisko is telling them.

Defending the A-series often goes along with adopting a view called *presentism*, which claims that only the present exists. At the present moment, the television premiere of *Star Trek: The Original Series* lies over forty years in the past. Thus, for the presentist, it doesn't exist. The presentist can thus dissolve the threat of an A-series contradiction. Since events that aren't present don't exist, no event ever has the incompatible properties of being both present and past, or both present and future.

There's a lot to like about presentism, but there are also many problems with it. Here's one big one. Once we deny the reality of the past we can no longer make sense of any statements about past happenings. We would all agree that *Star Trek* premiered on September 8th, 1966. But if the past doesn't exist, what could possibly make that claim true? What could distinguish it from the false claim that *Star Trek* premiered on October 5th, 1966?

For us trekkies (even those of us who don't wear our Starfleet uniforms to the office), there's an even bigger problem with presentism: It makes time travel impossible. If only the present exists, then how could the *Enterprise* visit the year 1969 and be mistaken for a UFO ("Tomorrow is Yesterday," *TOS*)? How could Picard travel back and forth between past and future, one moment reliving the *Enterprise*'s first mission in the year 2364 and the next experiencing life as a retired old man tending to his vineyards in the year 2395 ("All Good Things," *TNG*)? And how could Sisko, Dax, and others members of the twenty-fourth-century Deep Space Nine crew be on Deep Space Station K-7 for the great tribble infestation of 2268 ("Trials and Tribble-ations," *DS9*)?

There's another option for answering McTaggart, though it too has its problems. Rather than attempting to bolster the A-series, we might attempt to rethink the B-series instead. McTaggart had claimed that the B-series can't accommodate certain fundamental temporal truths, like the fact that some events occurred in the past and that others will occur in the future. In response, one could claim that anything that appears to make reference to the A-series's notions of past, present, and future can be easily reformulated in terms of the B-series. For example, when Picard says that the *Enterprise*'s mission to Farpoint occurred in the past, all he means is that the Farpoint mission is earlier than the time at which he's speaking.

What's the main problem for B-theorists? They have to accept that time doesn't really pass. Since we sense the passage of time, this must just be a result of the way that we perceive the world. Though a B-theorist sees *time* as objectively real, she views the *passage* of time as existing only subjectively. This goes along with the fact that B-theorists usually reject presentism and adopt a view called *eternalism* instead. For an eternalist, the past and future are just as real as the present. In fact, for the eternalist, our entire timeline always exists. Eternalists think of reality as a sort of four-dimensional "cake," where time is just one of the "layers."

But eternalism seems to commit us to a kind of *fatalism*.[7] If the future already exists, and if it has always existed and will always exist in just that way, then it looks as if we have no power to change it. Data gives us a perfect illustration of what it means to embrace eternalism in "Time's Arrow, Part I" (*TNG*). His severed head is discovered in a cavern beneath San Francisco, buried there since the early nineteenth century. While

---

[7] For a discussion of the relation between eternalism and free will in the context of *Star Wars*, see Jason T. Eberl, "'You Cannot Escape Your Destiny' (Or Can You?): Freedom and Predestination in the Skywalker Family," in *Star Wars and Philosophy*, edited by Kevin S. Decker and Jason T. Eberl (Chicago: Open Court, 2005), pp. 3–15.

some of his shipmates get emotional about this discovery, Data takes the news in his usual impassive fashion:

> **DATA:** . . . it seems clear that my life is to end in the late nineteenth century.
> **RIKER:** Not if we can help it.
> **DATA:** There is no way anyone can prevent it, sir. At some future date, I will be transported back to nineteenth-century Earth, where I will die. It has occurred. It will occur.[8]

Later in the same episode, Data reminds Picard that one can't "cheat fate."

Tomorrow Is Yesterday

For those of us who aren't androids, eternalism may be a bit harder to swallow. But if we're going to believe in the existence of entities like the Bajoran Prophets—beings who can "see" the future—it looks like we might have to buy it.[9] Kira Nerys helps us (and Sisko) see why. In "Destiny" (*DS9*), a team of Cardassian scientists is scheduled to come to Deep Space Nine to help set up a subspace relay through the wormhole. A Bajoran holy man, Vedek Yarka, comes to Sisko, pleading with him not to let this plan proceed, since an ancient prophecy predicts that the mission will have disastrous consequences. Later, as Sisko is grappling with his decision on whether to let the project proceed, Kira tries to convince him that the vedek is right:

> **SISKO:** I'm a Starfleet officer, and I have a mission to accomplish. If I call it off, it has to be for some concrete reason, something solid, something *Starfleet*.
> **KIRA:** All right, how about this? The Prophets . . . the aliens who live in the wormhole, as you call them, exist outside of linear time. They know the past, present and future.
> **SISKO:** Agreed.

---

[8] It's interesting that we see this expression of eternalism in an episode entitled "Time's Arrow," since the adoption of eternalism requires us to reject the claim that time has an arrow.

[9] For the non-Bajorans among us, belief in God (who, according to classical philosophical theism, exists atemporally) would also commit one to eternalism.

KIRA: It seems perfectly reasonable that they could've communicated their knowledge of the future to a Bajoran named Trakor. He wrote that knowledge down in the form of a prophecy and now, three thousand years later, we are seeing those events unfold. To me, that reasoning sounds concrete, solid. I'd even call it "Starfleet."

The picture given to us by eternalism helps us to understand the way the Prophets experience the world—events simply *are*, but they don't flow into one another. Given their non-linear perspective, much of the way that we experience the world is inconceivable to them. In some ways, this might be a plus. For example, we learn in "Emissary" (*DS9*) that the Prophets can't understand *loss*. Since the past for them is no different from the present, nothing is ever lost to them. Sisko has a hard time explaining to the Prophets what it means to experience a loss:

PROPHET: (*appearing as Jennifer*) Lost? What is this?
SISKO: In a linear existence, we can't go back to the past to get something we left behind, so . . . it's lost.
PROPHET: (*appearing as Jennifer*) It is inconceivable that any species could exist in such a manner. You are deceiving us.
SISKO: No. This is this truth. This day, this . . . this park . . . it was almost fifteen years ago, far in the past. It was a day that was very important to me—a day that shaped every day that followed. That is the essence of a linear existence. Each day affects the next.

Most of us probably wouldn't mind being unable to experience the loss of a loved one; missing out on this isn't really missing out at all. But having a non-linear existence comes with some downsides as well. The Prophets can't boldly go where no one has gone before—the notion of "before" is meaningless to them. They can't live long and prosper—the notion of living "long" is also meaningless to them.[10]

---

[10] These claims are based on the supposition that if the Prophets have a non-linear existence, then they exist outside of time. Strictly speaking, however, beings like the Prophets might exist in time, yet lack the capacity to understand the passage of time.

We might also wish sometimes that we could escape from time; we might chafe against the constraints of our linear existence. But, as the ever-wise Picard tells us, it would be a mistake to view time as our enemy. Time isn't a predator, stalking us all our lives. Rather, "time is a companion who goes with us on the journey, reminds us to cherish every moment, because they'll never come again" (*Star Trek: Generations*).[11]

[11] Thanks to Kevin Decker and Jason Eberl for comments on previous versions of this paper. Thanks also to Gabriel Rocklin for starting me on my *DS9* obsession, and to Frank Menetrez for (among many other things) introducing me to the wonders of all things *Trek*.

16

"Your Big Chance to Get Away from It All": Life, Death, and Immortality

THEODORE SCHICK

The history of philosophy is replete with different views of what makes you *you*. Lela, one of Dax's former incarnations, embraces one of these views when she asks, "What is a person but a sum of their memories?" ("Facets," *DS9*).[1] She suggests that what makes you the person you are is the memories you have, and nothing more. Yet one of Dax's best friends, Dr. Julian Bashir, seems to disagree. In "Life Support" (*DS9*) he refuses to replace more than half of Vedek Bareil's brain with a positronic matrix, claiming, "If I remove the rest of his brain and replace it with a machine, he may look like Bareil, he may even talk like Bareil, but he won't be Bareil." For Bashir, who you are apparently depends on the stuff out of which you are made. Change enough of that stuff, and you cease to exist.

This is bad news for those who look forward to a disembodied existence in the afterlife because disembodied spirits don't have physical brains. So if your identity is tied to a physical object, you can't exist if that object doesn't exist. Bashir's view is also bad news for those who hope to achieve eternal life by downloading the contents of their brains into a computer. Unless that computer is composed of neurons like those in your brain, any person resulting from such a download would, at best, be a copy of you. It wouldn't be the "real" you because it doesn't have your brain.

---

[1] Commander Sisko makes a similar claim in "Emissary" (*DS9*).

Lela and Bashir hold different views of personal identity—of what makes you *you*. As a result, they have very different opinions on what actions are morally permissible. Every system of morality, every idea of justice rests on a theory of personal identity because both morality and justice depend upon common sense notions of personal responsibility. It would be unfair to reward or punish *you* for what somebody else did. Morality requires that praise and blame attach to the person who did the right or wrong act, while justice requires that the person receiving the judgment be identical to the person who did the deed.

Like philosophy, *Star Trek* also explores many different theories of personal identity. Each episode that deals with this issue is like a "thought experiment" putting various theories of personal identity to the test by examining their implications in an imaginary situation. The results of these experiments can help us decide which theories are the most plausible, and which common sense ideas the most reasonable. So let's enter the laboratory of the mind and see what *Star Trek* can teach us about the nature of personal identity.

"We Are Merely a Different Kind of Machine"

The captains of the *Enterprise* often seem to agree with Bashir that our bodies are essential to us. In "What Are Little Girls Made Of?" (*TOS*), the *Enterprise* responds to a message apparently sent by Nurse Chapel's fiancé, archeologist Roger Korby, who has been missing for five years. When Kirk and Chapel beam down to Exo III, they discover that Korby's an android. It appears that during his explorations, he suffered a fatal accident and, with the help of the android Ruk, used an ancient technology to download his mind into an android body. "It's still me, Christine," he explains to Chapel. "Roger. I'm in here. You can't imagine how it was. I was frozen, dying. My legs were gone . . . I had only my brain between life and death . . . I'm still the same as I was before, Christine, perhaps even better." Kirk doesn't buy Korby's analysis of the situation. He doesn't believe that Korby survived the procedure. As he tells Spock, "Dr. Korby was never here." Since the android Korby seems to have the human Korby's memories, beliefs, and desires, Kirk's view seems to be that our bodies make us who we are: we can't exist without our bodies.

Captain Picard sees things similarly. In "The Survivors" (*TNG*), the *Enterprise* discovers a dead planet containing only two life forms: Kevin and Rishon Uxbridge. All other life on the planet had been destroyed in an attack by the Husnock. Kevin survived the massacre because he is a member of an omnipotent and immortal race known as the "Douwd." He came to live among mortals after he fell in love with Rishon, who was killed in the attack. Kevin used his unlimited powers to resurrect her. According to Picard, however, the woman Kevin resurrected is not Rishon. Picard tells her: "I can touch you. I can hear your voice. I can smell your perfume. In every respect, you are a real person with your own mind and beliefs, but you do not exist. You died, along with the others, defending the colony." Apparently, Picard believes that the current Rishon Uxbridge is a copy of the original—not Rishon herself. Since the copy of Rishon apparently has all of the qualities of the original that made Kevin love her, Picard's claim only makes sense on the grounds that our identity resides in our bodies.

Other episodes seem to suggest that it's not our entire body that's essential to us, but only our brain. In "Spock's Brain" (*TOS*), his entire brain is removed from his skull and used to regulate the functions of a vast underground society. But while in this disembodied state, Spock appears to still be Spock. He retains his memories, his personality, and his character. Kirk addresses him as Spock and he responds to that name. The rest of his body, which is mechanically controlled, isn't considered a person at all. This suggests that our identity resides in our brains: where our brains go, we go.

This also seems to be Bashir's view. In "Life Support," he had no qualms about replacing Bareil's damaged organs with artificial ones. But the brain was a different matter. As one of his teachers in medical school used to say, "The brain has a 'spark of life' that can't be replicated." Echoing his teacher's view, Bashir refuses to replace more than half of Bareil's brain with positronic implants claiming that if he did, "That 'spark of life' will be gone. He'll be dead. And I'll be the one who killed him." Bashir doesn't deny that there'll be a person in Bareil's body after the procedure; he denies that the resulting person will be *Bareil*. Without at least half of his brain intact, Bashir apparently believes that Bareil won't exist any longer.

Both the body theory and the brain theory deny that you can survive the death of your body, for they maintain that having a particular physical constitution is essential to you. Once that constitution is gone, you no longer exist. So according to both of these theories, a disembodied existence is impossible. Holders of these theories can look forward to an afterlife, however, through resurrection. For example, if someone (like God) gathered together all of the atoms that made up their bodies when they were alive and put them back into their original configuration, they would be reborn. Alternatively, they could try to preserve their dead bodies or brain through cryogenic freezing, say, in hopes that science will one day find a way to cure what killed them, as portrayed in "The Neutral Zone" (*TNG*). In any event, even if we are identical to our bodies or brains, it's possible that we will live again.

"Does Data (or Any of Us) Have a Soul?"

The notion that we're simply our bodies (or brains) contradicts other things we know about the *Star Trek* universe, however. If our identity resides in our bodies, it should be impossible to switch bodies and retain our identity. Yet that's exactly what happens in "Turnabout Intruder" (*TOS*) when Janice Lester uses an alien device to switch her "essence" with Kirk's. While the device is operating we see a ghost-like cloud leave each of the bodies and enter the other. After the switch, the person in Janice Lester's body declares that whatever makes Kirk "a living being special to himself" is present in that body. If she's correct, then both the body and brain theory of personal identity are mistaken. If the same person can occupy different bodies (or brains), then their body (or brain) can't be what makes them who they are.

The same problem arises in the case where two people occupy the same body (or brain). This occurs in "Power Play" (*TNG*). When beaming up from a moon that seemed to be the source of a distress call, Troi, Data, and O'Brien become possessed by alien intelligences. While their bodies were under the control of the alien beings, Troi, Data, and O'Brien were still mentally "present," but unable to control their bodies. As Troi explains afterwards, "It was as though my own consciousness was pushed to the side. I was watching everything happen— hearing my own voice—but not being able to control any of it."

If your body (or brain) can house more than one person, however, it can't be your uniquely defining feature.

The problem with the body and brain theories is that they identify us with a certain sort of stuff. What makes us persons, however, isn't the stuff out of which we're made, but what we can do with that stuff, as illustrated in "The Measure of a Man" (*TNG*). Commander Bruce Maddox, a cyberneticist, wants to disassemble Data to figure out how his positronic brain works. Data balks at this suggestion, claiming that he has a right to choose what happens to him. The question, he says, is whether he is "a person or property." Is he a person with the same rights and privileges afforded other people in the Federation, or is he the property of Starfleet, in which case they can treat him as they would the *Enterprise*'s computer? The case goes to court and Picard, as Data's defender, asks Maddox under oath what makes something a "sentient being," by which he means a person. Maddox identifies three qualities: intelligence, self-awareness, and consciousness. Data obviously possesses the first two, and Picard was able to justify enough speculation about Data's consciousness that the Judge Advocate General, Captain Phillipa Louvois, ruled in favor of Data. Being a person doesn't require being made of flesh and blood. Silicon based life-forms like Data (or even the Horta in "The Devil in the Dark" (*TOS*)) can be persons, too.[2]

"Is a Trill Responsible for the Conduct . . . of Its Antecedent Selves?"

English philosopher John Locke (1632–1704) realized over two hundred years ago that being a person doesn't require being made of a particular kind of "stuff." According to Locke, a person is a "thinking, intelligent being that has reason and reflection; and can consider itself as itself, the same thinking thing in different times and places."[3] For Locke, any rational, self-

---

[2] But not holographic ones. In "Author, Author" (*VGR*) the Doctor, who is a hologram, was ruled not to be a full fledged person. But the judge did grant that he could be considered an "artist" and thus entitled to the intellectual property rights of his novel, *Photons Be Free*.

[3] John Locke, *An Essay Concerning Human Understanding* (New York: Penguin, 1997), p. 302.

conscious creature that is aware of its own existence over time is a person. What it's made of or how it came into being is irrelevant.

After establishing what a person is, Locke goes on to develop the first full-blown theory of personal identity. Citing the possibility of body switches and double occupancy, he says:

> This may show us wherein personal identity consists: not in the identity of substance, but, as I have said, in the identity of consciousness, wherein if Socrates and the present mayor of Quinborough agree, they are the same person: if the same Socrates waking and sleeping do not partake of the same consciousness, Socrates waking and sleeping is not the same person. And to punish Socrates waking for what sleeping Socrates thought, and waking Socrates was never conscious of, would be no more of right, than to punish one twin for what his brother-twin did, whereof he knew nothing, because their outsides were so like, that they could not be distinguished, for such twins have been seen. (p. 308)

By "identity of consciousness," Locke means identity of experience memories. Experience memories are mental records of those sensations and perceptions we've had. So Locke's theory is often referred to as the "memory theory" of personal identity. In his view, if the present Mayor of Quinborough has Socrates's memories, then the present Mayor of Quinborough *is* Socrates, or, more precisely, the reincarnation of Socrates. So unlike the body or the brain theory, Locke's memory theory allows body switches.

It also allows for double occupancy—for more than one person to inhabit the same body. Locke gives the example of Socrates waking and sleeping. He claims that if Socrates sleeping did something that Socrates waking had no memory of, then we shouldn't hold Socrates waking responsible for it because he isn't the same person. The sleepwalking defense is legitimate in courts of law, and one of the most important tests for proving the claim of sleepwalking is lack of memory. What's more, scientists studying multiple personality disorder (now known as "dissociative identity disorder") have found that some personalities in those suffering from this disorder have no memory of what other personalities have done. So there may actually be bodies that house more than one person.

It should now be clear why Lela Dax supports the memory theory. Lela is a Trill—a joined species consisting of a sentient symbiotic organism and a humanoid host. The symbiont can be joined with many different hosts during its lifetime; the resulting persons have both the symbiont's and the host's memories. Since each incarnation of a Trill contains the prior incarnation's memories, however, the memory theory tells us that there's a continuous person present through all the incarnations.

Yet this view was called into question in the episode "Dax" (*DS9*). A former incarnation of Jadzia Dax—Curzon Dax—was accused of treason and murder. At the extradition hearing, Sisko tries to argue that Jadzia Dax isn't the same person as Curzon Dax because she has a different body and personality. But as Minister Peers, a Trill, points out, "the symbiont does carry memories of time shared with previous hosts." That seems to be enough to establish Jadzia's responsibility, if she were the guilty party. It turns out, however, that Curzon Dax didn't commit the murder and thus Jadzia doesn't have to be extradited.

"The Body Is Just a Shell"

There's a particular sort of body switch that many technophiles, transhumanists, and posthumanists look forward to: that of downloading their minds into a computer and living forever. Jay Sussman, formerly of the MIT artificial intelligence lab, states this hope succinctly:

> If you can make a machine that contains the contents of your mind, then that machine is you. The hell with the rest of your physical body. It's not very interesting. Now the machine can last forever. Even if it doesn't last forever, you can always dump it out onto tape and make backups, then load it up on some other machine if the first one breaks.[4]

The theory of mind behind this view is known as *functionalism*: the mind is what the brain does. It's often expressed in terms of an analogy: the mind is to the brain as the software of a computer is to its hardware. In other words, your mind is the

---

[4] Quoted in Grant Fjermedal, *The Tomorrow Makers* (New York: Macmillan, 1986), p. 8.

program running on your brain. It follows, then, that anything that ran your program would be you. If we could copy that program and get it up and running on another machine, you would have undergone a body switch.

Star Trek depicts a number of such body switches. In addition to Korby's attempt to download his mind into a robotic replica of himself in "What Are Little Girls Made Of?" there's Dr. Ira Graves's attempt to download his mind into Data in "The Schizoid Man" (*TNG*). Graves is a cyberneticist who is suffering from the incurable and inevitably fatal Darnay's disease. He was planning to download his consciousness into his own computer before he died. When he learned that Data had an "off" switch, however, he was able to use it and transfer his consciousness into Data.

Another example of a seemingly successful consciousness transfer from human to machine occurs in "Inheritance" (*TNG*). Data meets Dr. Juliana Tainer, who claims to be the former wife of his creator, Dr. Noonien Soong. While Data and Dr. Tainer are working together in an underground cave, it starts to collapse and they must jump a thirty-foot crevasse in order to escape. Dr. Tainer makes the jump with Data but lands hard, is knocked unconscious, and loses her arm. Data's suspicions that she is an android are confirmed. While attempting to reactivate Dr. Tainer, Geordi discovers a chip in Dr. Tainer's positronic matrix that allows Data to talk to a likeness of Dr. Soong, who reveals that he transferred Dr. Tainer's consciousness into the android body after she suffered a fatal accident. "Soong" tells Data:

> When I realized nothing could be done for her, I built an android. I tried to perfect my synaptic scanning technique so that I could transfer Juliana's memories into a positronic matrix. Didn't know if it would work, but I had to try. I couldn't stand the thought of losing the only woman I ever loved.

When Soong activated the Juliana robot, she looked up at him and smiled: the memory transfer worked. She didn't know that she was android, and Soong never told her. This puzzles Data: "Then you do not believe she should know the truth?" Soong answers: "The truth is, in every way that matters, she is Juliana Soong." If Soong's new synaptic scanning machine did succeed in transferring her memories to the android, then, according to the memory theory, Soong is correct: the android is Juliana.

Other *Star Trek* episodes explore the memory theory's implications for justice systems. Locke derives the following implication from his memory theory of personal identity: if you don't remember doing something, you didn't do it. He recognizes that this sort of plea isn't accepted in courts of law, but that, he claims, is because we can never be sure that the defendant is telling the truth. It follows from this view that if we could erase a person's memory of committing a crime, we could no longer hold them responsible for it. Once the memory is gone, they would no longer be identical to the person who committed the crime.

This technique of criminal rehabilitation is employed in "Dagger of the Mind" (*TOS*). On the Tantalus penal colony, Dr. Tristan Adams developed a device known as a "neural neutralizer" that selectively erases people's memories. Adams explains, "Part of our cure, if you will, Captain, is to bury the past. Why should a person go on living with unbearable memories if there is no necessity?" The neural neutralizer is the ultimate brainwashing tool: not only can it erase memories, but it can also implant new ones. In this way, it can create totally new persons. But it can also destroy old ones. If you are your memories, then it follows that if you lost all of your memories, you would cease to exist. That's exactly what happens to Adams. After a fight with Kirk, he's left alone in the room with the neural neutralizer which empties his mind of all his memories. When Kirk returns, Adams is dead.

Death by memory wipe also occurs in the episode "Sons of Mogh" (*DS9*). Disgraced and dishonored for being the brother of Worf, who sided with the Federation against the Klingon Empire, Kurn falls into a deep depression and loses the will to live. He attempts to end his life with Worf's help in a Klingon ritual known as Mauk-to'Vor, but Dax intervenes before the ritual is completed. Worf comes to believe that suicide isn't an honorable thing, but still wants to put his brother out of his misery. Dax offers him a way out of his predicament: "What if there was a way to kill him without really killing him?" Dax's plan is to have Kurn's memory erased and his features and DNA altered so he can begin a new life. Worf agrees to the procedure. According to the memory theory, however, Kurn is just as dead as if he'd been killed the old fashioned way because his experience memories no longer exist.

"A Double Dumb-Ass on You!"

The view that you are your memories isn't without its problems, however, as the *TNG* episode "Second Chances" reveals. As the result of a freak storm, two versions of then Lieutenant Riker are created: one that remains on the planet for eight years and one that gets beamed up to the starship *Potemkin*. Both versions have Riker's consciousness, but both cannot be numerically identical to Riker, because two different things can't be one and the same thing.

When assessing theories of personal identity, there are two notions of identity that need to be kept distinct: *numerical* identity and *qualitative* identity. Two things are qualitatively identical just in case they share the same qualities or properties. In "Allegiance" (*TNG*), aliens kidnap Picard and put a duplicate of him in his place. As one of the aliens explains: "Our transporter is able to replicate living matter, including the brain's many trillion dendritic connections where memory is stored." So the duplicate Picard is qualitatively identical to the real Picard, but he's not numerically identical to him because he's not the real Picard, who only the viewers know is in captivity. Qualitative identity is a relation that can be had by many different things. Numerical identity, on the other hand, is a relation that a thing can have only to itself. A thing at one time is numerically identical to a thing at another time just in case they are *one and the same* thing.

The two Rikers are qualitatively identical because they share the same properties. They aren't numerically identical, however, because they are two separate people. So the question arises: which, if either, is numerically identical to the original Riker? The memory theory can't answer this question because both Rikers share the same memories. If sharing memories were enough to make a person at one time numerically identical to a person at another time, then the two Rikers would be numerically identical. But that's impossible. So there must be more to being numerically identical to someone than sharing their memories.

Maybe having the same body is more important to our identity than it first seemed. Only one of the two "Rikers" can be made out of the same *matter* as the original. If Geordi could trace the path of the original transporter matter stream, he could determine who the real Riker was and who was the copy. If the matter from the original was distributed equally between them, however, knowing where it went wouldn't be much help in determining their true identities.

The possibility of reduplication or fission isn't the only problem facing the memory theory. There's also the possibility of fusion—of merging two (or more) people into one—which is the subject of the *Voyager* episode, "Tuvix." As a result of a transporter malfunction, Tuvok and Neelix are merged into one being dubbed "Tuvix," who possesses all of the memories and abilities of both. After several weeks, the Doctor discovers a way to restore Tuvok and Neelix. Tuvix balks, however, claiming that such a procedure would result in his death. Despite Tuvix's protests, Janeway restores Tuvok and Neelix, sending Tuvix to oblivion.

To restore Tuvok and Neelix, the transporter had to recruit new matter because Tuvix's body didn't contain enough for both. So just as in the case of Riker's double, the transporter had to function as a replicator, imposing a person's pattern on matter that wasn't part of the original person. But, given that the transporter can function as a replicator, there was no need to destroy Tuvix. Janeway should have been able to spare him and recreate Tuvok and Neelix out of completely new matter.

The replication and reintegration capabilities of transporter technology raise some intriguing possibilities. For example, with a properly outfitted transporter, you could make clones of anyone that would be both physically and psychologically identical to the original (like the aliens did in "Allegiance"). Every ship in the Federation could have its own Data. You could make clones of yourself that explore different parts of the galaxy. At some point in the future, these clones could be reintegrated into one, so that "you" would have all their memories and experiences. You could even integrate other people's experiences into your mind. If Tuvix is any indication, doing so would be like a undergoing a permanent Vulcan mind meld or a Borg assimilation. You could even look forward to a time when all the experiences of all the sentient creatures in the universe are merged into one vast super-mind. In that case, the Hindu claim that "everyone is one" would then be a reality.

The transporter could also be used to achieve immortality. When your aging body starts giving out, you could transfer your consciousness into a younger version of your body as was done to Dr. Pulaski in "Unnatural Selection" (*TNG*). But you wouldn't be limited to using your own body: you could have the transporter fashion any type of body and place your consciousness into it—which is what Sargon and his people intend in "Return to Tomorrow" (*TOS*). If you would like to see what it's like to be a member of the opposite sex, another race, or even another species, that would be possible as well. By trying out different bodies, you would be like the symbiotic Trill who live in many different bodies during their lifetimes.

If you downloaded your program into two different bodies, however, neither of the resulting persons would be numerically identical to you because, as we've seen, two can't be one. So strictly speaking, neither of the two Rikers is numerically identical to the original. Do we want to say, then, that Riker did not survive the transporter malfunction?

"I Feel Exactly What You Feel"

Philosopher Derek Parfit says, "No." For him, numerical identity isn't what matters in survival. What matters is *psychological continuity*, much as Locke said. If we retain our memories, desires, and character it doesn't matter whether we're numerically identical to anyone who lived before. In that case, we have all that's really important.[5]

To see what Parfit's getting at, suppose that your mind was successfully transferred into two clones of your original body. The two resulting people would look and act just like you used to. The existence of these two replicas would certainly be disconcerting to your friends and relatives, especially if they met both of them at the same time. But because they're both psychologically and physically indistinguishable from the old you, your friends would have every reason to be just as interested in them as they were in you.

Even though neither of your clones is numerically identical to you before the procedure, it wouldn't seem to them that they

---

[5] Derek Parfit, *Reasons and Persons* (Oxford: Oxford University Press, 1986).

had just come into existence. Both would believe that they were you, for both would have all of your memories, desires, and character traits. Of course, it would be difficult for both of them to get everything they wanted, especially if you were married, employed, or a homeowner. Which one, for example, would sleep with your spouse? Which one would get your job? Which one would pay your bills? If you had planned to be cloned in this way, however, you might have established a procedure for deciding these issues which was agreeable to both of you. In any event, from both a third-person and a first-person point of view, being duplicated, even though it results in your no longer being numerically identical to your former self, is certainly better than dying.

What about the views with which we started? According to Parfit, Lela's view of personal identity makes more sense than Bashir's because we're more like the Trill than we realize. Your body now is almost as different from the body you had in kindergarten as Jadzia Dax's body is from Curzon Dax's. Not only is it made out of different atoms, but it looks very different as well. So you aren't qualitatively identical to the person you were then. But you're numerically identical to that person because you're psychologically continuous with him or her. There's an overlapping chain of memories, beliefs, and desires connecting you to that person. So even if you were to change your gender, as the Trill are capable of doing ("The Host," *TNG*; "Rejoined," *DS9*), you can remain numerically the same person provided you don't completely sever the psychological bonds that connect you to your former self.

17

Spock's Vulcan Mind Meld: A Primer for the Philosophy of Mind

MAHESH ANANTH

> **KIRK:** What would you say the odds are on our getting out of here?
> **SPOCK:** Difficult to be precise, Captain. I should say approximately 7,824.7 to one.
> **KIRK:** Difficult to be precise? 7,824 to one?
> **SPOCK:** 7,824.7 to one.
> **KIRK:** That's a pretty close approximation.
> **SPOCK:** I endeavor to be accurate.
> **KIRK:** You do quite well.
>
> —"Errand of Mercy," *TOS*

The original *Star Trek* series and films were always a treat for me when I was growing up. All the characters were unique, yet their personalities complemented one another, as was often evidenced by their ability to work together cleverly to escape one harrowing situation after another. I must admit, however, that I especially enjoyed the character of Spock. Not only were his feats of superhuman strength impressive to my ten-year-old self, but his "logical" answers to problems, mathematical calculations, and overall assessments of various situations also astounded me. All of this was wonderfully balanced with the humorous jabs that Dr. McCoy and Scotty took at Spock.

These facets of Spock's character, however, pale in comparison (at least for me) to his ability to use his powerful *mind* to interact with and manipulate the *minds* of other people—and other creatures! Such as when Spock, using his ability to mind meld, "brainwashed" his fellow shipmates into believing that the bullets that were about to penetrate their bodies weren't real ("Spectre of the Gun," *TOS*), communicated with the rock-like Horta in order to determine why it was killing mine workers on Janus VI ("The Devil in the Dark," *TOS*), or caused Captain Kirk to forget about an android woman with whom he'd fallen in love ("Requiem for Methuselah," *TOS*).

Spock's mental powers bring into play a number of interesting questions about having a mind: What is the nature of the mind (in general and within the *Star Trek* universe)? Despite our reverence for the principles and methods of science, is it possible to make sense of the mind without reducing it to *mere* physical brain stuff? How can Spock possibly interact with other minds in the way that he does?

Dualism by Way of the Death and Rebirth of Spock: Is Scotty Beaming Us Up Too High?

GILLIAN: Sure you won't change your mind?
SPOCK: Is there something wrong with the one I have?

—*Star Trek IV: The Voyage Home*

In *Star Trek II: The Wrath of Khan*, Spock is killed as a result of exposure to large amounts of radiation. Just before he decides to sacrifice himself as a means of saving the *Enterprise*, Spock grabs a disagreeable Dr. McCoy by the shoulder and not only renders him unconscious, but also places a very important memory in McCoy's mind. In effect, Spock transfers "his mind" (in Vulcan, *katra*) to McCoy. The assumption here is that the mind is, in some way, different from the body such that Spock can transfer a copy of his "mental being" or identity to McCoy.

Subsequently, in *Star Trek III: The Search for Spock*, Spock's body is sent off to a newly formed planet, which assists in bringing him back to life in a rapid succession of developmental stages—he moves from being a baby to an adult in a very short amount of time as a result of the scientifically engineered Project Genesis. The problem, however, is that Spock's body is brought back to life, but his mind is largely missing. In order to make Spock "whole" again, a mind transfer between Spock and McCoy occurs on Spock's home planet, Vulcan. The result of the transfer is that Spock regains his mental identity or spirit, which he had previously stored in McCoy's mind.

Star Trek embraces the idea that the mind can exist distinct from the body—at least for periods of time. Within the philosophy of mind, the mind's ability to exist independently of the body can be explained by the view called *dualism*.[1] On this view, the mind and the body are radically different kinds of entities; the body is extended physical matter, while the mind is thought to be a certain kind of non-physical entity. The famous philosopher René Descartes (1596–1650) offered the following argument in defense of dualism:

> There is a great difference between mind and body, inasmuch as body is by nature divisible, and the mind is entirely indivisible. For, as a matter of fact, when I consider the mind, that is to say, myself inasmuch as I am only a thinking thing, I cannot distinguish in myself any thinking parts, but apprehend myself to be clearly one and entire; and although the whole mind seems to be united to the whole body, yet if a foot, or an arm, or some other part, is separated from my body, I am aware that nothing has been taken away from my mind . . . this [is] sufficient to teach me that the mind or soul of man is entirely different from the body.[2]

Descartes claims that the mind is very different from the body, because the mind can't be carved-up or separated into parts like the body can; the mind, on Descartes's account, is non-physical. This kind of argument helps support Spock's mind transfer event.[3] Indeed, dualism makes sense of most of Spock's psychic skills mentioned at the beginning of this chapter, because it's just such a split between mind and body that would

---

[1] The particular version of dualism I'm discussing here is *interactionism*—the idea that the mind interacts with the body. For a recent analysis of various versions of dualism, see Howard Robinson, "Dualism," in *The Blackwell Guide to the Philosophy of Mind*, edited by Fred Adams, Kenneth Aizawa, John Bickle, and Stephen Stich (Oxford: Blackwell, 2003), pp. 85–101.

[2] René Descartes, *Meditation 6*, in *The Philosophical Works of Descartes* (Cambridge: Cambridge University Press, 1972), p. 196.

[3] This is one of a number of arguments that Descartes gives in defense of dualism in his *Meditations*. This one has been chosen because it appears to fit well with the events associated with Spock's mind transfer. It should be noted, however, that this particular argument from Descartes isn't very persuasive because it assumes the existence of the very phenomenon, specifically the mind, which requires prior justification. If one doesn't believe in the mind's existence, then one won't be persuaded that it can't be divided.

allow his mind to influence and interact with other minds, whether those of other humanoids or rock creatures. Still, there are a number of objections to dualism that appear to render it a less than persuasive account of mind, especially in the light of our non-*Star Trek* universe.

First, there is *the argument from parsimony* (also known as Ockham's razor).[4] This is the view that, when confronted by competing theories, it's most reasonable to embrace the theory that has the least number of commitments to what kinds of basic things exist unless it's absolutely necessary to do otherwise. Another way to put this is that the *better* theory is the *simpler* theory. For example, if there's a theory of how warp drive (traveling faster than the speed of light) functions that requires two fundamental laws about the nature of light and an alternative theory that requires only one fundamental law about the nature of light, defenders of parsimony would insist that the theory that requires only one fundamental law is superior to the other theory so long as the one-law theory is able to explain everything that the two-law theory is able to explain. Thus, the argument from parsimony would require that the theory of one fundamental law about the nature of light should be accepted over the theory with two fundamental laws.[5]

Some philosophers argue that *materialism*, the idea that the mind is nothing more than physical stuff, is a better theory than dualism because it postulates only physical stuff, while dualism postulates both physical and non-physical stuff. Thus, following the principle of parsimony, one should reject dualism in the light of materialism, because the latter postulates only one type of stuff. This assumption of parsimony in defense of materialism suggests that Spock's mental powers are nothing more than complex ensembles of brain activity—anything Spock can do

---

[4] A version of this argument can be found in Paul Churchland, *Matter and Consciousness* (Cambridge, Massachusetts: MIT Press, 1988), pp. 18–21.

[5] 'Fundamental law' refers to laws of nature that occur with almost strict regularity in the course of events in the universe. So, a theory that includes only a law about how light must bend in the universe during warp drive would be superior to a theory that not only includes the same light-bending law, but also a separate law about the influence of gravitational forces during warp drive. For some of the philosophical debates concerning the nature of such fundamental laws, see John W. Carroll, *Laws of Nature* (Cambridge: Cambridge University Press, 1994).

with his mind is a product of the physical stuff between those wonderfully pointed ears of his.

One reply to the above objection, known as *the argument from subjectivity*, is that it's absolutely necessary to reject materialism because the subjective quality of experience can't be explained through a purely materialist account. Even after all the neurological details are made available, there'll always be the awareness of "what an experience is like" for which an explanation will be needed. For example, even after Vulcan neurobiology explains Spock's state of anger when Kirk insults his parentage ("This Side of Paradise," *TOS*), Spock's awareness of being in a state of anger remains. This is the *subjective aspect of mind* that many scholars think can be neither ignored nor explained away. Given the undeniable reality of subjectivity, dualists insist that the effect of Ockham's razor can't be applied without ignoring an integral feature—namely, the very quality of subjective experience. So, a dualist claims that Spock's mental powers are part of his non-physical mind.

As compelling as this reply may seem, it won't move those who embrace the materialistic tradition of science—as Spock, the senior science officer, does. The primary reason is that it ignores *the problem of mental causation*, which is raised when we consider that it seems impossible for a non-physical entity to interact with a physical entity. How do the non-physical mind and the physical body interact with each other?[6] At least for our discussion, this question must be answered because almost all of Spock's mental feats require that his non-physical mind interact with either his own physical body or the physical body and non-physical mind of another.

Second, to say that there has to be a connection between the physical body and the non-physical mind is to offer what could be seen as rather naïve in the light of modern science. The idea that a hypothesis could be tested to see if it's true or false is a first principle in science. However, it may be difficult for us to offer such a hypothesis as to how the non-physical mind interacts with the body. Anything less than satisfying this demand would be considered scientifically immature. Even

---

[6] For further discussion, see Jaegwon Kim, "Lonely Souls," in *Soul, Body, and Survival: Essays on the Metaphysics of Human Persons*, edited by Kevin Corcoran (Ithaca: Cornell University Press, 2001), pp. 30–43.

Spock might hesitate here in the light of his own scientific and logical training.

Third, one of the most forceful criticisms of dualism is that it violates the principle of conservation of energy—the idea that while energy can be transferred from cause to effect, the total energy doesn't increase or decrease. To see the problem posed by *the argument from the conservation of energy*, both directions of the "two-way street" of dualism need to be considered.

To start, imagine that the non-physical mind has a causal influence on the body. For example, Spock wills, by way of his Vulcan mind meld, that Captain Kirk forget the woman who broke his heart. First, there'd have to be a transfer of energy from the non-physical mind of Spock to the physical body of Kirk. The problem is that Kirk's body (specifically his brain) will gain energy, but Spock's mind won't lose energy because it has no physical characteristics and thus no energy to transfer to Kirk's brain. The result would be an overall increase of energy in the universe, and this would violate the conservation of energy principle.

Alternatively, proceeding down the other direction of dualism's two-way street, assume that Spock's brain causes a mental event to occur. For instance, his brain generates the non-physical mental phenomenon, usually called a "belief," that he can communicate with silicon-based creatures. What's happened is that Spock's physical brain has expended energy to produce a non-physical belief. Again, the problem is that Spock's non-physical belief can't "capture" the energy transfer initiated by his brain, resulting in energy loss. Rather than an increase of energy in the universe, there's now a decrease in the total amount of energy as a result of this cause and effect event. The conservation of energy, yet again, has been violated. Thus, regardless of which way one moves on the two-way street of dualism, energy is either created or destroyed. The upshot is that this is scientifically implausible, rendering dualism an implausible theory of mind.[7]

---

[7] A variation of this conservation of energy argument can be found in Richard Double, *Beginning Philosophy* (Oxford: Oxford University Press, 1999), pp. 115–17.

Eliminative Materialism: Is Scotty Beaming Us Down Too Low?

SPOCK: The late Landru, Captain. Marvelous feat of engineering. A computer capable of directing the lives of millions of human beings.

KIRK: But only a machine, Mr. Spock. The original Landru programmed it with all his knowledge, but he couldn't give it his wisdom, his compassion, his understanding, his *soul,* Mr. Spock.

SPOCK: Predictably metaphysical. I prefer the concrete, the graspable, the provable.

KIRK: You'd make a splendid computer, Mr Spock.

SPOCK: That is very kind of you, Captain.

—"Return of the Archons," *TOS*

In *The Next Generation*, Lieutenant Commander Data is a cybernetic android, who most closely approximates the character of Spock. Indeed, much like Spock, he can compute information at incredible speeds, displays impressive logical skills, and exhibits tremendous physical strength. However, Data isn't considered truly human because of his robotic nature, which is driven by his sophisticated "positronic" brain. It's generally thought that beings like Data don't posses a human mind because his computer brain simply cannot generate "the awareness of what it is like." Note, however, that Spock was able to communicate with a silicon-based rock creature, the Horta, which exhibited intentional behavior and expressed (to Spock by way of his mind meld) emotions—that is, the Horta had a mind of some sort. The problem is one of consistency: How can we make sense of a silicon-based creature (the Horta) possessing a mind in the original *Star Trek* series and another largely silicon-based creature (Data) not possessing a mind in *The Next Generation?*

In the wake of the above criticisms of dualism and the tension between whether or not metal-based creatures have minds, *eliminative materialism* could be viewed as a plausible alternative. Paul Churchland best captures the eliminative materialist position:

> When neuroscience has matured to the point where the poverty of our current conceptions [of mind] is apparent to everyone, and the superiority of the new framework is established, we shall then be

able to set about reconceiving our internal states and activities, within a truly adequate conceptual framework at last. Our explanations of one another's behavior will appeal to such things as our neuropharmocological states, the neural activity in specialized anatomical areas, and whatever other states are deemed relevant to the new theory. (pp. 44–45)

Churchland suggests that a sufficiently sophisticated neuroscience, which we currently don't have, will provide all the answers we'll ever need to understand such psychological terms as 'mind', 'consciousness', 'subjective experience', 'desire', 'belief', and 'emotion'. Restated, such terms will be *eliminated* in favor of both neurochemical and neurophysiological explanations. For example, rather than thinking of fear as the conscious or mental state of a Ferengi at the approach of an angry horde of Klingons, it might be more accurate to say (assuming a certain picture of Ferengi neurology and neurochemistry) that, according to Churchland, "the neurotransmitter, glutamate, transmitted the unconditioned response of fear through the central amygdala of the limbic system." In their dogged attack on anything that might resemble a dualistic theory of mind, eliminative materialists are driven to the conclusion that psychological phenomena (beliefs, intentions, consciousness, or emotions) are illusions.

For instance, to claim that Dr. McCoy is angry at Spock is to say, in common ways of speaking, that he's in a mental state of anger. In contrast, to say that Data is puzzled by one of his shipmates' decisions is to say that his computerized brain (or a particular region of it) can't make logical sense of the decision—there's no need to invoke a psychological state in the case of Data because his responses are entirely understood in terms of the computing dynamics of his positronic brain. In fact, Data provides just such a description of how he "feels" friendship: "As I experience certain sensory input patterns, my mental pathways become accustomed to them. The input is eventually anticipated and even *missed* when absent" ("Legacy," *TNG*).

An eliminative materialist would claim that McCoy's anger is nothing more than the neurobiological activity of a certain region of his brain—much like Data! So, eliminative materialists would reject the "folk-psychological" description that McCoy is in a certain mental state because they reject the existence of mental states; rather, according to eliminative materialists, there's only complex brain activity. Notice that this resolves the problem of silicon creatures and robots having minds—they don't and neither do any other organisms.

There are numerous replies to the eliminative materialist position. A famous criticism is provided by Thomas Nagel:

> Fundamentally an organism has conscious mental states if and only if there is something that it is like to *be* that organism—something it is like *for* the organism . . . We may call this the subjective character of experience . . . Any reductionist program[8] has to be based on an analysis of what is to be reduced. If the analysis leaves something out, the problem will be falsely posed. It is useless to base the defense of materialism on any analysis of mental phenomena that fails to deal explicitly with their subjective character. For there is no reason to suppose that a reduction which seems plausible when no attempt is made to account for consciousness can be extended to consciousness.[9]

Nagel's reply is just the same as that provided in the dualism section: "the awareness of what it is like" cannot be reduced or eliminated from an account of the mind or consciousness because this would be to eliminate the very phenomenon that requires an explanation. To claim that McCoy's mental state of anger is nothing more than a particular subset of brain processes is to eliminate the mental state of anger; yet, even after all the biology is provided, McCoy's "awareness of what it is like to be angry" persists. In addition, if we were to ask McCoy to explain what it's like to be angry, he'd be hard-pressed to provide a description that didn't reference other mental states—a difficulty Geordi LaForge experienced when asked to do so by Data:

---

[8] *Reductionism* within the philosophy of mind is a kind of explanation wherein higher-level mental phenomena are explained by their underlying constituent parts. Eliminative materialism is a kind of reductive explanation that insists that the constituent parts are all there really is: Mental stuff doesn't really exist. For example, to say that Kirk was sad when hearing of his son's death, according to the eliminative materialist, is to claim that certain neurological processes were occurring in Kirk's brain—and that's all there is to being sad.

[9] Thomas Nagel, "What Is It Like to Be a Bat?" in *Philosophy of Mind: Classical and Contemporary Readings*, edited by David J. Chalmers (Oxford: Oxford University Press, 2002), p. 219.

GEORDI: Well, when I feel angry first, I, uh... first I feel... hostile.

DATA: Could you describe feeling hostile?

GEORDI: Well, yeah, it's like feeling . . . belligerent, combative.

DATA: Could you describe feeling angry, without referring to other feelings?

GEORDI: No, I guess I can't. I just . . . feel angry.

("Descent, Part I," *TNG*)

To ignore this aspect of the mental is to ignore the core feature or property of the mind. Since this is exactly what follows from the eliminative materialist position, many philosophers of mind have considered it a dubious approach and have rejected it straightaway—even though it's in keeping with current principles and practices of science.

Emergentism: Now Can Scotty Beam Us Up?

McCOY: Please, Spock, do me a favor and *don't* say it's "fascinating."

SPOCK: No . . . but it is . . . interesting.

—"The Ultimate Computer," *TOS*

Neither dualism nor eliminative materialism appears to be a viable approach to understanding the nature of the mind. Dualism has the benefit of taking mental phenomena and mental causation seriously, but does so at the expense of jettisoning some basic scientific principles. Alternatively, eliminative materialism plays by the rules of science on what counts as a legitimate explanation, but implausibly insists that mental phenomena must be abandoned if we're to take neuroscience seriously. Given these difficulties with both theories, is there an alternative that's sensitive to the demands of science without eliminating mental phenomena? The answer, argue some philosophers of mind, is "yes" and the details are found in a theory known as *emergentism*.

Emergentism is the view that, as natural systems increase in complexity, there's a threshold of dynamic intricacy where new properties come to exist. These novel properties, argues the emergentist, are natural, but are able to transcend (in some sense) the physical complexity from which they arise *and* are able to function in ways that can't be explained by simple physical laws.[10] For example, Nomad ("The Changeling," *TOS*) and V'Ger (*Star Trek: The Motion Picture*) demonstrate both defensive and mental capacities that go well beyond their original programming and hardware. On this view, the mind is an emergent feature of the brain, but can't be understood purely in terms of the physics of brain functioning. A recent proponent of emergentism, John Searle, offers the following account:

> [Consciousness or mind] is an *emergent feature* of certain systems of neurons in the same way that solidity and liquidity are emergent features of systems of molecules. The existence of consciousness can be explained by (1) the causal interactions between elements of the brain at the micro level, but consciousness [mind] cannot itself be deduced or calculated from the sheer physical structure of the neurons without some additional account of (2) the causal relations between them.[11]

Similarly, he says:

> If we are careful, we can give a clear sense to the idea that consciousness [mind], like solidity and liquidity, is an *emergent property* of the behavior of the micro-elements of a system that is composed of those micro-elements. An emergent property, so defined, is a property that is explained by the behavior of the micro-elements but cannot be deduced simply from the composition and the movements of the micro-elements.[12]

Emergentism has the following five characteristics:

1. The only things that exist in the world are material particles and the wholes they make up.

2. Unique properties do emerge out of the complex interaction of material parts of systems.

---

[10] For a detailed discussion of both the history and the recent renaissance of emergentism, see Jaegwon Kim, "Making Sense of Emergence," *Philosophical Studies* 95 (1999), pp. 3–36.

[11] John Searle, *The Rediscovery of the Mind* (Cambridge, Massachusetts: MIT Press, 1994), p. 112.

[12] John Searle, "How to Study Consciousness Scientifically," *Brain Research Review* 26 (1998), p. 385.

3. Emergent properties can't simply be reduced to their material parts.

4. Emergent properties are both unpredictable and unexplainable from the laws governing the parts that are their origins.

5. Emergent properties have new powers that may have a causal impact on the material constituent parts from which they have arisen.

Notice that emergentism is designed to take advantage of aspects of both dualism and eliminative materialism without accepting either position entirely.[13] Specifically, emergentism embraces the methods of science *and* our everyday experiences, including mental causation. For example, McCoy's desire for a mint julep has the novel causal power to activate his motor cortex to move his legs in the direction of the nearest bar.

It appears that emergentism is a way of making sense of the mind without being stuck with the problems of dualism and eliminative materialism. For just as liquidity, transparency, and solidity are emergent properties of complex chemical structures, the mind is an emergent feature or property of the brain. It seems, then, that with emergentism there is a persuasive theory of the mind that will allow me not only to keep my childhood fascination with Spock's mental skills, but to do so without discarding either "the awareness of what it is like" or mental causation.

Unfortunately, however, things aren't so easy and straightforward. An eliminative materialist would deny that emergentism is in line with the facts of science. For instance, characteristics 1 through 5 can't easily fit into our existing scientific worldview. Liquidity, for example, is an emergent feature of water, but it *can* be explained in terms of the interaction between hydrogen and oxygen molecules in a way that the mind can't for the emergentist. Moreover, the causal powers of liquidity *can* also be explained by the same interaction of molecules and the relevant chemical bonding laws. Finally, if the mind emerges out of brain processes, is irreducible to such processes, and is still able to

---

[13] I'm not suggesting here that Searle necessarily accepts these five characteristics of his version of emergentism, but they could be inferred from his analysis.

influence matter and be influenced by matter, then this appears to be the very position embraced by dualism—indeed, some have claimed that emergentism is a version of dualism in disguise, rendering it an implausible theory of mind.[14] The point is that emergentism doesn't seem to be a naturalistic theory of mind—what we were searching for in the first place—even though some of its proponents claim the contrary.

At issue here are two distinct types of predictions. Eliminative materialists insist that a sufficiently sophisticated neuroscience in the future will vindicate the idea that the mind is nothing more than complex neurobiology. Alternatively, emergentists insist that future science will reveal, presumably by way of new natural laws, the existence of the mind and its unique characteristics (including subjectivity). At this point, one must decide which prediction is most worth accepting. Current science may seem to vindicate the claims of eliminative materialism, but given the ebb and flow of science, future science may very well substantiate the emergentist view.[15]

I think that the joy I had as a kid about Spock's special skills has diminished to the extent that I must embrace a theory of mind—namely, emergentism—which allows me only a modicum of comfort. Nonetheless, given the alternatives of dualism and eliminative materialism, I'll cling to the possibility of emergentism until a time when it's rendered more than moribund by future science. All in all, philosophy has forced me to proceed cautiously and critically about what beliefs are worthy of retaining and I'd have it no other way. Indeed, I can see no better way to live long and prosper.[16]

---

[14] Kim makes just this criticism. See his "Mental Causation in Searle's 'Biological Naturalism'," *Philosophy and Phenomenological Research* 55 (1995), p. 192. Also, William Hasker bites this bullet in his *The Emergent Self* (Ithaca: Cornell University Press, 1999) and calls his theory "emergent dualism."

[15] See Vilaynur S. Ramachandran, *The Emerging Mind* (London: Profile Books, 2003).

[16] I thank Jay Ayer, Ben Dixon, Jason Gatliff, Bernard Rowan, Tonya Scott, and Ven Srinivasan for discussing earlier versions of this paper. Also, for their patience and thoughtful discussions and suggestions, I would like to offer a special thanks to my Spring and Fall 2006 undergraduate Introduction to Philosophy students on whom an earlier version of this paper was tested.

18

Harry Mudd Always Lies

JERRY KAPUS

Compelled by anger, hatred, and vengeance, civilizations cannibalize themselves through warfare. Retaliation and counter-retaliation seems the only reality, and raw and deadly passions destroy any sense of justice. In this situation, what can possibly bring peace and restore meaning to life? A philosopher gives the answer, and naturally, it's a peculiarly philosophical answer.

Surak is the philosopher, Vulcan is the civilization, and *logic* is the answer. Surak's answer is that the best life is lived in accordance with logic and an absence of emotion. Surak's philosophy, developed during Earth's fourth century, saved Vulcan civilization during a period called the Time of the Awakening ("The Savage Curtain," *TOS*; "The Forge," "Awakening," "Kir'Shara," *ENT*).[1]

Although we humans may scoff at the Vulcan lifestyle as perhaps dull and sterile, an attitude that motivates many of Dr. McCoy's gibes at Mr. Spock, the life of logic, or reason, is one that resonates throughout the history of western philosophy on Earth. Well before the time of Surak, Stoic philosophers emphasized the importance of a life based on reason and control of emotions; later, Immanuel Kant (1724–1804) grounded the moral life solely in the exercise of rationality; most recently, Ludwig Wittgenstein (1889–1951) reduced all philosophical

---

[1] For further discussion of the role of logic in Vulcan history and life, see Chapter 2 in this volume.

problems to problems in logic.[2] Although we may not wish to imitate completely Spock's unemotional demeanor, we would agree that it's important to think logically. This leads naturally to several questions: What is logic? Why does it matter? Can human thought be reduced to a set of logical operations? What is the relationship between truth and logic?

"A Dazzling Display of Logic"

KIRK: Everything that is in error must be sterilized?
NOMAD: There are no exceptions.
KIRK: Nomad, I made an error in creating you.
NOMAD: The creation of perfection is no error . . .
KIRK: I am the Kirk, the Creator?
NOMAD: You are the Creator.
KIRK: You are wrong. Jackson Roykirk, your creator, is dead. You have mistaken me for him. You are in error. You did not discover your mistake. You've made two errors. You are flawed and imperfect. And you have not corrected by sterilization. You have made three errors . . .
KIRK: Exercise your prime function!
NOMAD: Faulty. Faulty! Must sterilize. Ste-ri-lize.
— "The Changeling," *TOS*

Not only is Captain James Tiberius Kirk a man of action, he can also deploy a syllogism with deadly force. In "The Changeling," Kirk faces off with Nomad, a space probe from Earth originally created with the mission of seeking out new life. As the result of a meteor collision and subsequent merging with an alien probe with the mission of collecting and sterilizing soil samples, Nomad acquires the new mission of seeking out and sterilizing imperfect biological organisms. Since Nomad is driven by an artificial, computerized intelligence, the standard of perfection naturally includes perfection in logical reasoning. Not surprisingly, Nomad's scan of Spock's mind finds it to be well-ordered, whereas McCoy is found irrational. Fortunately, before Nomad

---

[2] See A. Long and D.N. Sedley, eds., *The Hellenistic Philosophers*, Volume 1 (New York: Cambridge University Press, 1987); Immanuel Kant, *Groundwork of the Metaphysics of Morals* (New York: Cambridge University Press, 1998); and Ludwig Wittgenstein, *Tractatus Logico-Philosophicus* (New York: Routledge, 1974).

can execute its mission against the *Enterprise* crew, Kirk reasons with Nomad to the conclusion that it's imperfect and must be sterilized. In the vacuum of space, Nomad commits suicide. Logic is nothing to trifle with.

Kirk's lethal reasoning with Nomad demonstrates his understanding that logic is the study of "good" reasoning. Logic is concerned with identifying, explaining, and evaluating the structural features of an argument that provide a good logical connection between evidence or premises and a conclusion.[3] Obviously, we need to say more about what's meant by a "good logical connection" if we're to avoid giving a circular explanation. We want to avert sterilization.

To bring the idea of a good logical connection between premises and conclusion into focus, let's examine the argument that Kirk presents to Nomad. We first need to separate the argument's *structure* from its *content*. Kirk actually presents two interconnected arguments in reasoning with Nomad. One involves convincing Nomad of its error. The other leads Nomad to the conclusion that it must sterilize itself. We can paraphrase Kirk's main argument as follows:

PREMISE 1: Everything that is in error must be sterilized by Nomad.

PREMISE 2: Nomad is in error.

CONCLUSION: Nomad must sterilize itself.

This is an example of a *syllogistic* argument structure. There are many other types of argument structures. Logic's goal is to identify and understand which structures properly allow premises to support a conclusion. The idea is, if our premises are true *and* we have a good logical connection between the premises and the conclusion, then this logical connection ensures that the truth of the premises leads inevitably to the truth of the conclusion.

Argument structures fall into two broad categories: *deductive* and *inductive*. The difference between the two depends on the

---

[3] For a detailed introduction to logic as outlined briefly in this section, see Patrick Hurley, *A Concise Introduction to Logic* (Belmont: Wadsworth, 2006).

degree of support that the premises provide to a conclusion. A deductive argument is one where the premises are supposed to give one hundred percent certainty to a conclusion; the premises, if true themselves, guarantee the truth of the conclusion.[4] This is the type of argument that Kirk presents Nomad with. An inductive argument is one where the premises give the conclusion a degree of certainty that is less than one hundred percent; the premises make the conclusion *probably*, but not *definitely* true.

In "The Ultimate Computer" (*TOS*), the crew of the *Enterprise* is replaced by the M-5 computer in order to test whether it can run a starship as efficiently as a human crew. This test involves the application of inductive reasoning. As Commodore Wesley explains to Kirk, "There'll be a series of routine research and contact problems for the M-5 to solve, plus navigational maneuvers and the war games problem." A test such as this would involve a hypothesis—a provisional conclusion to be tested— and predictions based on the hypothesis. If the predictions turn out to be true, then the hypothesis is confirmed. In the case of the M-5, the hypothesis is that it can run the *Enterprise* as efficiently as a human crew and the predictions involve its performance based on various problems presented. Assuming that the M-5 did solve the problems correctly, the inductive argument would have the following structure:

PREMISE 1: If the M-5 can operate the *Enterprise* as efficiently as a human crew, then it will respond appropriately to the problems presented to it.[5]

---

[4] In "Elementary, Dear Data" (*TNG*), Data states that he solved a problem by "reasoning, from the general to the specific." He then asks rhetorically, "Is that not the very definition of deduction?" The answer is no. Reasoning from general to specific is just one type of deductive argument structure. Deductive reasoning can also go from the specific to the specific. For example: I left my keys either in my jacket or on my desk; the keys aren't in my jacket; so, they must be on my desk. This is a deductive argument that goes from the specific to the specific. What defines deductive and inductive reasoning is the degree of support that premises are supposed to provide to a conclusion.

[5] To be more precise, the first half of Premise 1 should include not only the hypothesis being tested, but also auxiliary hypotheses involving relevant background theories and testing conditions that are needed to tie the hypothesis to the prediction deductively. In the case of testing the M-5, an example of a

PREMISE 2: The M-5 did respond appropriately to the problems presented to it.

CONCLUSION: The M-5 can operate the *Enterprise* as efficiently as a human crew.

The above argument is inductive since the premises give us some reason to agree to the conclusion, but they don't *guarantee* that the M-5 can operate the *Enterprise* efficiently in *all* cases. Each successful test by Starfleet of the M-5's capabilities would increase the probability of the conclusion's truth. As it turns out, Kirk, who feared the outsourcing of his job to a computer, holds onto his command. The M-5 fails the test, kills several hundred Starfleet personnel in its efforts, and provides Kirk with another opportunity to demonstrate the superiority of human over machine.

Logic is not only about identifying argument structures; it also determines standards for evaluating these structures. We can reason logically or illogically, as Spock often notes in regards to humans, and we need to understand the difference. A good deductive argument is one where the argument's structure guarantees the conclusion's truth if the premises are true. This is what's known as a "valid" argument structure. An "invalid" structure fails to provide this type of guarantee. In the earlier example, Kirk presents Nomad with a valid deductive argument.

A good inductive argument is one where the argument's structure makes the conclusion likely to be true if the premises are true. This is called a "strong" argument structure. But a "weak" inductive argument claims too much certainty for its conclusion, beyond what's justified by the premises. The example concerning the M-5 presents a strong inductive argument. So what does it mean to be logical? It means to reason using *deductively valid* and *inductively strong* argument structures.

---

relevant background theory involves the physics underlying the construction of the M-5. An example of a testing condition is that the M-5 is properly installed on the *Enterprise*. The inductive structure discussed here is called the "hypothetico-deductive method." The deductive part of the structure refers to the idea that the prediction should be a deductive consequence of the main hypothesis plus the auxiliary hypotheses. The overall structure is inductive since the truth of Premises 1 and 2 provides only a degree of probable support to the conclusion.

Logic, though, won't tell us if the premises in our arguments are actually true.[6] Logic tells us what follows from premises, assuming they're true. At some point, we'll need to ground the actual truth of our premises. If the premises of an argument are true, then the argument is called either *sound* or *cogent*. A sound argument is a deductively valid argument with true premises, while a cogent argument is inductively strong, also with true premises. Sound and cogent arguments are logic's ideals.

"I Am Not Programmed to Respond in that Area"

The evaluative standards of deductive validity and inductive strength reflect the intuition that good reasoning should be *truth preserving*. Deductively valid structures preserve the truth of the premises in the conclusion. Inductively strong structures preserve the truth of the premises in the conclusion to an appropriate degree. These standards reflect an intimate link between our understanding of the concept of truth and our understanding of good reasoning. However, there is a deep puzzle at the heart of the concept of truth. In "I, Mudd" (*TOS*), Kirk exploits this puzzle to free his crew from becoming lab rats.

Norman, an android, has hijacked the *Enterprise* to an unmapped planet, where Kirk again faces the affable and inept conman Harcourt Fenton Mudd. Harry, or "Mudd the First" as he has dubbed himself, reigns over a planet of advanced androids whose purpose is to serve his desires. Unfortunately for Harry, the one desire that the androids won't serve is his desire to leave "this bloody planet" since their purpose is also to study Harry as a human specimen. Harry has schemed to deliver the *Enterprise* crew to serve as his replacement for the androids' study of humanity. As is often the case with the best laid plans of mice, men, and Harry Mudd, the androids have their own plan. Recognizing the aggressive and greedy tendencies of humans, the androids decide to save us from ourselves. Rather than ferrying Harry to freedom, the *Enterprise* will ferry the androids across the galaxy with the purpose of "serving" humanity by

---

[6] The one exception to this is when a premise is a tautology: for example, "Either Kirk is or isn't the captain of the *Enterprise.*"

controlling humanity's self-destructive instincts. How can the androids be stopped? Kirk's answer is to celebrate humanity's capacity for illogical behavior by acting illogically in the hope of confusing the androids. This strategy reaches its peak when Kirk and Harry present Norman, the central computer control for the android population, with a paradox that challenges his understanding of truth and logic:

> **KIRK:** Everything Harry tells you is a lie. Remember that. Everything Harry tells you is a lie.
> **HARRY:** Now listen to this carefully, Norman. I am lying.
> **NORMAN:** You say you are lying, but if everything you say is a lie, then you are telling the truth. But you cannot tell the truth, because everything you say is a lie. But . . . you lie . . . you tell the truth, but you cannot, for you lie. Illogical. Illogical. Please explain. You are human. Only humans can explain their behavior. Please explain.

In attempting to reason through the implication of Harry saying that he's lying, Norman is sucked into a black hole of logical paradox, overloads his circuits, and crashes the entire android population.

The paradox that Kirk and Harry wield against Norman has a long history in philosophy and is appropriately called the "Liar's Paradox." Eubulides of Miletus (fourth century B.C.E.) is credited with the earliest formulation of the version of the paradox Harry uses. To generate the paradox, we don't need Kirk's statement that "Everything Harry tells you is a lie." All that's needed is Harry's statement that "I am lying." If we assume that Harry is telling the truth then this means that it's true that Harry is lying. However, if Harry is lying then what he's saying isn't true. Thus, if Harry's statement is true then it's also not true. Alternatively, if we start with the assumption that Harry's statement is false, then this implies that Harry isn't lying. However, if Harry isn't lying, then this implies that he's telling the truth. Thus, if Harry's statement is false, then it's also true. So it seems we're forced to accept the contradiction that Harry's statement is true if and only if it's false. Facing this contradiction, we may feel like crashing too.

Although we may think that the Liar paradox is nothing more than an interesting brain teaser, we can't simply choose to ignore the paradox since the contradiction threatens our logical principles of reasoning. Consider the following example of two standard reasoning rules: If Spock is a Vulcan, then it follows that either Spock is a Vulcan or Kirk is a Vulcan; and if either Spock is a Vulcan or Kirk is a Vulcan, and Kirk is not a Vulcan, then it follows that Spock must be a Vulcan. The first example is the *addition* rule, and the second is the *disjunctive syllogism* rule. Given that the Liar paradox says that the Liar sentence is both true and not true, we can reason as follows:

1. The Liar sentence is true.

2. The Liar sentence is not true.

3. Either the Liar sentence is true or Kirk is a Vulcan. (*addition* applied to 1)

4. Kirk is a Vulcan. (*disjunctive syllogism* applied to 2 and 3)

Something is rotten in ShiKahr when we can prove that Kirk is a Vulcan. What's rotten is that the contradiction of the Liar paradox together with some standard reasoning rules allows us to prove any conclusion we want. The fact that any conclusion whatsoever follows from a contradiction is called the "explosion problem."

The Liar paradox is interesting because it suggests that there's a fundamental problem in our understanding of the concept of truth. Alfred Tarski (1902–1983) brought this problem into focus through his rigorous work on truth in the twentieth century.[7] The central insight of Tarski's work is that the meaning of truth is given by statements of the form:

(T) "S" is true if and only if S.

"S" stands for any sentence that declares a fact. An example of a T-sentence would be:

(V) "Spock is a Vulcan" is true if and only if Spock is a Vulcan.

---

[7] See Alfred Tarski, "The Semantic Conception of Truth and the Foundations of Semantics" *Philosophy and Phenomenological Research* 4 (1944), pp. 341–376; and "The Concept of Truth in Formalized Languages," in *Logic, Truth, Metamathematics*, ed. J. Corcoran (Indianapolis: Hackett, 1983).

The fact that sentences like V are "trivially true" led Tarski to believe that each specific T-sentence reveals a bit of the truth about one part of the world. If so, then *all* of the T-sentences together would, like a laundry list, exhaust what we mean by "the truth." The problem is that T-sentences also play a role in generating the Liar paradox. To see this, consider a more straightforward formulation of the Liar than Kirk and Harry use:

(1) This sentence is not true.

In (1), we have a case of self-reference so that

(2) This sentence = "This sentence is not true."

The T-sentence for (1) is

(3) "This sentence is not true" is true if and only if this sentence is not true.

Using the equivalence given in (2) and substituting in (3), we obtain the contradiction that

(4) This sentence is true if and only if this sentence is not true.

Although the T-sentences capture something obvious about the meaning of truth, they also demonstrate that truth is an inconsistent concept igniting the explosion problem.

We're faced with a serious dilemma. Good reasoning is supposed to be "good" because it involves logical structures that are truth preserving. Yet the concept of truth appears to be inconsistent, and this in turn trivializes logic by allowing us to prove anything. We could aim our photon torpedoes at the connection between the T-sentences and truth, but the strong intuitive correctness of the T-sentences suggests that we exercise the Prime Directive in regards to them. Maybe Norman had the correct response: crash and take some time off from thinking.

If Norman's creators had been a bit more advanced, then they could have programmed him with a response to the Liar paradox that would have forced Kirk and Harry to go into warp drive with their logic skills. The response is that Liar-type sentences simply lack a truth value. This idea makes sense if one rejects the logical principle of *bivalence*, the idea that every statement must be either true or false. The principle of bivalence drives us to seek a definite truth value for Liar statements and thus leads us to a contradiction. Without bivalence, we could recognize that some statements don't have a truth value. Systems of logic based on this approach rely on a three-valued logic—true, false, and undefined—as opposed to the standard two-valued logic—true and false.[8]

Had Norman responded that Harry's statement lacked a truth value, he would have met Kirk and Harry's attempt at illogic with logic. Spock, with his acute Vulcan mind, would have had to pick up the logical slack. We can imagine Spock continuing the discussion:

> **SPOCK:** Fascinating. Your creators obviously had an advanced understanding of truth and logic. However, your response does not solve the paradox, rather it relocates the problem. Norman, analyze the following sentence:

(5) This sentence is false or it does not have a truth value.

> **NORMAN:** I am programmed to serve you. I will do as you request. If sentence (5) is true then what it says is correct and so sentence (5) is either false or it does not have a truth value. But both of these options mean that sentence (5) is not true. But if sentence (5) is not true then what it says is incorrect and so sentence (5) is not false and it has a truth value. But if sentence (5) is not false and it has a truth value then sentence (5) is true. But if sentence (5) is true then, illogical, illogical.

---

[8] See Saul Kripke, "Outline of a Theory of Truth" *Journal of Philosophy* 72 (1975), pp. 690–716. For alternative responses to the Liar paradox, see T. Burge, "Semantical Paradox" *Journal of Philosophy* 76 (1979), pp. 169–198; G. Priest, "The Logic of Paradox" *Journal of Philosophical Logic* 8 (1979), pp. 219–241; A. Gupta and N. Belnap, *The Revision Theory of Truth* (Cambridge: MIT Press, 1993); and D. Grover, "How Significant is the Liar," in *Deflationism and Paradox*, edited by J.C. Beall and B. Armour-Garb (New York: Oxford University Press, 2005).

In this extension of "I, Mudd," Norman still crashes under the logical weight of the Liar paradox while we're provided with a deeper understanding of truth and logic. However, we should notice that Spock's Vulcan commitment to the life of logic comes up short in ultimately calling itself into question. The Liar paradox isn't simply an amusing brain teaser. It suggests that our understanding of truth is inconsistent, and that like a supernova, it threatens to explode the connection between truth and logic by allowing us to prove any and every belief, no matter how illogical. As Spock would likely say, with a mixture of awe and trepidation, "Fascinating."

"You'd Make a Splendid Computer, Mr. Spock"

Within cognitive science, the study of how the mind functions, a common approach is to see the mind as something like a computer program that contains representational symbols—such as sentences or formulas—and computational rules that apply to these symbols. The representational symbols are similar to computer data structures, and the computational rules are similar to the algorithms comprising a computer program. The brain is like the computer hardware that implements the program. By analogy, the argument structures of logic would specify computational rules that the mind follows or should follow to reason well. It's easy to see how good reasoning, envisioned as a system of rules applied to sentences or formulas, could be thought of as nothing more than a specific kind of computer program. But is the mind nothing more than a very sophisticated computer program?

In "The Return of the Archons" (*TOS*), a computer named Landru controls the lives of the people of Beta III with the goal of promoting their good by ensuring peace and tranquility. Unfortunately, Landru achieves this goal by reducing the people to empty shells lacking the ability to make their own choices. Kirk and Spock convince Landru that its control of the people of Beta III is actually contrary to their good, which results in Landru's self-destruction. Before departing, Kirk and Spock engage in a brief philosophical discussion related to the question of whether being human involves more than performing computations according to some predetermined algorithms:

SPOCK: Marvelous.

KIRK: What?

SPOCK: The late Landru, Captain. Marvelous feat of engineering. A computer capable of directing the lives of millions of human beings.

KIRK: But only a machine, Mr. Spock. The original Landru programmed it with all his knowledge, but he couldn't give it his wisdom, his compassion, his understanding, his soul, Mr. Spock.

SPOCK: Predictably metaphysical. I prefer the concrete, the graspable, the provable.

Although Kirk invokes the notion of a soul to distinguish humans from computers, he appears to grant that much of human and Vulcan knowledge could be simulated by a computer. Yet an approach like Spock's emphasis on "provability" allowed John Lucas and Roger Penrose to argue against the idea that the mind can be identified with a computer program.[9] Their argument relies on the "incompleteness theorems" of Kurt Gödel (1906–1978).[10]

Instead of talking in terms of truth, Gödel focuses on what could or could not be deductively proven within a language capable of expressing arithmetic. Gödel shows that it's possible within such a language to construct a formula G that says of itself that G isn't provable—similar to the Liar sentence. Given this formula, Gödel derives his first incompleteness theorem, which states that if a formal system[11] is consistent and capable of expressing arithmetic, then neither G nor not-G is provable within the system. A formal system is said to be complete if for any given formula F in the language of the system, *either* F or

---

[9] See J.R. Lucas, "Minds, Machines, and Gödel" *Philosophy* 36 (1961), pp. 112–127; and Roger Penrose, *Shadows of the Mind* (New York: Oxford University Press, 1994).

[10] See Kurt Gödel, *Collected Works I: Publications 1929–1936*, ed. S. Feferman, S. Kleene, G. Moore, R. Solovay, and J. van Heijenoort (New York: Oxford University Press, 1986). For an informal presentation of Gödel's incompleteness theorems, see T. Franzen, *Gödel's Theorem: An Incomplete Guide to Its Use and Abuse* (Wellesley: Peters, 2005). We'll consider here only the argument involving Gödel's first incompleteness theorem.

[11] A "formal system" is a set of axioms and rules for drawing inferences that determine what can and cannot be proven within the system.

not-F is provable within the system. Since neither G nor not-G is provable if the formal system is consistent, it follows that the system is incomplete. Gödel's incompleteness theorem is important for mathematics since it shows that there's a limit to mathematical reasoning: there are some formulas which can neither be proven nor not proven within the system.

To see how Lucas and Penrose use Gödel's first incompleteness theorem to argue that the human mind can't be completely modeled by a computer program, we need to assume that a computer program can be viewed as a consistent formal system. A computer program that can model the human mind will be capable of doing—among other things—arithmetic. In this case, Gödel's theorem applies to the program, and there will be a formula G (G says of itself that it is not provable) which the program can neither prove nor not prove. Our minds, however, can see that G is true since G isn't provable and this is what G says. So we're able to do something that the computer program can't do: determine that G is true.

Lucas and Penrose's argument may appear convincing, but as Hilary Putnam and others have shown, their argument fails since it lacks a crucial premise.[12] In order to conclude that G is *definitely* true, it isn't enough to assume the consistency of any computer program put forth as a model of our minds. This assumption only allows us to conclude the conditional statement that *if* the program is consistent *then* G is true. To conclude that G is *definitely* true, Lucas and Penrose would first need to show that the program *is* consistent. As Putnam points out, though, any program put forth as a plausible model of our minds would be very complex and large, and it's unlikely that we could prove its consistency. Since it's unlikely that we could prove the program's consistency, we can't conclude that G is *definitely* true. Furthermore, the Liar paradox suggests that our actual thought processes may be inconsistent. If so, then Gödel's incompleteness theorem wouldn't apply to our minds, and so it can't be used to prove a difference between our minds and computer programs.

---

[12] See Hilary Putnam, "Review of *Shadows of the Mind*," *Bulletin of the American Mathematical Society* 32 (1995), pp. 370–73; Paul Benacerraf, "God, the Devil, and Gödel," *Monist* 51 (1967), pp. 9–32; and David Chalmers, "Mind, Machines, and Mathematics," *Psyche* 2 (1995), http://psyche.cs.monash.edu.au/v2/psyche-2-09-chalmers.html.

Although the appeal to Gödel's incompleteness theorem doesn't show that the mind outstrips the capabilities of any computer program, Lucas and Penrose do draw a distinction between what can be *known to be true* and what can be *proven using rules of reasoning*. In turn, this distinction suggests an important difference between minds and computers. Kirk asserts that the computer Landru lacked the understanding of the person Landru. On Kirk's view, a computer doesn't understand the meaning of the symbols that it manipulates. This is because a computer simply follows a set of instructions based on its ability to identify the symbols and the rules that apply to them. This can be done without understanding what the symbols mean or the purpose behind the rules. Presumably, the person Landru *did* understand the meaning of the symbols and the purpose of the rules that he programmed into his computer. Understanding is more than just symbol manipulation. It also involves knowing that symbols have contents that are about things in the world, and it involves understanding the purpose behind the rules applied to the symbols. The idea that symbols or thoughts are about things in the world addresses what John Searle calls the "intentionality of thought."[13] Understanding involves not only receiving input from the outside world, but also conscious awareness of the content of one's thoughts. Explaining the mind as a symbol manipulation system isn't the same thing as explaining *consciousness*. The idea that logic, and by extension computer programs, are nothing more than systems for manipulating uninterpreted symbols gives real poignancy to McCoy's claim that "you cannot evaluate a man by logic alone" ("I, Mudd," *TOS*).

"Logic Is the Beginning of Wisdom . . . Not the End"

In "I, Mudd," Spock facetiously explains to Norman that "logic is a little tweeting bird chirping in a meadow. Logic is a wreath of pretty flowers which smell bad." These characterizations are

---

[13] See John Searle, "Minds, Brains, and Programs," *Behavioral and Brain Sciences* 3 (1980), pp. 417–457. For a critique of Searle's view, see Paul Churchland and Patricia Churchland, "Could a Machine Think?" *Scientific American* 262 (1990), pp. 32–37.

part of a sequence of illogical puzzles aimed at causing Norman to crash, and are similar to the kind of self-referential loops exploited by Gödel. Our look at the Liar paradox left us with a pessimistic conclusion concerning the inconsistency of our concept of truth and the implication that this undermines our reasoning. It wouldn't be a stretch to take Spock's facetious remark about the nature of logic as if it were true: logic and being reasonable may not be all that it's supposed to be. We may wonder how Vulcans succeed in building their lives on a commitment to logic. However, this isn't the final lesson of the Liar paradox or Gödel's theorem.

Many philosophers have seen a close connection between the structure of language, the structure of knowledge, and the structure of reality. Motivated by the belief in this connection, some philosophers have sought to develop a universal language in which all truths could be clearly stated and clearly model reality. This motivation played a part in the development of modern logic. What follows from attempts to resolve the Liar paradox and from Gödel's incompleteness theorem isn't skepticism about reasoning, but rather the reasonable idea that the goal of a universal language is unattainable. It may not be possible to determine whether the Liar sentence is or isn't true, or whether a Gödel-type formula is or isn't provable within certain mathematical systems. But this is a problem only if we believe that there has to be a universal language in which we can, once and for all, express everything that's true. The Liar paradox and Gödel have laid out some of the limits of what can be said and known. Yet within these limits there's an abundance of important questions and problems that we can and should try to solve. Still, some people will be driven to strive for answers beyond these limits. Perhaps the only option left is to share Captain Kirk's trust in human *intuition*.[14]

---

[14] I thank Kevin Decker and Jason Eberl for their careful editing and comments on earlier drafts of this paper. I also thank Carole Berg, Joseph Kapus, Randy McKinney, John Muenzberg, Tim Shiell, and Stephen Scott for their comments.

Crew of the Starship
Enterprise NCC-1701-?

MAHESH ANANTH is Assistant Professor of Philosophy at Indiana University, South Bend. He studies and teaches ancient Greek philosophy, medical ethics, philosophy of biology, and philosophy of mind. He's the author of *In Defense of an Evolutionary Concept of Health: Nature, Norms, and Human Biology* (2007), and has contributed to *Batman and Philosophy* (forthcoming). Mahesh hopes to live long and prosper, but realizes that, since the academic life isn't likely to yield either, he can only hope to avoid being assimilated.

ROBERT ARP is the editor of *South Park and Philosophy: You Know, I Learned Something Today* (2007) and has contributed to numerous volumes on popular culture and philosophy. He's currently doing postdoctoral research at the National Center for Biomedical Ontology through SUNY-Buffalo. Since he loathes split infinitives, he wants to go where no man has gone before, boldly.

SHAI BIDERMAN is a doctoral candidate in Philosophy at Boston University. His research interests include philosophy of culture, philosophy of film and literature, aesthetics, ethics, existentialism, and Nietzsche. His essays appear in *Movies and the Meaning of Life: Philosophers Take on Hollywood* (2005), *Hitchcock and Philosophy: Dial M for Metaphysics* (2007), *South Park and Philosophy: You Know, I Learned Something Today* (2007), and several forthcoming volumes. Shai spends most of his free time tasking his co-author William J. Devlin, continuously calling him "Scotty," and demanding that he provide more power and more speed.

PAUL A. CANTOR is Clifton Waller Barrett Professor of English at the University of Virginia. He's written on such pop culture subjects as film noir, Martin Scorsese, *South Park*, and *The Simpsons*. His *Gilligan Unbound: Pop Culture in the Age of Globalization* was named by the *Los Angeles Times* as one of the best non-fiction books of 2001. With the intergalactic dissemination of his chapter in this volume, he hopes to realize his long cherished dream of becoming the Darmok and Jalad Professor of Tamarian at the University of Tanagra.

TIM CHALLANS is Associate Professor of Philosophy at the School of Advanced Military Studies. He's the author of *Awakening Warrior: Revolution in the Ethics of Warfare*, a book that may yet have some influence, even if only in the *Star Trek* universe. Even though Tim often says he was born four hundred years too soon—retiring from the Army as a Lieutenant Colonel instead of from Starfleet as a Commander—his bald head (and other Picard-like qualities) helped set a trend that will make Jean-Luc Picard attractive to some of the finest women in the galaxy.

KEVIN S. DECKER is Assistant Professor of Philosophy at Eastern Washington University. He's co-editor of *Star Wars and Philosophy: More Powerful than You Can Possibly Imagine* and has written on philosophical themes in Stanley Kubrick, James Bond, and *The Colbert Report*. He's passionate about Shakespeare, democracy, and hot pretzels with mustard. Should he live long enough, he envisions having the shortest-ever commission as a Starfleet captain because he'll undoubtedly indulge his preference for having a Gorn as his security officer, thus starting the Romulan Wars.

WILLIAM J. DEVLIN is Assistant Professor of Philosophy at Bridgewater State College. His research interests include philosophy of science, theories of truth, Nietzsche, and existentialism. He's written on such films and series as *12 Monkeys*, *The Terminator*, *Lost,* and *South Park*. Frustrated with being called "Scotty," William has devoted his life now to chasing his co-author, Shai Biderman, 'round the moons of Nibia, and 'round the Antares maelstrom, and 'round perdition's flames before giving him up.

JASON T. EBERL is Assistant Professor of Philosophy at Indiana University—Purdue University Indianapolis, where he teaches and conducts research in bioethics, medieval philosophy, and metaphysics. He's co-editor of *Star Wars and Philosophy: More Powerful than You Can Possibly Imagine* and has contributed to similar volumes on Stanley Kubrick, *Harry Potter*, and Metallica. When he was fifteen, Marina Sirtis told him at a convention that he didn't have a big enough chest to pose as Riker in a red *Next Gen* uniform. In 2006, at another convention, he almost made Jonathan Frakes choke on his drink when he told him the story.

JACOB M. HELD is Assistant Professor of Philosophy at the University of Central Arkansas. He's published on issues in philosophy of law and political philosophy in journals such as *Vera Lex, Public Affairs Quarterly,* and the *Journal of the British Society for Phenomenology.* He's also co-editor of *James Bond and Philosophy: Questions Are Forever* (2006) and the author of Rule of Acquisition 287: "If you seek latinum, avoid philosophy."

JERRY KAPUS is Associate Professor of Philosophy at the University of Wisconsin—Stout. He teaches courses in critical thinking, logic, epistemology and metaphysics, and philosophy of religion. He's published in the areas of logic, metaphysics, and philosophy of language. His current research interests are in theories of truth and meaning, and the role of truth in philosophy. Part of his philosophy for a long life is to avoid being a "red shirt" on one of Captain Kirk's landing parties.

HEATHER KEITH is Associate Professor of Philosophy at Green Mountain College, where she teaches Asian philosophy, feminist theory, logic, and the history of philosophy. When she's not skiing, horseback riding, hiking, or teaching, she writes articles on pragmatism, feminism, and Chinese philosophy. She co-authored an essay on the film *Contact* in *Movies and the Meaning of Life: Philosophers Take on Hollywood* (2005). She's always wondered how the short skirts on the women's uniforms survived until the twenty-fourth century, and she really, really wants a transporter for her birthday.

AMY KIND is Associate Professor of Philosophy at Claremont McKenna College, where she infuses her courses on philosophy of mind and metaphysics with *Trek*-related content. She's published in *Philosophical Studies, Philosophical Quarterly,* and *Philosophy and Phenomenological Research.* Despite any rumors to the contrary, she's never insisted that her students call her "Commander Kind," nor has she ever worn a Starfleet uniform to class.

SANDER LEE is Professor of Philosophy at Keene State College. He's the author of *Eighteen Woody Allen Films Analyzed: Anguish, God, and Existentialism* (2002), as well as other books and essays on issues in aesthetics, ethics, social philosophy, and metaphysics. He still wonders what the Breen look like under their refrigeration suits.

JASON BURKE MURPHY, from Saint Louis University, is a doctoral candidate in Philosophy—not a bricklayer, damnit! He works primarily on political philosophy and contemporary German philosophy. He's found that graduate students are a lot like "red shirts" and mind melding with them leads to "Pain! Pain!"

MARNIE NOLTON is currently completing her doctorate on the wormhole connecting political philosophy and theology at Murdoch University. Her research interests extend to cultural expressions of the religious, the textuality of tradition and identity, politics and religion, Altonian brain-teasers, and Ferengi ethics. Along these last lines, she's a firm believer that anything worth doing is worth doing for money, so she's paid to teach philosophy at the University of Ballarat.

TODD PORTER is a doctoral candidate in English at Saint Louis University. His research interests include the nineteenth-century British novel, the public museum, and gender studies. He isn't Guardian of the Holies, Speaker of the Holy Words, and Leader of Warriors, but he's seen the *Ee'd plebnista* and thinks it's a pretty good idea to share it.

WALTER ROBINSON is a Zen Buddhist priest who teaches East-West philosophy at Indiana University—Purdue University Indianapolis. He's also known in other places in the universe as Ritoku, which means "cultivating virtue." His interests include philosophical psychology of religion and telepathic time travel.

THEODORE SCHICK is Professor of Philosophy at Muhlenberg College. He's co-authored *How to Think about Weird Things* (2007) and *Doing Philosophy* (2006), and edited *Readings in the Philosophy of Science: From Positivism to Postmodernism* (1999). He's also contributed to a number of volumes in the Popular Culture and Philosophy series, on *Seinfeld, The Matrix* films, and *Lord of the Rings*. Although he's been likened to a Denebian slime devil, he prefers to think of himself as a long-lived Lyssarrian desert larva.

PHILIP TALLON is a doctoral candidate at St. Andrews University. He's published popular articles on Alfred Hitchcock, C.S. Lewis, and superheroes. Though a resident of Earth, he considers himself an alien species because he has a weird-looking forehead.

HARALD THORSRUD is Assistant Professor of Philosophy at Agnes Scott College. His research focuses on ancient skepticism and ethics. Even though he's never had the chance to mind meld with Surak, he's still convinced that logic is the beginning of wisdom, not the end.

JERRY L. WALLS teaches at Asbury Seminary. He's co-edited *The Chronicles of Narnia and Philosophy: The Lion, the Witch, and the Worldview* (2005) and *Basketball and Philosophy: Thinking Outside the Paint* (2007), and has authored a variety of professional and popular articles on topics ranging from foreknowledge and freedom to *Harry Potter*. Like Captain Picard, he's an avid fan of "tea, Earl Grey, hot."

Chronicles from the Final Frontier

Episodes listed in production, not airdate, order.[1]

Star Trek: The Original Series (1966–1969)

The Cage (unaired pilot—as if you didn't know that already)

Season One

Where No Man Has Gone Before
The Corbomite Maneuver
Mudd's Women
The Enemy Within
The Man Trap
The Naked Time
Charlie X
Balance of Terror
What Are Little Girls Made Of?
Dagger of the Mind
Miri
The Conscience of the King

The *Galileo* Seven
Court Martial
The Menagerie, Parts I and II
Shore Leave
The Squire of Gothos
Arena
The Alternative Factor
Tomorrow Is Yesterday
The Return of the Archons
A Taste of Armageddon
Space Seed
This Side of Paradise
The Devil in the Dark
Errand of Mercy
The City on the Edge of Forever
Operation: Annihilate!

Season Two

Catspaw
Metamorphosis

---

[1] Why? Because it's not the case that Dr. McCoy was the *Enterprise*'s CMO for two weeks, then left for a week while Dr. Piper took over, and then returned (and while he was gone they changed all the uniforms and back?!)

Friday's Child
Who Mourns for Adonais?
Amok Time
The Doomsday Machine
Wolf in the Fold
The Changeling
The Apple
Mirror, Mirror
The Deadly Years
I, Mudd
The Trouble with Tribbles
Bread and Circuses
Journey to Babel
A Private Little War
The Gamesters of Triskelion
Obsession
The Immunity Syndrome
A Piece of the Action
By Any Other Name
Return to Tomorrow
Patterns of Force
The Ultimate Computer
The Omega Glory
Assignment: Earth

Season Three

Spectre of the Gun
Elaan of Troyius
The Paradise Syndrome
The Enterprise Incident
And the Children Shall Lead
Spock's Brain
Is There In Truth No Beauty?
The Empath
The Tholian Web
For the World Is Hollow and I
    Have Touched the Sky
Day of the Dove
Plato's Stepchildren
Wink of an Eye
That Which Survives
Let that Be Your Last
    Battlefield

Whom Gods Destroy
The Mark of Gideon
The Lights of Zetar
The Cloud Minders
The Way to Eden
Requiem for Methuselah
The Savage Curtain
All Our Yesterdays
Turnabout Intruder

Star Trek: The Animated Series (1973–1974)

Season One

More Tribbles, More Troubles
The Infinite Vulcan
Yesteryear
Beyond the Farthest Star
The Survivor
The Lorelei Signal
One of Our Planets Is Missing
Mudd's Passion
The Magicks of Megas-Tu
The Time Trap
The Slaver Weapon
The Ambergris Element
The Jihad
The Terratin Incident
The Eye of the Beholder
Once Upon a Planet

Season Two

Bem
Albatross
The Pirates of Orion
The Practical Joker
How Sharper than a Serpent's
    Tooth
The Counter-Clock Incident

Star Trek: The Next Generation (1987–1994)

Season One

Encounter at Farpoint, Parts I
   and II
The Naked Now
Code of Honor
Haven
Where No One Has Gone
   Before
The Last Outpost
Lonely Among Us
Justice
The Battle
Hide and Q
Too Short a Season
The Big Goodbye
Datalore
Angel One
11001001
Home Soil
When the Bough Breaks
Coming of Age
Heart of Glory
The Arsenal of Freedom
Symbiosis[2]
Skin of Evil
We'll Always Have Paris
Conspiracy
The Neutral Zone

Season Two

The Child
Where Silence Has Lease
Elementary, Dear Data

The Outrageous Okona
The Schizoid Man
Loud as a Whisper
Unnatural Selection
A Matter of Honor
The Measure of a Man
The Dauphin
Contagion
The Royale
Time Squared
The Icarus Factor
Pen Pals
Q Who?
Samaritan Snare
Up the Long Ladder
Manhunt
The Emissary
Peak Performance
Shades of Gray

Season Three

Evolution
The Ensigns of Command
The Survivors
Who Watches the Watchers?
The Bonding
Booby Trap
The Enemy
The Price
The Vengeance Factor
The Defector
The Hunted
The High Ground
Déjà Q
A Matter of Perspective
Yesterday's Enterprise
The Offspring

---

[2] Yes, this episode is out of production order, but we can't have Tasha dying and then coming back to life the next week. There'll be a few other episodes listed out of production order for the sake of maintaining continuity within the series.

Sins of the Father
Allegiance
Captain's Holiday
Tin Man
Hollow Pursuits
The Most Toys
Sarek
Ménage à Troi
Transfigurations
The Best of Both Worlds,
    Part I

Season Four

The Best of Both Worlds,
    Part II
Family
Suddenly Human
Brothers
Remember Me
Legacy
Reunion
Future Imperfect
Final Mission
The Loss
Data's Day
The Wounded
Devil's Due
Clues
First Contact
Galaxy's Child
Night Terrors
Identity Crisis
The Nth Degree
Qpid
The Drumhead
Half a Life
The Host
The Mind's Eye
In Theory
Redemption, Part I

Season Five

Redemption, Part II
Darmok
Ensign Ro
Silicon Avatar
Disaster
The Game
Unification, Parts I and II
A Matter of Time
New Ground
Hero Worship
Violations
The Masterpiece Society
Conundrum
Power Play
Ethics
The Outcast
Cause and Effect
The First Duty
Cost of Living
The Perfect Mate
Imaginary Friend
I, Borg
The Next Phase
The Inner Light
Time's Arrow, Part I

Season Six

Time's Arrow, Part II
Realm of Fear
Man of the People
Relics
Schisms
True-Q
Rascals
A Fistful of Datas
The Quality of Life
Chain of Command, Parts I
    and II
Ship in a Bottle
Aquiel
Face of the Enemy

Tapestry
Birthright, Parts I and II
Starship Mine
Lessons
The Chase
Frame of Mind
Suspicions
Rightful Heir
Second Chances
Timescape
Descent, Part I

Season Seven

Descent, Part II
Liaisons
Interface
Gambit, Parts I and II
Phantasms
Dark Page
Attached
Force of Nature
Inheritance
Parallels
The Pegasus
Homeward
Sub Rosa
Lower Decks
Thine Own Self
Masks
Eye of the Beholder
Genesis
Journey's End
Firstborn
Bloodlines
Emergence
Preemptive Strike
All Good Things..., Parts I
   and II

Star Trek: Deep Space Nine (1993–1999)

Season One

Emissary, Parts I and II
Past Prologue
A Man Alone
Babel
Captive Pursuit
Q-Less
Dax
The Passenger
Move Along Home
The Nagus
Vortex
Battle Lines
The Storyteller
Progress
If Wishes Were Horses
The Forsaken
Dramatis Personae
Duet
In the Hands of the Prophets

Season Two

The Homecoming
The Circle
The Siege
Invasive Procedures
Cardassians
Melora
Rules of Acquisition
Necessary Evil
Second Sight
Sanctuary
Rivals
The Alternate
Armageddon Game
Whispers
Paradise
Shadowplay
Playing God

Profit and Loss
Blood Oath
The Maquis, Parts I and II
The Wire
Crossover
The Collaborator
Tribunal
The Jem'Hadar

Season Three

The Search, Parts I and II
The House of Quark
Equilibrium
Second Skin
The Abandoned
Civil Defense
Meridian
Defiant
Fascination
Past Tense, Parts I and II
Life Support
Heart of Stone
Destiny
Prophet Motive
Visionary
Distant Voices
Through the Looking Glass
Improbable Cause
The Die Is Cast
Explorers
Family Business
Shakaar
Facets
The Adversary

Season Four

The Way of the Warrior, Parts I
    and II
Hippocratic Oath
The Visitor
Indiscretion
Rejoined

Starship Down
Little Green Men
The Sword of Kahless
Our Man Bashir
Homefront
Paradise Lost
Crossfire
Return to Grace
Sons of Mogh
Bar Association
Accession
Rules of Engagement
Hard Time
Shattered Mirror
The Muse
For the Cause
The Quickening
To the Death
Body Parts
Broken Link

Season Five

Apocalypse Rising
The Ship
Looking for par'Mach in All the
    Wrong Places
...Nor the Battle to the Strong
Trials and Tribble-ations
The Assignment
Let He Who Is Without Sin...
Things Past
The Ascent
Rapture
The Darkness and the Light
The Begotten
For the Uniform
In Purgatory's Shadow
By Inferno's Light
Doctor Bashir, I Presume
A Simple Investigation
Business as Usual
Ties of Blood and Water
Ferengi Love Songs

Star Trek: Voyager (1995–2001)

Season Two

Projections
Elogium
Twisted
The 37's[3]
Initiations
Non Sequitur
Parturition
Persistence of Vision
Tattoo
Cold Fire
Maneuvers
Resistance
Prototype
Death Wish
Alliances
Threshold
Meld
Dreadnought
Lifesigns
Investigations
Deadlock
Innocence
The Thaw
Tuvix
Resolutions
Basics, Part I

Season Three

Basics, Part II
Sacred Ground
False Profits
Flashback
The Chute
Remember
The Swarm
Future's End, Parts I and II
Warlord

The Q and the Grey
Macrocosm
Alter Ego
Fair Trade
Blood Fever
Coda
Unity
Rise
Darkling
Favorite Son
Before and After
Real Life
Distant Origin
Displaced
Worst Case Scenario
Scorpion, Part I

Season Four

Scorpion, Part II
The Gift
Day of Honor
Nemesis
Revulsion
The Raven
Scientific Method
Year of Hell, Parts I and II
Random Thoughts
Concerning Flight
Mortal Coil
Waking Moments
Message in a Bottle
Hunters
Prey
Retrospect
The Killing Game, Parts I and II
Vis a Vis
The Omega Directive
Unforgettable

---

[3] "The 37's" was actually the premiere episode of *Voyager*'s second season, but there were three hold-over episodes produced in Season One.

Living Witness
Demon
One
Hope and Fear

Season Five

Night
Drone
Extreme Risk
In the Flesh
Once Upon a Time
Nothing Human
Timeless
Infinite Regress
Thirty Days
Counterpoint
Gravity
Latent Image
Bride of Chaotica!
The Fight
Bliss
The Disease
Dark Frontier, Parts I and II
Course: Oblivion
Think Tank
Juggernaut
Someone to Watch Over Me
11:59
Relativity
Warhead
Equinox, Part I

Season Six

Equinox, Part II
Survival Instinct
Barge of the Dead
Tinker, Tenor, Doctor, Spy
Dragon's Teeth
Alice
Riddles
One Small Step
The Voyager Conspiracy

Pathfinder
Fair Haven
Tsunkatse
Blink of an Eye
Virtuoso
Collective
Memorial
Spirit Folk
Ashes to Ashes
Child's Play
Good Shepherd
Fury
Live Fast and Prosper
Life Line
Muse
The Haunting of Deck Twelve
Unimatrix Zero, Part I

Season Seven

Unimatrix Zero, Part II
Imperfection
Drive
Critical Care
Repression
Inside Man
Flesh and Blood, Parts I and II
Body and Soul
Nightingale
Shattered
Lineage
Repentance
Prophecy
The Void
Workforce, Parts I and II
Human Error
Q2
Author, Author
Friendship One
Natural Law
Homestead
Renaissance Man
Endgame, Parts I and II

Star Trek: Enterprise (2001–2005)

Season One

Broken Bow, Parts I and II
Fight or Flight
Strange New World
Unexpected
Terra Nova
The Andorian Incident
Breaking the Ice
Civilization
Fortunate Son
Cold Front
Silent Enemy
Dear Doctor
Shadows of P'Jem
Sleeping Dogs
Shuttlepod One
Fusion
Rogue Planet
Acquisition
Oasis
Detained
Vox Sola
Fallen Hero
Desert Crossing
Two Days and Two Nights
Shockwave, Part I

Season Two

Shockwave, Part II
Carbon Creek
Minefield
Dead Stop
A Night in Sickbay
Marauders
The Seventh
The Communicator
Singularity
Vanishing Point
Precious Cargo

The Catwalk
Dawn
Stigma
Cease Fire
Future Tense
Canamar
The Crossing
Judgment
Horizon
The Breach
Cogenitor
Regeneration
First Flight
Bounty
The Expanse

Season Three

The Xindi
Anomaly
Extinction
Rajiin
Impulse
Exile
The Shipment
Twilight
North Star
Similitude
Carpenter Street
Chosen Realm
Proving Ground
Stratagem
Harbinger
Doctor's Orders
Hatchery
Azati Prime
Damage
The Forgotten
E^2
The Council
Countdown
Zero Hour

Season Four

Storm Front, Parts I and II
Home
Borderland
Cold Station 12
The Augments
The Forge
Awakening
Kir'Shara
Daedalus
Observer Effect
Babel One
United
The Aenar
Affliction
Divergence
Bound
In a Mirror, Darkly, Parts I
    and II
Demons
Terra Prime
These Are the Voyages . . .

Feature Films

Star Trek: The Motion Picture
    (1979)
Star Trek II: The Wrath of Khan
    (1982)
*Star Trek III: The Search for
    Spock* (1984)
Star Trek IV: The Voyage Home
    (1986)
Star Trek V: The Final Frontier
    (1989)
*Star Trek VI: The Undiscovered
    Country* (1991)
Star Trek: Generations (1994)
Star Trek: First Contact (1996)
Star Trek: Insurrection (1998)
Star Trek: Nemesis (2002)
Star Trek (2009)

Isolinear Data